Occupied Hearts

Love The Long Way Around

Based on a True Story
by Alice Parker

Dedication

*To the Families who shared their personal lives
with me for this story.
To Kazuyo Mizutani for all of her patience and
assistance with this story.*

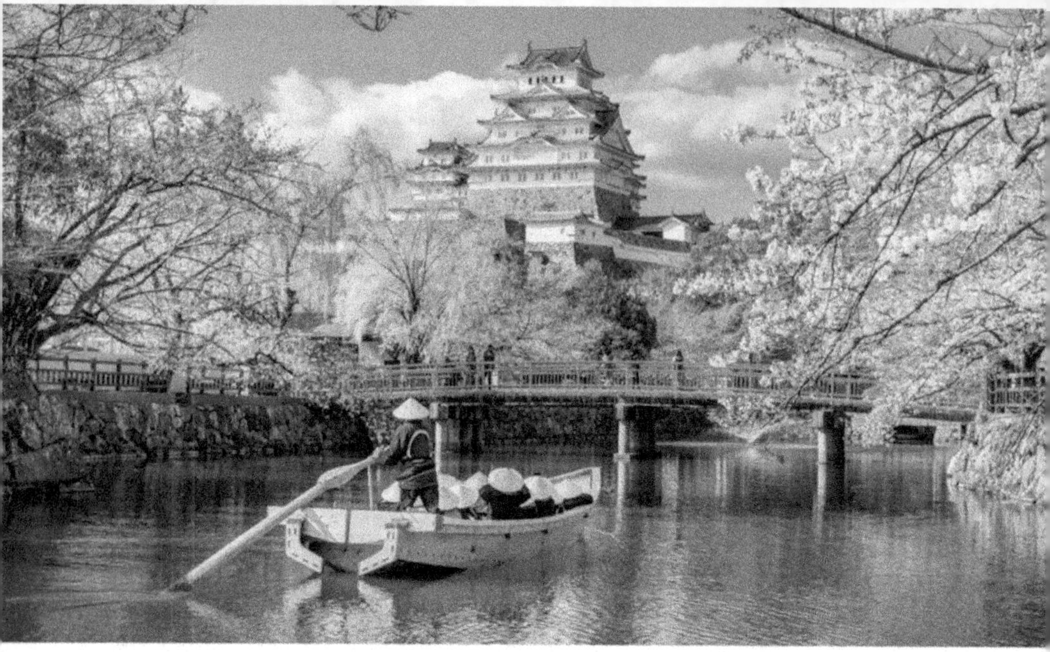

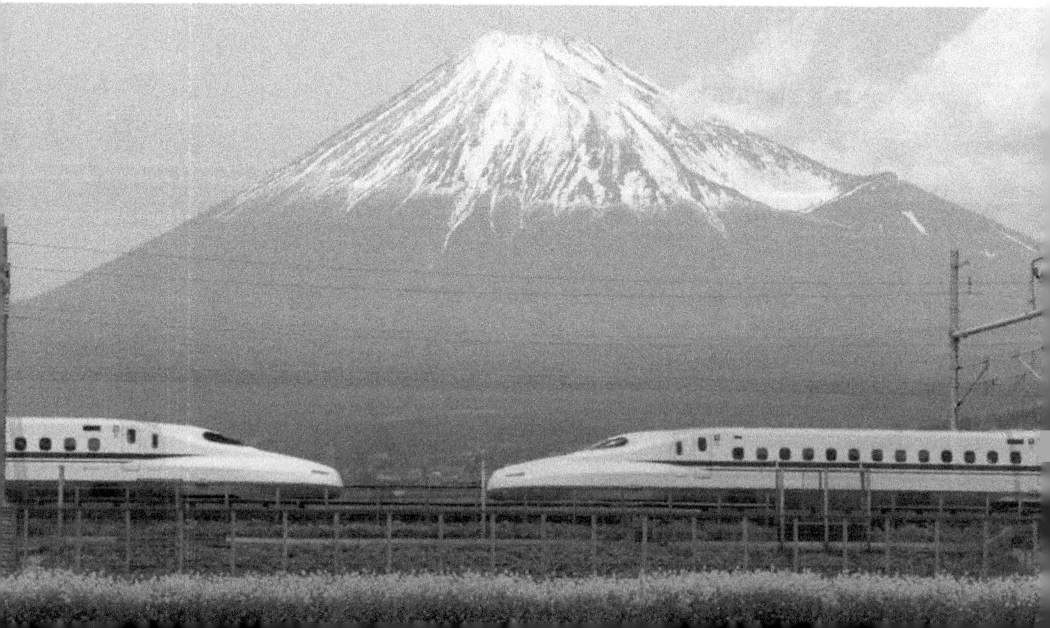

EXPLORA BOOKS
700 – 838 West Hastings St. Vancouver, BC V6C 0A6
www.explorabooks.com
Phone: (604) 330 6795

ISBN: 978-1-998394-15-9

Table of Contents

Prologue

How it All Began - Discovery of a Remarkable True Story

Three related Love stories, three Continents and three Wars

The modern hero, the modern individual who dares to heed the call and seek the mansion of that presence with whom it is our whole destiny to be atoned, cannot, indeed must not, wait for his community to cast off its slough of pride, fear, rationalized avarice, and sanctified misunderstanding. ... It is not society that is to guide and save the creative hero, but precisely the reverse. And so every one of us shares the supreme ordeal— carries the cross of the redeemer —not in the bright moments of his tribes' great victories, but in the silences of his personal despair.

Joseph Campbell ,
The Hero With A Thousand Faces

They are all heroes in this story, of various direct and indirect affects from war.

Nagoya, Japan

To most *gaijin*-foreigners, especially those who spent a few years there, Japan was the ultimate dichotomy. I arrived unceremoniously at Narita Airport outside Tokyo in February, 1988. For the next seven years it never ceased to amaze me, as I learned from the experiences it gave me, which I still think about to this day. I did not blame Japan for my luggage getting lost - though the singular situation of watching the 'group consensus' on how to handle it was a telling lesson of things to come. The numerous hours of turbulence caused my plane to be late, and me to miss my flight to Nagoya, was a blessing in disguise.

Yet, the whole trek into the city is quite a long, not so funny story I won't go into here, as like many of my Japan-stories, they need a drink to go along with them. Once accomplished, it gave me a chance to spend time with the representative from the language teaching company I was contracted to work for in Nagoya - kind of the 'Chicago' of Japan. The rep, a long-time veteran of living in Japan from Britain, gave me a brief introduction to cultural life over a late dinner of sushi-my first and beer. To say it barely scratched the surface, is obvious.

I appreciated the hand-holding for I knew only the generic version of Japan, none of the language, and had many wrong assumptions. At the same time, though I had worked many years in Downtown Chicago, I'd never faced such throngs of people at all hours - especially since they're all moving on the Left side. Also, as not a small, or flat-chested, white-woman - along with being blonde and blue-eyed - I'd learn racial and sexual discrimination quickly. I spent the night at the Rep's large, company apartment, as part of his job to house new teachers coming into Japan. He assured me, its size was a big perk of a country known for its match-box housing.

My first day, riding on the Shinkansen - bullet train - from Tokyo to Nagoya, I settled into the spotlessly-clean and quiet train. It glided over the elevated rails at an amazing speed, so I put my observation skills to work. I had two hours of uninterrupted sight- seeing of the continuously massive, utilitarian-looking cities spread out below the rails. I learned how every morning the futons - sleeping mattresses - were placed out the window, stretched across roofs or hung over terrace bannisters with humongous plastic clips to air-out in the slivers of sunlight slipping between the rows of apartment buildings. They gave a colorful, patched-work quilt-look to the bland, urban domiciles.

I had never seen a train conductor so nattily-attired in such a perfect uniform, and I soon noted that casual dress was not a big option among these traveling adult customers. The business man across the aisle wore what even I knew to be at least a thousand-dollar suit, two-hundred dollar shoes and impeccably tailored overcoat, neatly folded in a rack above his head. So, when he crossed his legs and revealed the brightly colored, stitched 'Mickey Mouse' on his dress black socks, I almost fell out of my seat, covering my mouth not to laugh out loud. *"I think I'm going to like this country,"* I whispered to myself. I later learned Mickey Mouse was second only to the Emperor Hirohito in being worshiped.

Yet in looking back, perhaps the most perplexing paradox, in this country with a thin Western facade built on eons of Asian moribund propensities, was the story of Paula. She and her twin brother Peter, were born illegitimately in Allied Occupied Germany and raised traditionally in Occupied Japan. With their American roots from a military father, neither of them were ever accepted into the Japanese culture, yet they were likewise uncomfortable in the U. S. This story did not just fall into my lap, nor did I stumble across it among all the other bizarre tales of long-term gaijin in Japan. I lived there years before I heard even a thumbnail-sketch of Paula's trek. It was exhaustive through every twist and turn of the labyrinth, to find her own niche in Japan. Of course, as every heroine needs a hero, hers came from a most unlikely and unacceptable source - according to her mother - a Vietnam veteran. Yet, as an avid history-culture buff - my major study in graduate school - I yearned to learn this saga, its worth to investigate and retell with their permission.

My story-quest started out in an unlikely manner, from a late summer evening bike ride in a park near my apartment with my Japanese friend Kazuyo, who spoke excellent English. I'd lived in Nagoya perhaps four months and exploring the area on bicycle was both an adventure and a way to unwind after working late, since the national stress was contagious to a born workaholic. One did not have to speak the language to see how boring and childish the television was, while the cultivated gaijin habit of escaping into American videos also had no real appeal to me.

So, I paused that evening to watch the little action taking place in the park, most of it probably habitual: a young man jogging the circular path, an older woman walking her dog and students, still in their uniforms, cutting through the park on their way home from the *juku* - the necessary cram-school, so many junior and senior high school students attended for passing University entrance exams. I'd just remarked to Kazuyo how great it was to be out after ten o'clock at night and not have to worry about avoiding any kind of crime.

I am sure, my English talk and me, obviously a gaijin, had warranted the elderly man to stop and speak to us. He was an internist at a small hospital nearby, and passed through the park on his way home. Once he learned I was new to Nagoya, he was quite keen to ask about my acceptance of the conservative, central Japan city, that was also the industrial backbone of the nation. He spoke for several minutes about the pros and cons of it all, and was about to bid us good night, when I commented on his proficient English ability. I so rarely heard it from any Japanese, much less an older one.

iv

He smiled proudly, as he attributed it to the American military during their extensive 'Occupation' of Nagoya, noting too, in the same breath its total destruction by their 'capable' fire bombs. Still learning that Japanese covered shame with a smile, yet this paradox was incomprehensible to my senses. He actually seemed happy at having had the opportunity to learn and work with the military, as it rebuilt his city. He then commented almost every park in Nagoya had been some kind of Japanese military manufacturing plant. He spoke sort of gratified, as if all retribution for their part in the war had been paid off with the deaths, and the new surroundings had removed the military evidence. Somehow in my mind or perhaps his, he'd taken all facets of the war and wrapped them up in a neat package. The past was forgotten, the present to be enjoyed.

For several minutes after he left, still absorbing what, and most importantly how, he'd revealed to me the city's history and attitude toward the war. It suddenly sank in, not only had I never heard of Nagoya before my contract to work there, but I knew very little of the Allied Occupation of Japan. Unfortunately, at that time, my work schedule restricted following up on expanding my knowledge of any of it, but my curiosity, which was probably deeper than average, had been piqued. Over the next few months, as time permitted, I visited the city castle and several historical-cultural museums in the area.

Each one, in its own subtle way added information to me, not only of facts, but how they were presented. Tightly edited would probably best describe the English notations, even giving them the benefit of translation difficulties, their perspective not a totally accurate recounting of the war America rained down on them. A part of me did understand.

On a short vacation later, a side visit to Hiroshima made indelible the devastation the atomic bomb wrought on Japan, but also some national, historical amnesia. Again, I felt like the society had an uncanny Catch-22 way of presenting itself as a victim, which without a doubt it was, of a most horrendous nature. Yet, not wanting to accept or acknowledge its participation in creating the war. I'd heard in the early days of Occupation, the children were taught that Pearl Harbor came *after* Hiroshima, not before. Publicly people were silent on the topic. I decided to do some reading and research to see exactly what role Nagoya did play in the war, and how the Americans changed it during the Occupation.

Luckily, I had a library available from a private American missionary school, started in the early 1900s, and continued to be active until Pearl Harbor, which was known to few Japanese. Many of the missionaries stayed during the war, some imprisoned, then opened again after the surrender. Able to check out or read there, many older English books regarding before and during the Occupation. They were written by those living in Japan, and not those whitewashed by the military under General MacArthur.

Interestingly, the more I learned and shared with other gaijin and Japanese friends, the more they began to reveal to me. In time, my experience of the culture and people increased, along with connecting to the web of gaijin in Nagoya. Weird stories involving long-term gaijin abounded, if one knew who to ask. It dawned on me the Japanese were more comfortable talking about *their* war and Occupation experiences with a foreigner. So, as my curiosity developed further, I gathered stories by interviewing these people who had survived some devastating situations, only known to those misplaced by war.

Several years later, I smugly felt quite versed on Japanese culture. I then attended a small party at a friend's apartment, where I learned I'd barely scratched the surface of the Japanese conundrum. I overheard a fascinating topic, and joined a discussion with Paula at the center. I'd talked to her several times in the past, but never personally spoke with her extensively. I knew she had lived for many years in Japan, and only six months prior I'd attended her Sayonara - going away party, when she moved permanently back to the United States.

Paula had just returned to Nagoya because of the death of her grandmother. She explained to several of us, respectfully and patiently, about the Buddhist ceremony for the funeral, and how everything was done by exact daily, monthly and yearly rituals. She commented she really should not have been at a 'party,' but wanted to see her friends, as the adjustment to Michigan was more difficult than anticipated.

I listened quite intently, since I'd studied Buddhism, but the burial concept was a bit confusing, as I'd never quite comprehended that her mother and grandmother were Japanese. I somehow had the misconception from other gaijin, she was a part of the last batch of missionary children who grew up in Japan after the war. The *surface-friendship syndrome* - know someone only from the work relationship

- was a common malady among the many transit gaijin, and produced much misinformation. We all hesitated to do twenty questions on each other, when you might not see them often or even again. Besides, we were all put through those basic questions constantly as a teaching tool to the students. Privacy actually became sanctified to us.

Border-lining on prying, I acknowledged my ignorance and asked for clarification. Paula smiled so benignly, if I'd not known her Japanese background, I'd have thought she was patronizing me. She hesitated, more as if not wanting to take up my time by talking about herself. Then she acquiesced with delight, that someone would take such a personal interest in her. She plunged in to tell a brief synopsis of the cultural-allegory which had been her life, she mesmerized even a jaded me. Her epic story and its evolvement, in conjunction with the enigmatic Occupation, became a challenge, as I became compelled to chronicle it.

I made a definite point to get details for a future contact in regards to my Occupation research. In a very Japanese manner, she discounted her story as insignificant, until my second insistent request. The definite Japanese-native attributes she displayed were not lost on me. They were smooth, unconscious and not the overly affectations of some gaijin, who wished to emote their assimilation into the culture.

Not sure what funeral etiquette I might break by my pursuit of Paula before she returned to the States, I checked with several mutual friends before I called. I also questioned these same friends for more clear-cut details regarding Paula and her family. A few years earlier, in the course of riding the trains to the corporations where I taught my business programs, I'd met her husband, Mac. As smiling and gregarious as he was, there was something pensive, yet slightly defensive, as he explained some of the idiosyncrasies I questioned about the Japanese.

Over the term of my work contract, we often saw each other and I came to depend on his information. My love-hate relationship with Japan - I loved the people and hated the society/government that controlled them - had already taken hold of me. We met occasionally also on the city subway once my contract ended. It was on such an evening I first met Paula as they traveled home. She barely said a word, yet his attentiveness to her surprised me. It was not as if there was any danger, other than squashed by the masses, and it was more my problem as I stood and they sat. Not unusual, even on the most crowded trains, a Japanese would get up and move rather than sit next to a gaijin. So, I did get to sit next to Paula.

They eventually made it to one of my parties, and I noticed how Paula felt more comfortable talking with the Japanese guests rather than the gaijin. There were only a few people she knew there, so when not speaking to them, she intently watched the interactions of both gaijin and Japanese. Then Paula seemed to keep herself busy in the later hours of the evening picking up and cleaning dishes rather than socializing. Since long-term gaijin had to be a bit bent or different to live in Japan anyway, I ignored it at the time. Later thinking it over, all the pieces started to form into a life-sized puzzle that would be long in my finishing.

I met with Paula and her mother Sakiko in a Western family- style restaurant about a week after the cremation ceremony. I'd brought along my friend Kazuyo, who had become my excellent interpreter for my research on several interviews where the person's English ability may be of question. I did not know if her mother Sakiko would even agree to being interviewed, but I wanted her to know I had a trusted person to whom she could speak in Japanese, if she preferred. The meeting went quite well, though the proprieties by Paula were clearly defined. Kazuyo even commented later, Paula was more traditionally Japanese that she was, though the age difference could explain some of it, as Paula was closer to my age and Kazuyo ten years younger than me. Also, Kazuyo had lived overseas and was working for an American company in Japan. Still, an interesting remark and supported my own feelings in regard to Paula's character.

Surprisingly, Sakiko not only agreed to the interview, but invited us back to her home which was only a short distance away. I was glad Kazuyo had the time and interest, for her feedback was quite valuable to me. The house was decorated ornately with heavy wooden furniture, inlaid with intricate shell designs. I related it more to what was a popular Chinese style rather than the traditional simplicity of Japanese decor. But, I also knew it was a strong statement of money, for although it had been purchased years before, it had been expensive.

Sakiko's English was very good, in fact she rather enjoyed using slang, even if it was a bit dated. An interesting contrast, as she ceremoniously served the green tea. We set a time and date for Kazuyo to interview her, yet when the appointment came, Sakiko occupied

Kazuyo's time without ever relating her story. I was rather taken aback Sakiko chose to be insulted by being interviewed in Japanese, or more so she kept Kazuyo, relenting to let her leave.

Obviously, she enjoyed the captured audience, as she showed off her photos and served food on her finest china. Sakiko did not want Kazuyo to record anything. She felt quite capable of being interviewed by me, and gave Kazuyo the impression she did not want a second- banana to interview her. After several false starts, and as more pieces of the puzzle came together from other sources, I interviewed Sakiko. She truly was a 'piece of work,' enigmatic like no other person I'd ever met before, and by no means anti-climatic in her past, present or future life.

A few months later, during a trip back to the States, I arranged to fit a few days into my schedule to interview Paula and Mac at their home in Michigan outside of Detroit. The bonus came in that Peter, Paula's twin, was there and to my surprise, her son John. I interviewed them all individually, so they could speak freely of their feelings. That accomplished, my only large missing piece was the information on Paula's biological parents. She had a copy of her birth certificate, yet she refused to research it. Mac encouraged her many times, and even suggested they travel to Germany together to do it. He knew on his own, the military could have easily tracked down her father, as she had his name and the records were publicly accessible.

Paula, silently adamant about not seeking them out, finally admitted her hesitation came from not wanting to hurt Sakiko, the only mother she ever really knew. Mac and I fruitlessly tried to persuade her that Sakiko did not need to know, and finding her birth parents in no way should change their relationship. Yet, all of us, knowing how controlling Sakiko was, knew she'd not accept that. She'd say she had not been loved or appreciated, as the mother who sacrificed so much for Paula. Sakiko truly played the ultimate Queen of the guilt-tripping mothers of the world.

In her early years, Sakiko instilled in Paula that her birth parents had abandoned her and Peter. Having read enough war-torn books and seen too many heartbreaking movies, I did not want to believe this was Paula's story. There was a certain amount of selflessness attached to a mother in those desperate situations who gave up her children to a better life, rather than half-survival in dismal, or possible death circumstances, especially when twins were involved.

An adult can struggle, forage food and creature comforts, but an infant has no ability to sustain itself. In truth, the twins may not have survived in Germany, as the Iron Curtin was about to fall, but without the airlifts of food begun. With this thought, my curiosity got the better of me, again. Gladly, I made a copy of the information on Paula'a birth certificate when Mac offered it to me. I always believed the best stories had as much truth in them as could be found.

One of the rewards of the intricate web of gaijin floating into Japan from all over the world, was the opportunity to meet so many of them. As the case so many times, I met Dieter on the trains to do classes for Toyota. From Munich, he studied Japanese at Nanzan University and taught a class in German to employees being sent to various cities in Germany. Over the course of our hour-long ride twice a week for four months, we became friends. When he returned home, we kept in touch and on my next trip to Europe, we had several days together. I got to meet his new bride, a Japanese living in Germany and several of their friends including Bettina. She was fascinated by an American lifestyle, in contrast to Japan or Europe. She asked if we might correspond, so over the next year, we also became friends.

When I planned another trip to Paris, she responded to the opportunity to meet again, especially since she studied French. I thought too, of a stop in Frankfurt, since it was the hometown of both Bettina and Hanalore - Paula's birth mother. Intrigued by my research, Bettina, and more gaijin friends in Japan with a fluency in German, tracked down records of Hanalore in Frankfurt. Bettina then agreed to interpret the eventually-arranged interview.

A good thing I had to plan my vacations far in advance, for it took several months to work it all out. Interestingly, when asked, Hanalore likewise did not want to meet Paula. It had all been buried so long ago, she could not bear to see her child - though now a grown woman - she'd given up. My part in this story, definitely developed into more than just the writer, as there was more than a chill down my spine. I felt Hanalore would weave a tale more heart-wrenching than any I'd seen on the silver screen. Part of me began to worry about what I'd actually gotten myself involved with, from my curiosity and fascination of lives tossed around during a foreign Occupation.

* * * * * *

Chronicled are three related love stories and almost too ironically, the American men all have military backgrounds, though thoroughly different in their nature, as well as time and place. Uniquely, too, each on a different continent, within a different culture and war. Yet, they each came a long way to find their unexpected love. But, the aftermath and ugliness of war was identical, as it sharply controlled the destiny of each of them to overcome. Sadness, fear, and loss occupied each of their hearts, and yet what ultimately brought them together in love.

The story starts in Germany, with the hero seemingly doing the right thing, whether for his country, his men or his home family. Perhaps if he'd known the full circumstances surrounding the woman he loved, it would not have been an unrequited romance. But then, I would not have a story.

The second love story in Japan is harder to describe, for it had little romance, but a fulfilling of one's fixated-dreams with the obsessed person who best fit the image. Occupation created a different kind of survivor. And, the Korean Conflict a different kind of war. In many ways, a sadly, tragic story, dragging on, as a faded, illusive- vision denied.

The last love story, though in America, it is framed by Vietnam. It parallels the first almost too frighteningly, until a happy ending was bravely secured, by fighting against all odds. A hero needs a heroine to save who believes in him, even if the fire-breathing dragons are only cultural dinosaurs. Determined to succeed where he was not wanted, until they needed him.

* * * * * *

In the Epilogue, I've reflected on my own, and other friends' cultural experiences, as well from seven years in Japan learning it. I left in mid-April, 1995.

Part I: From Occupied Germany to Occupied Japan

From Occupied Germany

Chapter 1 Love Found and Love Lost

Hoffnung

Es reden und träumen die
Menschen viel, Von bessern
künftigen Tagen,
Nach einem glücklichen goldenen
Sieht man sie rennen und jagen.
Die Welt wird alt und
wird wieder jung,
Doch der Mensch hofft immer
Verbesserung!

Hope

People are talking and
dreaming a lot
Of better days coming
For a happy golden aim Ziel,
You see them run and
hunt. The world
becomes old and
becomes again young,
But man always hopes
for improvement!

Friedrich Schiller,
The Robber

Late April, 1945 - Germany

Behind the gigantic, protective boulder and in the confines of the ditch, Terry pulled off his time-worn helmet to run his large, rough fingers through his thick, brown, wavy hair. He paused a moment to feel the fresh air, took a deep breath, wiped the dirt off his face with his shirt sleeve and thought what he'd give to have a bath ... and if his wish could be extended to include clean sheets, he'd be a very happy man. He didn't want to seem greedy by including in his dream a warm, supple, loving body - female in form, though vague in all other respects - to share it all with. Spring days could do that to the strongest men and even under a cloudy sky, but he also knew that it was too farfetched for this realm of the war.

Terry pushed the helmet back on, changed his grin of enjoyment, not to betray himself, to the usual smile of confidence he wore for his men. The hulk-like, six-foot body moved ten feet with a swiftness befitting a ballet dancer. His darting, deep-set blue eyes, though desperately needing sleep, surveyed every inch of ground and where each of his men were, before taking up his new position. They depended on that, as well his razor sharp decisions for each creative strategy. This war gave few chances to lapse into any kind of daydream, and live to experience it.

Terence Paul O'Brian had quickly risen to the rank of sergeant in the U.S. Army for his bravery and leadership skills. "Just like keeping the cattle in check back home in Colorado," he joked, while he patted his men on the back to calm their nerves, yet kept an ever watchful eye on them. He was one of them, but rank required him to be emotionally separate, so he would never hesitate to send them out to face possible death. Still, under that tough skin, in private moments he'd been moved to tears after so many of his men died, in those last days of fighting against the desperate Germans. Retreat could affect a man's ego, and many Germans had been indoctrinated at a young age. Maybe it was pride and loss of the dream they must die for, or bravely defend. As their trials of terror came to an end, many suicidal Germans took out several of Terry's men with their hopeless defeat.

Grabbing their joys where they could, his comrades tried to forget the realities of war while happily celebrating Terry's twenty- fifth birthday, which almost became his last. The Germans had laid a veritable, killing carpet of land mines, awaiting the aggressive Allieds. As careful and protective as Terry was with his men, it was he who stepped backwards right onto a landmine. The god of fate had been there only minutes later, in the form of a Colonel's jeep, which his men had not hesitated to stop and throw him into. The loyalty he'd garnered from them separated him into being a casualty instead of a statistic. He would have very easily and quickly bled to death from his mangled right leg and arm. When they informed the rookie-officer that Terry was a verified hero with a Purple Heart and Silver Cross, the Colonel could not refuse the side trip to a field hospital. Besides, his driver was already moving to arrange the body across the rear seat. The blood poured out from his head to his toes.

* * * * * *

Through a veil of drugs, Terry wafted in and out of a coma, strangely filled with a melodic voice, woven around glimpses of a blonde- framed face, and piercing blue eyes. This was a dream better than any before, though there were no puffy clouds or birds singing. He could not identify the smells he sucked into his nostrils, but his sense of touch definitely worked, maybe even overtime. His skin felt fresh like he had been swimming in the creek out by the north pasture, and he no longer had the taste of salt on his lips from the constant sweat, a result of the fear pumped by adrenaline. His mind once again created the body, surely intertwined with his. The softness beneath him just had to be a bed. The gentle, sturdy hands slowly and softly caressed his body were now around his most private, vulnerable ... and long neglected manhood. Ah, in his dreams, he could rise to the challenge. *"Ruhig, Junge!"* - "Down, boy! You not ready for that YET!" *"Sie sind, Nach nicht, GUSUND!"* His eyes popped open, as fear replaced the sexual adventure, thinking he had somehow become a prisoner of the Germans. Hanalore reacted with a similar startled jerk, as her comatose patient literally came alive in her hands. When Terry pulled backwards, the pain shot up his right side, and he yelped before he could control the reaction. *"Nien ..."* Hanalore, quickly looked around her to make sure no one had heard her slip into German, and changed to English - "No, do not do that! You must not move!"

The accent was somewhat heavy, but the words, thank God, were recognizable. "You speak English?!" Terry slowly slumped back to his previous position, as his injured right arm and leg were strung from some kind of wire system, so the pressure and pain were relieved. He could not survey the entire situation, as he did not want to take his eyes off the phantom-figure that had materialized before him. He still feared this lovely ghost might become his worse nightmare.

There'd been no thought of this scenario, as he had figured he'd either live or die. Wounded men had been taken away by a medic and rarely seen again during the last battle days. He'd never even been in an army hospital, especially a German one. His time in the war had been all battle fronts or training centers, and not much else in between. He'd often said it had been like being on a continuous roundup in bad weather that never ended. In his limited short life, he'd little but the ranch and the war with which to compare things. The cattle could be irritating, but they rarely killed you. The ranch may have built his stamina, but the war had constantly abused it.

Hanalore slowly removed the washcloth from under the sheet and began to rinse it in the basin. "Yes, ... of course. This ... American hospital now and ... I freed hear ... me say German." She squeezed most of the water out

4

of the cloth and began to return to the washing, but it was a totally different situation now that he was awake. For weeks she dreamed of this moment and what she'd say to him, but she'd never had this reaction by him in any of her rehearsals. She'd try to get the English and her feelings just right. His strong, marvelous body, she'd come to know so well, distracted her concentration. And, that masculine face she had carefully shaved, stared up at her in curious-caution. She wanted to tell him how she'd daily watched his beautiful hair grow back on his head, so one could barely see where the scar from his surgery was. Hanalore had often peeked under his eyelids, to search for life in the deep, blue eyes which lay hidden beneath and surrounded by the long, dark lashes.

Terry felt like he stretched his ears to hear and understand her words and their meaning. Was she telling the truth? He took a few deep breaths and tried to grasp the whole situation that seemed to involve him and his racked up body. In the corner reaches of his mind, the compassionate, tender touches of her gliding hands and the whispered, soothing words had become embedded in some feral memory, yet he was unsure of himself. The benign smile on her creamy face and the chipmunk cheeks spoke of innocence that could not do him harm, even if he attacked her. But then, in his limited physical state, she really did not have much to fear of him. He reviewed again her words enough to question, "Freed? Are you a prisoner?" Maybe the kindness was a forced state, and she was only doing it to save her own skin. He didn't know the rules on POWs- prisoners of war not in prisons.

"Uh … fired, is word? I sorry, I still learn your talk. American doctors talk very fast … very strict with German nurses. We treated … not same as American nurse. But, I real nurse, too. We not do all jobs." She lifted the sheet and finished cleaning him with more studious regimentation, so to be taken as a professional doing a job thoroughly. He felt his body tense a little now with embarrassment, then realized this was not the first time for

5

her cleaning his body. He finally began to relax, as he surveyed the shape and curves of her. The body was definitely at variance with her ingenue or immature reaction. How much had been a dream, and how much was the real thing before him?

Hanalore concentrated on cleaning his good arm, yet felt his eyes penetrating every inch of her body. She could not help the blush that began to rise from the heat in her chest. Without daring to look at him, she could feel as the searching stare moved and scanned her. As he studied her, a blonde, curly lock stubbornly did not stay put under the cap, she wanted to stop and push it back in place, but didn't dare. Even with the antiseptic surroundings, the fresh scrubbed smell covering her skin infused his nostrils, as she leaned in and began to wash his face. He'd never had such a sensuous feeling and as it covered his body, he had no idea what was happening to him. How long had it been since he'd seen and felt a real, considerate woman, not just a prostitute fawning attention for the money?

Hanalore picked up the clean hospital gown and unfolded it, so she could carefully slip it over the parts of his body not restricted to the elevated contraption. She quickly glanced at Terry to give a reassurance of her every action. At this point previously, when he was still in a coma, she'd often gently run her small fingers though his lightly-haired chest. Her mind suddenly questioned if he might have some recollection of such a sensual act? Terry's eyes were glued to her every move, trying to figure out just how she might feel about him.

Not sure if it was fear or what, she subconsciously began to flush again and pulled in her lower lip, as she habitually did when nervous. With great consideration of each movement, she slowly lifted his good left arm to work it through the sleeve. Terry asked as quietly and controlled as possible, "What's your name, angel?" He could not help sounding corny, she was the angel he'd seen in his dreams.

Hanalore lifted his head, supporting it now closer to her own body, to pull the string-tie behind his head. She then secured it to the empty sleeve, giving the strung-up right arm its limited mobility. She swallowed deeply, bit her lower lip again and answered clearly, also very controlled, "My name Ha-na-lore … Hanalore Frederick. I … your nurse for weeks … you here many weeks." She situated him as best she could, straightening the covers and sheets, so nothing would disturb his comfort or the cables. Brave now enough to finally look straight at him, she tried to smile, if only briefly. "I get doctor. He be happy you wake. I see you … tomorrow, I go home." She turned from him to leave.

Terry still ingesting her name and all the words, as she disappeared out the curtain that was around his bed. "Wait, Hannah or Hana … Laurie? Don't go now!" Terry slumped back feeling once again the wincing pain any quick movement brought. *"Wouldn't you know,"* he thought, *"I wake up to an angel and let her slip away."* Terry only sulked a moment when the curtain was quickly flung back to reveal a stern, older looking man with an even harsher looking dark- haired nurse at his side. The insignias were American and the doctor's booming voice and probing hands returned Terry to his real life situation. They were obviously glad he was awake, as well as alive.

* * * * * *

Hanalore Frederick truly was a determined survivor. She qualified this fact simply that she currently existed, outlasting the war's capable annihilation of Frankfurt, and more so by her persistence during the Allied Occupation. Not giving up the struggle was a characteristic that did determine the factor of life or death, even without bombs dropping. Being trained in medicine was no guarantee to life or a job. She knew how lucky she was and never took advantage of her situation. Following the rules in war or under the Occupation was key to survival, but also getting along with the Americans. Many of the staff were uncomfortable having any Germans working around them, and some didn't hesitate to let the Germans know it. But, it was part of the Occupation program, so she did her job as efficiently as possible and did not disrupt anyone or cause any upset.

Distracted by the way the long-anticipated encounter with Terry went, in the locker room, she still quickly changed out of her uniform, white socks and shoes. She placed the shoes on the bottom of the locker and shook out the socks before she stretched them over the shoes to air out. The uniform, the only one she had, she washed only when necessary by hand and never wore it out on the street. It could signal to people that she had a job, maybe money or even food hidden on her. She folded her uniform neatly and put it into her homemade bag, while her mind replayed his words with the sound of his long awaited voice.

Surprised, his was more husky, than low, but not gruff or demanding she thought. And strong, too, like his body that had stayed muscled after the weeks of inactivity. Since coming to work at the hospital, she'd been able to see several American movies they had for the patients. Gary Cooper, yes, that was the voice he reminded her of - strong and independent, like some cowboy. He looked like him, too, she decided. She took her old dress off the hook in the locker and pulled it over her head. She sat on the bench to slip on the dark socks and patiently folded the material so the holes were covered to prevent any blisters. Finally, she arranged the cardboard piece into her shoes over the holes, and carefully wiggled her feet into them, so as to not disturb its placement. She sat a moment taking a deep breath and then pulled in her lower lip, as she then stood to consider what all had happened with Terry finally waking up.

Hanalore hugged the bag to her full breasts and blushed again thinking of how he'd got the erection. She'd only seen a few before, which she knew were involuntary

from muscle spasms of the unconscious men. But this time, she was actually, sort of touching him
- something she'd never done before. She felt her face go into a full bright flush. She hoped he did understand she was only doing her job
- the job she was supposed to do for him - clean him thoroughly.

She probably had a dozen soldiers under her care, some constantly coming and going, but none had ever stirred her the same way. She pulled her sweater on over her worn dress, then tucked the left-over, partial loaves of bread tightly under each arm. She arranged herself and them beneath the sweater, so her precious gifts from the hospital chef could not be seen or slip out. Off into the late summer afternoon she walked, her steps a little lighter thinking of Terry coming out of his coma and even talking to her. Hanalore waited for an open spot to slip out of the gates of the courtyard into the passing crowd, not wanting to be conspicuous, as to where she had come from. The American guards nodded to her, then stared as she blended into the pathetic and pitiable sights that had become so familiar to them.

The streets were full of lonely people or sometimes families, keeping warm or cooking around a fire with all of their possessions close at hand. The cooking in an old army German helmets was common, and only a comedic sight to the Allied Powers. Other citizens wandered with pushcarts made from discarded baby carriages, searching for any kind of usable items. Hanalore slowly weaved her way through the maze of post-war life. Bicycles were a rarity, as tires alone were worth a small fortune. She held her nose and breath, as she speeded up her passage by the makeshift-boilers set up in the open lots to make 'new' rubber tires from old bits and pieces. Some neighbors sat on the broken concrete steps exchanging shared shoes, as the one person was going in and the other going out. Hanalore barely noticed those who wore mismatched shoes, or ill-fitting ones like her own. Only the Americans wore shiny new ones. She made a large circle around other neighbors who were spraying their children for lice. Dysentery and typhoid had swept the country with the breakdown in sanitation control from the bombings and fires. A bar of real soap, not the lye substitute, was a treasure not to be wasted. Luckily for Hanalore, it was another benefit of working in the American hospital.

With Terry occupying her mind again, Hanalore lost her maneuvering concentration and almost ran into several old men stopping short to gather cigarette butts. Once they had enough, they could be exchanged for a loaf of day-old bread, or a small bag of potatoes. New cigarettes-never a pack, but singles - were used as payment in most bars, especially those out-of-bounds to servicemen, since the bar owners could not accept the military script.

Just as Hanalore turned the corner to her street, she saw the usual collection of ragged people sleeping in the doorways with their loaf of bread tucked into the layers of clothes. She stepped over and around people, trying not to tread on the few possessions some had gathered around them. She could not bear to catch the sadness in their eyes, or feel the guilt for still having an apartment to come home to from a real job. She told herself that it was just fate to be accepted, she was a lucky one.

Hanalore dug deep into her bag for her key and finally got the creaking door opened, then quickly locked it behind her. Only two more flights of stairs, as she held tightly to the railing, since the small, dim light on the third floor barely gave her any protection from the broken steps. Hanalore knocked twice before inserting and turning her key. She did not want to frighten her mother, who had lived through many years of the door being broken down by the Nazis, or the Gestapo searching forbidden people or valuable items. The sparse room reflected very little of a prosperous, pre-war life, with her mother standing at the stove and her brother Helmut studying his high school books at the kitchen table. The valuable decorative items and all collectibles may be gone, but at least the roof had few leaks.

Hanalore handed the bread over to her mother, who refused to accept their current meager life. She stared and noted in German, "Two pieces barely make more than a half-loaf." She then held the cut ends to her nose to see if they had picked up any body odor from her daughter. Hanalore didn't wait for her mother's lack of appreciation of the precious donation. The woman slightly snorted and returned to her cooking. She was rarely grateful for the few prizes, as well the money Hanalore contributed to their little family. The woman came from the more pleasured-class with arrogance inbred, and she would not let it go. Though her officer husband was honored early in the war from his death, she considered their life now to be annoying, as if any moment it would all return to what she had known before. Whatever Hanalore did for them, she felt it was owed, as well as rather lacking.

Helmut had fewer memories of a happy family life, so with his dark eyes shining, he anxiously asked about the new American world which so impressed him with their power. "What happened at the hospital today?" Hanalore barely shared her good news regarding Terry, when their mother demanded the table to be cleared for dinner. She nodded to Helmut they'd talk later, for Mrs. Frederick considered it extremely disrespectful and dishonorable to talk admiringly about the Americans. The fact it was the American's money which supported them was of no consequence. Money was money, and it didn't matter where it came from, as long as it was there. She wasn't for Germany, per se, she was just against change that affected her badly.

The next morning Hanalore tried to use a drawing pencil of Helmut's to put some color on her eyebrows, since she had no makeup. She searched everywhere for some sort of lipstick, but her mother's old ones were a terrible color on her. She carefully brushed her long curls over and over to control the stubborn thick hair to fit into a more sleek style. She searched through the bathroom drawers and boxes for some kind of cream that might do the trick, the only thing she found had been her father's and it smelled terrible. She gave up, tying a scarf tightly around her head hoping it might help somewhat. She surveyed herself once more standing on her tiptoes to see in the the cracked mirror. She checked her bag before going out the door as quietly as possible, since she was leaving earlier than usual and did not want any questions. She had to understand herself, as she'd barely slept all night, yet only wanted to return to the hospital.

The summer sun had been glowing less than an hour and cast its strange shadows through the fragmented buildings, but the rumpled streets were already busy with early-bird survival. Hanalore saw dozens of women lined up, or sitting on piles of rubble with buckets, as they waited for the U.S. military trucks to dump the unwanted food from the army's cold storage. Any kind of sweets - cakes, pastries, cookies - were priceless, because of the lack of flour and sugar, so these items would often go to the black market rather than to the family. These people knew a lot of their survival was dependent on the American base in Frankfurt. The women may have seemed relaxed and polite with friendly conversation now, but the military had learned to bring extra guards to keep the fighting under control once the leftovers were being discarded.

Hanalore picked up her step, not wanting to witness the disheartening scene. She was surprised that even at this hour the sidewalks in some places were so crowded. Groups of people would hang out staring into butcher shops or bakers. Others, more knowingly wise, stayed by the back doors or alleyways to be the first at grabbing the meat scraps, bones, leftover crumbs, bits of sugar, or raw flour. Handouts, leftovers or rifling through garbage was a daily, endless job if one was to survive.

Hanalore had to cross the street to avoid the usual emotional mob scene. As the Prisoners of War returned, women would go to the station carrying photos of their loved ones, searching the arriving passengers, afraid they would not recognize their man after war. When they were not found, the women would pitifully pull and tug at each survivor, shoving the photo at them, begging for recognition and testament of their loved one's existence. Hanalore pulled her sweater tighter around her old dress, as she clutched her bag closer to her body, she felt she was more fortunate having only lost a father, not a lover or husband. The last block to the hospital, she almost ran to escape the horrors of life outside the American gates. She barely acknowledged the friendly greeting, thinking how much easier it was to deal with blood and pain within a sterile atmosphere, in which most of the men were eventually healed and even became happy.

Hanalore stood on tiptoe again to carefully examine in the small mirror how her uniform fit, smoothing out wrinkles, tugging here and there over her curves, wishing she had more of the sleek body she saw in the American magazines. She fussed, tucking her curls into hr cap and searched her bag and then the floor for any hairpins. Finding two, she tried several different ways before accepting her fate of too many blonde curls. She never realized how pretty she was or how many men noticed her. She decided to take care of her other patients first, so once she got to Terry she would not have to rush. Today, she would be more confidant with her English, as she had rehearsed the night before.

* * * * * *

And so it all began, with Hanalore and Terry both hesitating, yet smiling openly, and then pulling back. Subconsciously, they both were dealing with the word 'enemy' and the painful reminders of their personal losses. But, each also could not contain the growing feelings of attachment, responding to deeds of kindness, and eventually laughing out loud with each other. Hanalore's gentleness seemed to feed Terry, as he grew stronger and returned to his affable self and loving life, although it had

13

not given him anything easily. Hard work was a major part of his foundation, along with doing the right thing toward people, especially family and friends who needed him. Making a livelihood out of a ranch, on the plains of Colorado, was no easy trick for his father.

Terry moved from the bed to a wheelchair and the dearth of visits from his men dwindled down to only those who waited for their points to accumulate and be shipped home. The new arrivals coming in for the Occupation had nothing in common with him, as they only knew battle from hearsay and many tried to earn respect by doing their fighting in the bars. Doctors would not give him a date to look forward to, as there would be more operations on the bones and skin grafts to smooth out the disfiguring scars. His body repelled and depressed him, as much as the view from the balcony that Hanalore had taken him to see. Yet, somehow she looked upon her city and his full recovery with the same great hope. She saw him as a whole, perfect white knight who sacrificed himself for his belief in a great cause. Her empathy for his pain, she carefully covered with the wide smile between the chipmunk cheeks.

Terry winced at her stories of German sufferings under Hitler and visibly cringed as she spoke honestly. She expected no pity, of her fears of the Soviets, for she'd had no weapons to repel the hunger, mistreatment or pain. It all reminded him of what his mother said about women waiting and helpless in their ignorance of what was happening. He would become angry when he thought of Hanalore's lovely, supple body being manhandled, or even violated by the German or Soviet soldiers. She'd told him over and over, "No, No! I saved. I hide, I cover me many old clothes." He could not imagine someone with her appeal escaping it all. Only with slight sadness, Hanalore told Terry how it ended for most of the arrogant soldiers. "Many army men … no home or family. Many wounded … like you, camp in parks or stand street corner … beg." Terry could see the sadness in her eyes, not defending or asking for sympathy, but as one human being to another.

"But people … you know .. do." she made a spitting sound, "and not give coin in cup."

Terry thought of how untouched America had been and all of the glorious homecomings he'd read about in the newspapers. "I don't think Americans would ever do that to their soldiers, even if we lost the war." He smiled broadly, letting his pride out. But historical ignorance of the South after the Civil War would have proven him wrong. "Of course, we've never lost a war and I doubt that we ever will. Even Japan will be finished soon, … I'm sure." He pondered a moment on what he'd said and ran his hand slowly through his hair. "But then, I've had enough of war and wouldn't want to fight any more. Four years was enough." Hanalore watched his face, and suddenly intuitive that men somehow interpreted war in a different vein than women. There was just some big part of the picture men did not see, nor want to get the meaning of the bigger picture. It was all about winning and losing, and not the after-affects to all lives.

Every possible day held trips to the balcony, eventually out to the courtyard and finally the grounds of the hospital. Hanalore's broken English improved with practice, as she'd tell Terry about her life in Germany before the war, then coping with the aftermath. He began to see the common person's endurance and perseverance in a totally different category, than the hell-bent-for-glory tenacity he'd seen in the efficiently-cruel German soldiers. It became sort of an awakening rather than a cultural experience. Of course, the lingering touches they more and more often exchanged, influenced a humanity perspective in them both. People are people, and should not be hated on a generalized basis, if they must be hated at all.

As they watched through the safety of the iron fence, Hanalore attempted to explain what the people - men, women and children - were doing around the bombed-out buildings, since the reclaiming of bricks was a lucrative free market, but a competitive hard job. "Each brick must good clean, no concrete or *martar* … mortar, but must not break." It was an amazing assortment of tools or objects that were used to break the debris from the individual bricks. Some people had little wagons or carts to stack their bricks on, while others just used gunny sacks or other heavy material to carry them away. With the dozens of bulldogs within view, it seemed that they would never run out of a ready supply to dismantle. People would horde their precious stacks,"One brick," she moved her hands to show how they equaled, "buy food."

On another day, they laughed as many people took obvious joy in dismantling a German war memorial, with its metal soldiers. Almost daily they would see the children and old people gathering firewood, whether from burned-out lumber or trees ravaged in the park. From the balcony overview, Terry could see there was no respite for anyone, and the pulse of the city became a part of his routine, relished as much as he did Handler herself. The neighborhood had a paradox or two, with the children using rusted-out Soviet tanks to stage a resourceful puppet show. But, the only new buildings being built were strictly for the Allied military. There was little rebuilding of any professional nature, as everywhere the hodgepodge, and quite ingenious. Laughter came easier, than Terry or Hanalore had experienced in a long time.

Summer was ending, and fall's chilly wind blew mixed blessings from the god of fate. The doctor said that this may be his last operation, and soon Terry would begin extensive physical therapy for his rehabilitation to go home. Hanalore was joyous, as she shared the good news with him on their now familiar balcony, as they talked about the city's slow improvements also. Their routine was rather set and Terry knew every hall and turn to and from his room. He had planned his play for over a week now. The other bed had been empty for weeks, so they were virtually alone.

Pushing him back to his room, Terry waited, as she propped his room door open, then pulled the curtain around the bed for privacy. The door had to be kept open.

Hanalore helped him up and scooted him over into the bed. She'd carefully slipped his legs under the covers and prattled with conversation, as she pulled them up to tuck him in. Suddenly, he swung his left arm around her and pulled her down onto his chest. Surprised, he had actually knocked the breath out of her. She quickly laughed at his recuperative strength, but had not pulled away from him. His doctors, too, would have been amazed at how adept and clever he'd become with only one good arm, his left one at that. The cast on the right arm would have probably slowed down a less tenacious man.

Terry then slowly pulled her down to him, to kiss the full mouth he had studied and desired for so long. He held her tightly, kissing her deeply until she relented, responded and finally rewarded him, with the passion he knew she'd kept just beneath her proficient, uniformed body. As he released her lips, but not her body, he whispered as much to himself, as to reassure her, "I knew my dreams hadn't been lying to me. You feel it just as much as I do." The active hand tried to touch, explore and absorb as much as possible of her, to feed every sense-deprived, craving. His eyes, face and body were full of love and excitement that radiated the room. The way he held her, it was as if he would never let go.

Hanalore's imaginative dreams had also been fulfilled and released, too. She wanted only to kiss him, again and again, all over his body, yet she slowly lifted herself up and away from Terry. She pulled her lips in, as she took a deep breath, and tried to keep the tears from welling up in her eyes. She gently began to stroke and smooth his covered chest and pat his right arm. "You should not do ... you could hurt your arm ... and ... we can not *fattenize* with soldiers." As her words said one thing, slight, uncontrolled twitches continued in her body, as his firm hand moved from her thigh to buttock area, almost massaging the muscled firmness.

The moment could not be broken by even her slightest show of rejection, for Terry knew this was love like he'd never known before. He gently pulled her back down to him and chuckled lightly, "It's 'fraternize' love, and you're not doing it to me, I'm doing it to you, so it's OK." He kissed her again, but could feel her fear keeping her from letting her emotions go again. "What's wrong, babe?"

It never occurred to him, how he'd slid so quickly into terms of endearment. "You afraid I'm going to rape you or something?" His large hand was now cupping her firm posterior closer to him. "I think you've still got some advantage over me. Although," he glanced down at the bed, "with your cooperation, we could put something together." His laugh was filled with pure devilment, and he seriously started to figure out just how they could arrange the casts, so he would not be in pain, or bruise her with one of them. He was a clever man, and a horny determined one. He did not want to wait any longer, now that he knew how she felt for him.

"Terry, I can not do," Hanalore mumbled, as she pulled up from him. "They fire me. I have mother and brother … support. I cannot … they can not know. What I do … no job and you go back America? You wife and family … wait you. My family here … need me. I can not do." The tears were pouring from her eyes, which were filled as much with love, as they were with alarm. Hanalore pulled his arm away from her waist, stepped back and ran out of the room.

Terry laid there a bit stunned, as the validity of another world outside this one in Germany came crushing down. It took his breath away. He had not thought much about his wife or parents in the months of pain and recuperation. Hanalore had been the sole one in his focus. She was his world, as everything in it was related to her and pure loneliness without her. For weeks now, his nights had been filled with dreams of her, and him as a whole man making love to her. She helped him write the letters home, often saying kinder, more caring things than he would have thought to say. So, Hanalore should have known, they were just another routine, he rationalized, he was only going through the emotions of duty and guilt to them. How could she have thought he cared for Vera, when they had been separated over four years? She'd never been in his dreams, even in the early years and never the way Hanalore had been, even before she materialized.

Terry had married, not out of love, but at his parents insistence. It had seemed like a good idea to a twenty-year old - to have someone waiting for him to return to and the steadfast Vera had faithfully written to him every week or so. Dull though the letters were, how exciting could the ranch be with his simple family, and their even simpler life? His, in the war, had been pushed to the extreme, not lived, but fought for every minute of each day. His emotions, too, had become so taut, the ordinariness no mater how much he'd loved it, he doubted he could ever return to it with satisfaction. This was something his family, however they may try, would never be able to comprehend from the safety of a Stateside life. He had changed more than they would ever be able to accept, and they had stayed the same more than he wanted to know.

"Mere daily life existence," he mumbled, as he took a deep breath, "is unknown here, and certainly not expected." His own course of challenges to overcome, and Hanalore's depictions, gave him a relative cognizance of the average German surviving the war. Terry spoke out loud, "How can I go back? There's an excitement here, of building, … and rebuilding … a struggling nation. Something that is lost … no longer exists in America. I want to be part of this!" He swung his left fist down on his left leg, but the jar shot pain into his right one. "Ouch! Damn it! I shed my blood in this goddamn country, I want to make it right again. These are good people! They deserve a chance to make it and I want to help them." The acknowledgment of this newly found goal began to give his life a fulfillment, of a greater purpose for his part in the war and being wounded. The idea of a fated-future sent a shiver, making the nerves inside the arm-cast tingle with shock. Unconsciously, he rubbed the cast, as if to soothe them, which increased the reaction further.

Terry waited patiently the next day for Hanalore to show up in his room. He had his speech all rehearsed and refined. He felt more than anything, his sincerity would show through. It did not take long for Terry to convince Hanalore of his love for her, and also his concern for her desperate, embittered country. He told her honestly, the reason he did not love his wife or want to return to his parents and their ranch, though he was the one to inherit it. Hanalore was a bit confused, for she could not imagine someone wanting to stay in her poor, divided country filled only with rubble, ruin and heartache. "War trials soon start ... much guilt and many evil men. They shame us," she moved her arms around groping for words, "... world." What advantage could his staying possibly bring him, she questioned with her eyes and face to him, but when no answer except his love for her came, she had to believe he wanted to stay.

In the process of 'denazification' many Germans were made to attend showings of filmed Nazi atrocities. It was thought, their 'seeing would be believing." Once the program sequence was completed, even those who had been questionable before were given the needed papers to work. "All ugly people learn ... no one think Germans kind ... much pre - juice and ... and dis ...*ccrim*... *inion*." He smiled, nodded understanding she had been studying the right English words.

Hanalore pulled in her lips, and bit her teeth at her emotional frustration of not being able to express herself fully. Her English was much better, but still upset, as she felt so strongly about what the world believed all Germans had participated in and done. She was wringing her hands tightly together, using every muscle to keep from bursting into tears. He had touched a protected spot of sealed dreams. Hanalore had fantasized of leaving it all behind and starting a new life, clean and un-tattered by the repugnance of war's leftovers. She was not just looking for America to escape to, but someplace not ugly or dirty, and filled with people starving. Best of all, would be someone who loved her, as much as she loved him..

Terry could never truly comprehend how the daily grind of survival was as debilitating as his own years as a soldier. "I don't feel that way, you know that." He reached out to gently take both of her hands into his one, and brought them to his chest. "You have taught me so much about Germany and what the people went through ... are still going through." His hand moved up her arm and pulled her closer. "Besides, I only want to be close to you, and be able to touch you all the time." He struggled to lift himself up. "You have no idea how much I desire you ... I want you. I've never felt this way about any woman before. You must believe me and how much I love you." He kissed her lightly and then the passion over took them, as they lowered to the bed, her fears and hesitation melting. His touch gave her an escape to a new ethereal place - warm, beautiful and loving.

Once Hanalore was on the night shift again, Terry quickly aroused her passion to share his bed. His advance preparation of logistically figuring out their positions, enabled him to seduce her before she really knew what he was doing. Her apprehension was swept away by the physical power of the encounter and he was quite surprised she was a virgin. She did not exactly understand his enjoyment and satisfaction of the fact, but she was happy she shared it with him. She was taken aback also by her own sensations of joy at her body being so fulfilled, for she had never heard other women speak openly of sex being something to enjoy. She felt almost guilty at having been given such a unique gift and blushed whenever she thought of Terry's body and hers together. She paused often after leaving him, as the rapturing and tingling replayed the event.

The miracle of love gave power to his healing, and though torturous as it was, he plowed through the physical therapy with the sole goal of being able to walk side by side with Hanalore. In the meantime, she carefully planned each weekend for trips out of the depressing Frankfurt and into the beautiful countryside, that had been spared the cruel, precise bombings. She'd borrowed a car from a hospital friend, as Terry enlisted Army friends to get gas-ration coupons. As more tracks were repaired, they expanded to train trips further out into the country. It quickly became apparent to the staff and doctors what was going on, but they turned a deaf ear and blind eye, for Terry's recovery was happening so rapidly. It truly was love making him whole again.

Hanalore took Terry to her beloved-Heidelberg, where she'd gone to the university and spent so many happy times along the Neckar River, with the castle on the hill. With the crisp fall weather, in the bright sunshine glistening off the multi-colored trees, it could not have been a more colorful, or romantic backdrop for the lovers. Only about an hour away by car, she'd point out the lovely vineyards on the slopes of the river and teach him short phrases of German. *"Ich hab' fein Herz in Heidelberg ver loren,"* *"Mein Liebchen"* and finally, *"Ich liege dict. -* I lost my heart in Heidelberg; My love and I love you." Now, it was her turn to tease him about his pronunciation and do the translations, as she took him to her favorite haunts and little, fairy tale- like family restaurants.

He could not get enough of the *Spatzle* - noodles; *Weiner Schnitzel mis Salat -* breaded veal with salad, or his favorite, *Wurst mis Senf -* sausage with mustard. The local people, having been spared the horrors of devastation, had little animosity to the American uniform, and he being crippled, softened whatever cursing thoughts some may have harbored. To the couple, the cobblestone streets, gingerbread houses with bric-a-brac, picturesque window boxes and the wonderful aromas were all magical. They laughed and loved like there was no tomorrow, or responsibility, or accountability, but to love.

Terry was like a millionaire to Hanalore, for as his Army salary accumulated, he generously spent it on her and her family. This was heaven on Earth, a happiness even in her dreams she was not prepared to have. To celebrate Terry's graduation from crutches to a cane, Hanalore planned for them to take the boat down the Rhine, from Koblenz to Bingen to see the Lorelei Rock. She convinced the doctors to let him stay out over night. On the boat, the changing myriad of colors and sights gave each sense a renewal after the drab, heartless- ness of Frankfurt. Energy filled each breath, as the breeze tossed her blonde curls and Hanalore pointed out with glee, the highlights of the cruise in child-like English words. She emotionally told Terry the old tales of Lorelei's songs and myths that so filled the region. Sad stories, and also those with the happy endings she detailed, dramatically sprinkled with German, as he listened with love anew.

Hanalore, too, wanted to tell him her story, her happy news, but she was afraid he'd not welcome the idea of being a father. For she now knew for certain that she was carrying his child. Part of her knew, at least wanted to believe this was something that would bring him more happiness than anything else she could have given him. Her chance to share the moment passed unspoken several times, for Hanalore could only get as far as saying Terry's name, then nothing more. She glowed like Terry had never seen her before, yet his own naiveté never considered or attributed it to any other thing, than their love for each other. He'd even teased her about seeming to gain weight, and with his help for buying extra food, she must have been indulging. The country boy's inexperience made no connection between the consequences of their love-making and the natural evolution of life.

After eight o'clock that Sunday night, when they finally returned to the hospital, Terry was glad to get to his bed to rest after all of the fresh air and exercise. Hanalore tucked in and kissed the exhausted Terry, who for once had no desire for anything more. Though off-duty herself, she stopped by the nurse's station to officially check him back in. There, the older dark-haired American nurse, whose obvious jealousy of Hanalore, as she'd dealt with her many times before, was on duty. With embittered glee, she informed Hanalore Terry's transfer papers had come through.

"He can finish his physical therapy near his home and *wife* in America." She smiled so invidiously, that Hanalore pulled back, fearing the woman had become possessed by some evil spirit. "I guess it's '*Avid da sein*' for you." Her dark eyes narrowed, as she leaned toward Hanalore, like she was coming in for the kill, "And, you probably thought there was more to it than just sex." She grunted and stood back, "You're not any different than any other poor whore, except we gave you a white uniform." She turned around as Hanalore reeled and grabbed hold of the counter, to keep from falling down in a faint. It was not from the remarks, for she'd heard those before from her mother and brother, as they snatched the food from her arms, that Terry's money had bought.

Hanalore got control of herself, took a deep breath and bit hard into her lip, for her whole body became rigid. Only her eyes darted quickly, as she carefully examined the paper to see the exact date he'd be pulled away from her. Wednesday, noon: *"We have two and a half days,"* she thought. *"If I told him of the baby now, there really would not be enough time to do anything about it and he may think it was a plan to trick him."* She sucked in her lips, and took yet another deeper breath. Her hands were shaking so hard, she had to press her palms against the counter again, to steady them enough to finish reading the papers. In reality, it was common knowledge the U.S. military's policy on its soldiers marrying any German - for whatever reason - was not good then.

The pressure in her head felt as if the top would fly off and all of her brains would fall limply to the ground. She decided not to add her burden to the lonesome-cowboy from Colorado, although she knew deep in her heart that he did love her. Hanalore, always a great believer in fate, she now replayed the dramatics of her short life - perhaps this fairy tale romance was not in her destiny. Maybe the fantasy and fairy tales of the last few weeks were all she was ever going to get. This was not only as good as it would get, but that it was over. Her fairy tale was finished without a happy ending. There was only the crime of loving a married man, and punishment of it for the little German girl. Had she really believed something so beautiful could have come out of something so ugly as this war?

Hanalore looked up at the back of the matronly nurse, who was going through files, as if she was no longer standing there, and forgave her. Sometime in the past, perhaps she too, had lost a love and had been left alone. Hanalore held her head up high. Her decision had been made, and she was once again composed with strength from an unknown source. She'd managed to save a little money her mother and brother did not know about. She'd have this child of Terry's ... so she'd have him with her always. She would do that, she *could* do that. Look at all of the widows who were managing somehow. She was truly better off than them, since she had a good job. While she would have to stop working for a while, she could still return to nursing soon after their child was born. She suddenly felt sorry for Terry, for he would never know the joy of his own child, and would never have the happiness their life together could have given him. He'd talked so much about what he saw for the future of Germany, while his interest and letters about his family in America dwindled down to a resentful few. She was young, strong and filled with love and determination to see this through.

As she re-buttoned-up her ragged coat, Hanalore walked out of the hospital and hope began to flourish, as she cupped her hands under the little emerging mound on her belly. "Vera - Terry's wife - must know," she mumbled to herself. "She must sense he does not love her. He does not even say love anymore, I have to write it for him." She stopped in her tracks, as she realized out of her own guilt for being so happy, Hanalore had continued the charade of love in the letters to Vera. She'd be expecting a man who could not wait to be in her arms again. What a cruel, ironic joke Hanalore had played on herself, with no help or participation from Terry.

She stumbled home slowly, among the other straggling people, as she bumped into several, then tripped on the cracked sidewalks and over scattered broken bricks. Hanalore stopped at the darkened steps of her building, and with freshly-open eyes surveyed the abhorrent gray and black surroundings. Would she have to finally accept the hopelessness of the war's devastation? Though she was sobbing, neither her mother or brother said a word to her. The truth of lost dreams was clearly on her face. Had she just hungered too much for the illusion?

With the news, Terry was in total confusion over the euphoric prospects of being with Hanalore forever, before he stopped to consider what he needed to do to protect it all. Then, his commander was trying to understand if he'd lost his mind, while staring at him leaning on his cane. "Sergeant O'Brian, I know you've been through a lot of trauma and your war record here is exemplary …" He held up the folder, filled with glowing details of Terry's medals and the honors he had garnered, and not known what to say to the adamant soldier. He was not sure if Terry was suffering from some kind of recovery stress, or delayed battle fatigue. He had never had a man refuse to go home with his honorable discharge. He took a deep breath and continued,

"I'm sure once you get Stateside, with your wife and family, you'll want to stay there. But, if you should decide you still want to become part of the Occupation Forces, by God, we're not going to refuse a man of your caliber here. We need all the good help we can get!"

Terry hesitated telling the commander the truth, as he was afraid for Hanalore's job and any implication of her. He couldn't even say he had no interest in returning to his family, or to America either, at this time. "But, Sir, don't you see, I could save the Army all that time and money, if you'd just let me stay now." He'd broke out in a sweat at the fear off losing Hanalore, and he could feel little beads forming above his lip, as drops slid down his temple. He slipped off his hat, tucking it under his injured arm and nervously ran his left hand through his hair.

"Oh, no son, the really big brass would jump on me, like … well you just wouldn't believe it. And, if you changed your mind next week or next month, I could really…"

"No, Sir, I wouldn't change my mind." Terry had said it bit too loudly, and then regained some composure. "I know I wouldn't …" It was useless. The commander was shaking his head, the rest of the explanations as to regulations and so forth, fell to the wayside in a mumble of words lacking any cognizance to the soldier's brain and heart. Terry would have given anything to be able to kick himself, although that was almost impossible and probably quite painful. How could he have been so stupid? How would he ever tell Hanalore?

A Mona Lisa-like smile sat on Hanalore's face, as she patiently listened to Terry reiterate about his attempts to remain in Germany. Since her face had not changed in over five minutes, and she had not uttered one question or protest, he began to wonder if she did not care. The resignation Hanalore processed through her mind and body had almost systematically, as well as mysteriously, removed all her feelings for the situation. She hated the idea of being helpless, yet her secret knowledge of carrying the child of her love, somehow pacified what could have developed into anger, from all the disappointment and hurt. Stoicism was not her forte or belief, yet she would not trap, or try to hold him with the guilt of an unborn child.

Finally, with the sheer frustration mounting, Terry had to ask. "Don't you love me, Hanalore? Don't you care that I'm leaving?" He'd been leaning on his cane and now collapsed onto his bed. He could not bear the thought she could have been like the other guys had said …'just out

27

for the money, and willing to do whatever she had to for it.' He raised his voice in almost a panic, "God I hate the madness this war has done to this country!" He did not know if he was going to cry or strike out at something. Terry, the hero, had never been so out of control of any situation, or scenario in his life. It had always been steered by strategy, with a blueprint of success.

Hanalore, a little frightened by his outbursts, took several deep breaths, while squeezing her hands together for more strength. She then looked straight at the broken man, and calmly answered. " I love you … more my life … and I always love you. I can … not … stop you … leave me." She looked down, as she pulled in her lips and stiffened her body to keep from crying. She'd sworn to herself he would not see her cry, and she'd never consider begging him to stay, by revealing about the baby. She tightly held her cold hands together, pressed against her little belly, as if protecting the child from the scene, like a girl before her chastising-father.

Terry grabbed her to him, but she pulled back as the curtains were not around the bed and his door was open, as required. "No, doctor see us … I can not." He wanted so badly to believe her words, yet there was something in her demeanor, a hidden behavior that seemed to say she was faking the emotion or hiding something. It must be him, with his scrambled brains and feelings. Perhaps this was her way of controlling the shock of them being separated. In his frustration, he pounded the pillow, but knew this was due to his own ineptitude with the circumstances. He should have gotten a divorce, as soon as he knew she loved him.

"As soon as I get home, I'll get a divorce and sign back up to come over here. We'll get married and then we can be together." Hanalore at last smiled directly at him, and into his eyes. It sounded perfect, there was a glimmer of hope, a last chance for being saved, just like the happy fairy tales she always wanted to live. She wanted to believe, for she knew he meant it. She swallowed hard and kept the smiled pasted on her face. She must not give up faith, she deserved a little happiness.

Hanalore Frederick was still a survivor. She told herself she had overcome the war, famine, and marauding soldiers, so she would persevere and come through Terry's leaving. She stood at the far end of the air field where she could get access, and clutched the wire fence with her strong, little hands. In the distance, she saw the soldiers lined- up and waiting to board the military aircraft. Slowly, Terry hobbled up the stairs with his cane, stopping at the door to search into the direction where Hanalore said she'd be. He carefully balanced himself and gave a strong wave, then threw a kiss. Her hands spread and pressed against the metal in response to catching it, and pushed her face hard into the fence. The sobs dumped out and drained all of her stout strength, until she slid down to the ground into a fetal lump.

* * * * * *

At first, the letters came every few days, and were filled with glowing love and optimism about their soon being together once again. By this time, he had filed the return paperwork and the military processing machine was chugging slowly forward. His main requirement for them was to be fully released from his physical therapy, and one hundred percent physically ready to go back. Terry told Vera he wanted a divorce, yet she was resolute, saying she understood, for the doctors had warned her, his being through so much trauma, he'd need time to work things out. She steadfastly traveled the thirty-mile round trip to the clinic daily, to encourage him in his physical therapy. He'd insisted on staying at the Veteran's hospital, rather than being at the ranch with her and his family. He needed the space to keep himself focused on just getting back to Hanalore and Germany for his new life.

Then, three days before Terry was due to be released from the medical leave and reinstated under his new status, the gods of fate played another nasty trick on him. His father suddenly died of a massive heart attack. Terry had no choice, but to take over the ranch as the deeply embedded responsibility to his family kicked in. His next younger brother had decided to make the Army Air Force his career, so had stayed with the Occupation Forces in Japan. His next youngest brother had just begun college, and his sister was still in high school. Terry was the only one *available* to support the family, by keeping the ranch going.

Though his last letter, said someday he hoped to return to Germany, Hanalore no longer let disillusioned airy-fairy tale hopes ensconce her. She did not have to read between the lines to know she'd never see him again, One of the things she had admired about him was his loyalty and responsibility to those he loved. She celebrated her twentieth birthday without him, but looked forward to the new year when she'd have their child to share it all with. Hanalore gently caressed her burgeoning tummy with her small, wiry hands. She closed her eyes, as the memories lapped back into her mind.

Whenever she was swept away by the memory of them together, it came first as waves building into a crescendo that tingled her skin and put a smile on her face. She glowed. floated and swooned until they crashed resoundingly in her ears, or dissipated with a collapse, like they had never existed. Tears welled up, and slowly pushed their way out of her tightly closed eyes. No matter how they flooded out, they couldn't fill the vacuum left by Terry. All she had left was the salt from the tears, and its bitter taste, as she bit hard into her lips. She would not live happily ever after, her love was gone.

Hanalore had been able to get home-care nursing jobs with referrals from the hospital, yet they were not the steady income she previously had. In a surprise act of kindness, her brother Helmont, got a part-time job. He then stood up for her, when their mother insisted Hanalore move out because of the shame she'd brought the family.

The U.S. Army set up tent cities for the homeless, though luckier Germans had taken over burned-out railway cars, trams and autos. Hanalore panicked, fearing she'd have to raise her child in the squalor and deprivation she knew would continue for years. She preferred to swallow her pride, along with her mother's rejection, to keep a clean room in her life. What she would do once the baby came, she did not even want to think about, as coping with it all daily, stretched her limits of physical endurance. Yet, each night she talked soothingly to the child within of the love from her, and from its absent father.

The bright Spring flowers blessed the senses when Hanalore went into labor. She carried with her, mental escapes to how Terry could have given their child so much more than just money, for she knew he would have wanted it. Through the haze of pain and drugs, Hanalore heard the doctor say, "Well, well Miss Frederick, you surprised me! You've got another one hidden up in there!" Then quieter he said, "Nurse, we need to get that baby out of there, before it loses any more oxygen." With one more final push, Hanalore passed- out from exhaustion. She was gently nudged awake, as the cleaned and wrapped baby was placed in her waiting arms, then wheeled into the ward room. She smiled at her beautiful, blue-eyed daughter, and delicately recognized those features she was certain were Terry's. Hanalore decided to name her Lorelei, so she'd always be a symbol of their happiest memories.

The kindly-looking American doctor came to her bed and pulled the curtain around it. With a hesitant look on his face he spoke softly. "Miss Frederick, your son is having a little difficulty, as he was stuck in your birth canal … but I'm sure he's going to be fine. Now, you relax and get some rest … that was some workout you had in there. I only wish … we'd known you were having twins. I'll see you later. Let me know what you've named them." He exited as quickly as he had entered, never knowing the joy and sorrow he bequeathed her.

Hanalore lay stunned on her bed and held Lorelei closer. It was not just a figment of the drugs, she'd really had another child, a son. She whispered in German close to Lorelei's face. "Oh, you have a brother to keep you company, play with and share life. And, as you are like me, then he must be like his father." She smiled with delight, feeling she had reincarnated Terry, and he would be with her always. "What shall we name him? Helmut? Dieter? Franz? His father's name is much too American. People will know his father is gone."

As quickly as the euphoria had come, it dissipated. Hanalore looked out the window at all the blooming flowers that had so recently given her faith in new life. "What shall we do little one? You, ... anyone would love to take care of, beautiful you. You are easy, you are only one little one. Who will help me with two? How can I ever manage with two?" She squeezed Lorelei up to her, until the infant began to squirm from the pressure. "And, I cannot separate you. You are twins, connected from birth. It would be a curse forever, if you were separated." Hanalore began to rock back and forth, as she wept desperately into her daughter's face. "Oh, God! What will I do? What will happen to my babies? Oh, Terry how could you have left me when I needed you ... when your son and daughter needed you?" Pent-up anger and hurt flooded her for days.

* * * * * *

Captain Frank Williams, oldest of seven children, had been orphaned before his thirteenth birthday. His mother, also orphaned at two and raised in an orphanage, did not hesitate to make arrangements after her husband died of pneumonia, to have the children placed in one, since she knew she was dying of cancer. Though several relatives offered to take one or two of the four brothers and three sisters, she did not want them separated. In later years, Frank would speak very highly of her and the orphanage, which kept his brothers and sisters together. He believed they had stayed close and still considered themselves to be a family. Their *home*, as he would refer to it, was St. Vincent's in Philadelphia. Originally founded for the care of German orphans, who had saturated that area of town in 1855.

Frank was also strongly influenced by the strict Catholic sisters, and though they were always concerned for the children, there were few displays of physical affection or love. Emotions were felt more inside than expressed or demonstrated, yet he never believed he had lacked for love. Once Frank finished high school at St. Vincent's, he became a theological student at St. Francis. Then, after graduating he decided against the seminary and joined the Army. The structured discipline and camaraderie, he believed it held, was a family.

In all honesty, Frank could judge himself not to be an outstanding man in physical looks or happy personality. His straight, brown hair was not a distinctive feature, nor his soft, plain face set upon his slight frame and short stature. His only real pride could be in his educational accomplishments. Yet, he did not just succumb to authority, he required it, for he was truly an insecure, indecisive man.

There was a security in the military, vaguely like a never-ending family, but more with clothes, shelter and a set regimentation for all things, he thought. Most importantly, he'd never be alone, but he also always needed to do good, and share his knowledge.

If the rules were followed, Frank rationalized, he would be rewarded with a life where problems had prescribed solutions laid out. One only needs to learn the boundaries and limitations, he propounded, and one can live easily within them. He would have no fear dealing with the unknown, he believed, since historically the military had experience in all fields. And, most importantly, he told himself, they had written the rule books to cover all of life in the military, if not outside.

To the military's advantage, Frank had learned early not to question what those in authority decided - mother and the nuns had never been wrong. Besides, if he had become a priest, he would have had to deal with people on a personal basis, and help them make decisions regarding feelings or emotions not prescribed clearly in the Bible. Yes, he concluded, but not in a sacrilegious way, of course, the military had a much better rule book for life.

First, Frank was in the Signal Corps School and then sent to Panama. It was exciting being in a foreign country, for a quiet man with no personal knowledge of other distinct cultures. Living in the military compound limited his experiences with the common citizen or daily societal life, but the filtered existence was sufficient for the easily impressed man. Although, needing glasses from all of the voracious reading, Frank took up boxing with the unique idea it would break him out of his introverted attitudes. Unfortunately, the malaria he contracted put him out of commission in more ways than sports - he was left sterile.

With the outbreak of World War II, Frank signed up for Flight School and transferred to the Army Air Corps with his training at Scott Field in Illinois. No problems with the stringent studies, but his eyesight eliminated him from becoming a pilot. He felt the experience was successful when he married the shy and sensitive Charlotte, a divorcee with a daughter. It meant a lot to Frank to have the opportunity to raise the child as his own, though she was already in grade school. Frank never did see action during the war, as the military seemed to prefer to send him from one training school to another. The military's generosity in feeding his quest for knowledge constantly reaffirmed to him his wise choice of careers. First, there was Officer Candidate School, then in 1943 he was sent out to the Presidio, in San Francisco, to learn Chinese. A true scholar at heart, Frank found his niche with Chinese, as no language or culture could have consumed him more, as its contents were practically endless. People could, and did, spend a lifetime studying the ancient, convoluted-beliefs of the Far East, only to become more mesmerized. The culture became an opiate for his mind, while he delved in trying to comprehend Asia through his books.

So, Frank was quite disappointed when at war's end, the military saw fit to send him, not to China, but to Germany. He and Charlotte arrived in Frankfort in the late Spring of 1946 and had their first taste of war. Without having experienced the full thrust of battle, the resulting destructive power and its desolation in the aftermath, was overwhelming, even depressing. And, especially so for Charlotte, as her daughter had to remain with her parents back in Illinois, since there was no adequate English school for her age group. Being small, yet slightly plumpish, she appeared more matronly for her years. Thus, many of the military wives were surprised by her fragile feelings and nervous reactions in dealing with the unknown, strange environment. Charlotte's small dark eyes seemed as tightly wound up, as her short, brown curled-hair. Those eyes appeared to pop-out of her face when startled, like a mouse watching for danger in every movement around her. Though the army encourage having domestic help to feed the local economy, Charlotte could not adjust to having people around doing things for her. Yet, she never could get the hang of the gas heaters or dealing with the market for food, or other daily necessities.

Frank busied himself with the requirements of the Occupation troops. And, Charlotte turned over the running of the apartment to their help, to occupy her time with daily volunteering at the local hospital, visiting the American soldiers and helping the staff. The writing of letters, fluffing pillows and trying to make small talk was eventually not fulfilling her nurturing needs. So, she jumped at the opportunity when she learned of the military-sponsored orphanage. Though it was not officially recognized or directly supported, for the Allied governments had no intention of admitting the *guilt* of their over-zealous men in uniform, it was readily acknowledged these were their children. The tugs of motherhood began to pull on her, not only for the lack of having her own daughter to care for, but acknowledging she truly desired to have more children. She never wanted to admit the embarrassment to family or friends that Frank was sterile, so she quickly saw this as a safe way to have pregnancy, birth and a family. With time and distance to cover her story, she could present an adopted child as their own.

Once Charlotte proposed the idea to Frank, he gave his full support, for he knew the realities of orphanage life, though fed and adequately clothed, there was nothing like a personal family. Charlotte spent her days surveying the children while she cleaned, fed and played with them. There were many children to choose from, but she could not decide on which one would make their family *perfect*. She knew most men wanted to have the pride of a son to raise, yet she had so loved the joys of a daughter. By the end of the summer, her dilemma was instantly settled.

Charlotte watched as the young, blonde German woman came in with the two bundles in her arms. She'd gone to assist with the babies, as another woman handled the paperwork. Charlotte could not help overhearing the story, told in a combination of German and English, through the heavy crying. Being older and a mother herself, Charlotte could have soothed Hanalore with sone kind reassurances, for she'd left a daughter behind, if only temporarily. But, the quiet woman was without reservations, self-centered in her search for a family, and her own needs.

Charlotte slowly open the first blanket, as the feisty arms and legs were kicking up a storm from being restrained. She could tell immediately, this curly blonde baby was quite a bouncing girl. The bright blue eyes, that had been on the verge of fussing, showed a slight smile. "Oh, you must be about three months old, aren't you?" She lifted Lorelei out of the cover, placing her on her shoulder, and turned to the other bundle that was more passive. Yet, the dark eyes were wide-awake, searching for something familiar to attach to. Charlotte leaned and whispered, "Well, I know who you're like ... my Frank with all of his contemplative moods and deep concentration." Dieter turned his head to the new voice that seemed to be talking to him.

Hanalore was still in tears, as she began to beg the register not to separate the twins. "Please, if not want both, I come back ... take back. They can not separate, they twins, they must together ... always." Hanalore grabbed the nurse's hand pleading. "I beg you, please ... American family, so live in America and know happy, good life. The father a good ... American, he ... he ... love them."

Charlotte never looked directly at the sobbing Hanalore, listening to her pain was enough. She did not want to see it, nor let it distract from her own joy. She knew Frank would not question her judgment. Besides, if they did not take them, who would or could? It was basically the military families, and especially the American ones, who had adequate food, as well as the housing and money to support two, new babies at this time.

It took only a few weeks for the twins' paperwork to go through, unlike Terry's previous struggle almost a year before. The military may not prevent a problem, but they could correct it. In the meantime, Charlotte spent every moment at the nursery exclusively with 'her' twins. They moved them to the big, new house once Frank had their room ready, and all the necessary accouterments were put into place. He could not have been happier himself with how it had all worked out. The military had truly given him a family.

All was set once Frank had them Christened at the Catholic church, and their new *Christian* names of Paula and Peter officially registered on the new birth certificates. Charlotte's own personal statement was made when she sent the birth announcements out to all of their friends and family in the States. To authenticate it, she added a small note saying she'd been pregnant before their sailing over, and the trip had been quite difficult for her. Frank never said a word to her, for he avoided confrontation at all costs, though he'd planned to tell his family the truth once they returned to America.

The empty nest now full, if not brimming over, and Charlotte devoted herself to the twins, Paula and Peter. Though Frank got her a nanny to help, Charlotte seemed to be drained by the constant care the two needed. She began to wonder how the young German mother had ever thought she could have done this by herself. In just a few months, the twins grew before her eyes as Paula's quickness, and more affable character became obvious when compared to Peter. Perhaps on his own, it would not have been so noticeable, but Paula did everything before the average child would have. Charlotte began to be obsessed with Peter's slowness in responding, "I know that child isn't right Frank, and that German woman probably knew it, too. That's why she wanted to get rid of them."

Frank adored Peter and could not believe Charlotte would feel as if she'd been swindled or cheated-out of her *perfect* family. Finally, he got the military pediatrician to trace down the history of Peter. He tried to calmly tell her, "Apparently, there was a delay in the birth canal, as they didn't know she was having twins. It caused a lack of oxygen to the brain, and Peter is *slightly* retarded."

The doctor gave reassurance the child still fell in the *average* range for education and physical development, but nothing could soothe Charlotte. "If you will just love him and be patient with him, he will be as normal, as any other child." To a woman with such anxiety over even the mundane things, something that would take extra effort seemed beyond her ability. It was as if she were ready to give up on Peter's life without even trying. She was now their mother, and didn't want people to think *she* had created a defect.

By the time Frank got home one evening, Charlotte had already had several drinks and was pacing the floor while yelling at the crying Peter in her arms. "Our hoped for family, was not meant to be," she ranted and lifted the baby up in utter disappointment. Before Frank could reach her, she'd thrown him down and collapsed herself. Once Frank examined Peter and had the housekeeper tuck him into bed, he tried to tend to Charlotte, thinking she'd merely fainted or passed out from her drinking. When he was not able to rouse her with cold water to her face, he called for the ambulance. This was not the way it was all supposed to go. Their plans for Thanksgiving had already been made and Frank looked forward with great anticipation to their first family Christmas.

Not until Charlotte's second week in the hospital, did the doctors finally discover what was wrong with her. They lamely told Frank she had bone cancer and absolutely nothing they could do for her there. "There's one military hospital in Texas, it's done some work in this area since the atomic bomb, but I've no idea what their success rate it." Frank was crushed and now desolate. Where was his God? Where was his rule book now? He'd asked for so little out of life, and never refused what other people wanted him to do. He'd only hoped to have a family he could be happy and all loving together. A simple man, whose life seemed to get complicated around him without any answers, as he didn't know what questions to ask.

When truly necessary, the military could react quickly. Thanksgiving was spent in Texas and Christmas in Illinois with Charlotte's family, so she might have her last days surrounded by those she loved. By the end of January, she was gone with Frank totally lost. What was he to do with the twins he'd come to love so much? He could not have gone on himself, if it had not been for Charlotte's parents - big, heavy-set Elsie and short, wiry Cliff.

They took over like country-people do, for they had been through hard times on the farm, so knew how to handle whatever came their way. Elsie would gather the twins into her generous, buxom- bosom, the softness alone made the twins feel safe and protected, like a well-worn, down comforter. The military gave Frank a year to recuperate, while stationed once again at Scott Field. With warmer weather, he took the twins to visit his brothers and sisters, who were still in the Pennsylvania and New Jersey area.

By the Spring of 1948, Frank got his next traveling papers. He was to stop off in California for a crash course in Japanese, for he was being sent to Japan to work with the Occupation forces there. Frank made a slight protest, saying his fluency was in Chinese, but the military felt the civil war going on in China was out of bounds for someone who had never seen battle. Besides, they rationalized, all those languages and people are basically the same - Chinese, Japanese. What difference did it matter where they sent him. Resolving to accept the assignment, Frank decided to at least ask if they knew anything about where he was going to be sent - Tokyo? Okinawa? "Nagoya," the officer replied, "the best kept secret in Japan. It was the industrial base during the war, where they made all them 'Zeros.' And, we just want to make sure they don't decide to make any more there …got it?" Frank returned home trying to be happy about the new assignment. At least he was going to go to the Far East - the Orient - the land of mystery and hidden secrets. Cliff and Elsie could only concur with whatever Frank and the Army had in store. They were more than happy to keep the darling twins for as long as they were needed to do so. While Paula raced around the house into everything, Peter quietly spent time with the gentle pets, still talking his own version of baby talk. Cliff and Elsie had the time and patience to give them both all the love and attention they needed. Charlotte's daughter Mary, now in junior high school, was gone most of the day, but would occasionally spend time with Paula. It was a simple, happy life without real strife.

That evening after dinner, Frank dug through some old boxes of books, until he found the few he had on Japan. Yes, the kanji based characters of Chinese would help him to learn, but the pronunciations and sentence structures of the two languages had nothing in common. He tried to think of it as a new learning adventure, and then he remembered the rapidly growing twins. Hopefully, he would be able to have them join him soon, and maybe he could even find a mother for them once again. "Growing up and living in another culture would be an *opportunity* they should *not* be deprived of," he soundly announced to himself. Frank reassured himself, once again the military always did the right thing for him. He returned to his books for solace. The Far East had been his secret dream. Now, he was truly going to have *his dreams* come true.

To Occupied Japan:
Chapter 2 Survival of the Savviest

Westerners think in terms of black or white - like a suitcase, defined and limited. Eastern logic is like the *furoshiki,* the cloth the Japanese carry for wrapping all sorts of things. It can be large or small according to needs, and afterward can be folded up and put in the pocket. Within almost every Japanese, metaphysical intuition and instinctive animalistic urges lie side by side

- from Buddhism. That's why they can brutalize their philosophy and philosophize their brutality.

John Toland,
Occupation

Lafcadio Hearn and His Contagious Syndrome

Lafcadio Hearn was born in Greece of a Greek mother and Irish father, so technically he was a British citizen. He was living in New Orleans when he first learned about Japan and to fulfill his life-long fascination with the exotic, he felt he must go there. So, in 1890, he went to Japan and was so readily satisfied with it, he married a Japanese woman, took a Japanese name and became a naturalized Japanese citizen. Sadly, Hearn liked the old Japan more than the Japanese did. Japan was modernizing at a rate so rapid, one could say in today's terms, they pushed the 'fast-forward' button and it stuck. He became extremely distressed at the destruction of Japan's traditional culture, as to him it was thrown off like an old rag.

He gushed in a letter to a friend after he had settled-in, "I love their gods (meaning Shintoism, with eight million gods), their customs, their dress, their bird-like quavering songs, their houses, their superstitions, their faults. We are the barbarians! I do not merely think these things; I am as sure of them as death. I only wish I could be reincarnated as some little Japanese baby, so that I could see and feel the world as beautifully as a Japanese brain does."

Unfortunately, although he lived in Japan the rest of his life, Hearn was doomed to frustration. The more he saw Japan 'Westernize' in dress, architecture, and spirit, the more depressed he became. He arrived in love with a Japan not only fast disappearing, but may never have existed in the first place. The Lafcadio Hearn Syndrome was by no means a thing of only the past Meiji era, but a continuance for those who believed, or just wanted to believe in a more romantic, mysterious, or exotic place *than where they were raised.*

Swashbuckling life styles, whether they be of King Arthur's Court, Robin Hood, the gun-toting cowboys of the old American West, or Samurai, were what some people preferred. They would rather live vicariously, in the past or otherwise, than in their own time. In 1894, Hearn wrote to a friend asking, "What is there, after all, to love in Japan except what is passing away?"

Nagoya - A Historical Perspective:

With great acerbity, it has been said, "Nagoya is to Japan, what Japan is to the world." For Nagoya is known to be an incredibly closed, uniquely provincial metropolis. Those in the know, acknowledge that the real *old* money of Japan is held by conservative Nagoyans, who maintain the highest savings rate in Japan. They are said to be much tighter with their money, do not follow the costly fashion trends, or buy the newest designer product - except when it comes to their extravagant weddings. Nagoyans, also it is said, rarely attempt to become friends with Japanese from other areas. They have formed a society of their own, in which they maintain both a superiority and an inferiority complex toward people from other regions of Japan. Their attitude is therefore analogous to that which Japanese people have to the rest of the world, or so other critics say. They are more cautious than the mixed heritage groups of Tokyo, and portray more often the ambiguous, indecisive 'wait-and-see' attitude. One can only imagine, if they are unaccepting of Japanese outsiders how they would be to actual non-Japanese - the gaijin.

A *Nagoya* Family, perhaps typical:

Early in January, 1926 - a birth year which was shared half way around the world with a German girl named Hanalore - a daughter was born in Yokkaichi, a smaller industrial city southwest of Nagoya. Sakiko was not to be raised or named by her birth mother, but by her father's brother Seiichi ad his wife Haruko. The childless couple had been promised the infant, regardless of its sex, and they were happy just to have a child. Poverty in the birth family was not the cause of the give-away, but obligation to share what they were able to have so easily, one after another. The practice of in-family adoption was quite common to *save-face* (a primary issue in Japan). Those who could not produce even one child, were looked down upon as not being supportive of the Emperor's growing empire. Often the husband was strongly urged to be rid of the wife who could not produce at least a daughter, if not a son. Male-based infertility was not considered.

In many ways, this was a more humane practice, to pass these children of prolific families on to relatives lacking in such, rather than sell them to the child broker to be used as indentured slaves or prostitutes. Though infanticide was another application assisting many overburdened families during these drastic and backward times, the strongest among them did not have the barbarity for it, and had to pay to have it done. In China, the outskirts of most cities had fenced pits with appropriate sized-holes, or in rural areas with deep ravines at crossroads, was where the unwanted babies could be tossed. This was their belief of what was expressed in Buddhism for reincarnation, but stretched a little to accommodate the circumstances. Both Japanese and Chinese wanted to believe that by returning the soul quickly, it would have another chance of a better family placement in a new life.

The late 1920s were not the best of times, financially or politically, yet no one wanted to consider that it would get worse. The cities tried bravely to march forward into the Westernized Twentieth Century with strong statements, and sometimes practices of Democracy. On the other hand, the Japanese in the small cities, towns and villages still had at least one foot stuck in the Seventeenth Century
- the Gold Era of the Samurai and Shoguns. They were pulled down and back by all the shackles attached to their feudal past, where the lines of one's heritage, birthright, and sex were clearly marked.

When Sakiko started middle school in Nagoya, where her 'parents' lived, she found out she was adopted, because a birth certificate was needed for registering. Being an only child, her family had always visited with the other children, whom she thought were her cousins. The fact they all looked so much a like, and her age fit into the sequence, never dawned on her child's mind. The fun of the visits to Yokkaichi, for they had the room for the numerous running feet, was her only concern. Sakiko's proud, adopted mother Haruko, said nothing to explain the situation, yet she did not hide it once the secret was revealed. The country neighbors paid no attention, but constant comments in the Nagoya neighborhood which had been, still were.

It was the Japanese way, after all, *not* to explain, what was felt not necessary to talk about. So, Sakiko was expected to accept the situation as it was, without explanation, reason or cause. *"Shikata ganai"* or *"Shogan'nai"* - "Don't question, that's how it is." - "There is nothing one can do about it, that is how it is." Sakiko could feel the secretiveness of it and thus, interpreted it as something to be ashamed of, or embarrassed by. So, she definitely did not discuss the topic with her 'cousins' or anyone else. At all cost to personal peace of mind, or mere curiosity, one did not want to be the topic of gossip, derision, or social ostracism, simply because her parents had not been able to produce an offspring of they own for the Emperor. The good little girl adapted and accepted.

As Sakiko grew, the neighbors continued to comment, with snide remarks just barely audible. "It's a strange family that has but one child." "And, that one came along so late in life!" Or, those in the know, "The husband's brother produced eight of them in profusion." She held her head high while building her protective insulation on survival instinct. Sakiko's birth mother never gave a hint by interfering with any decision regarding her schooling, discipline, or other guidelines of parenting. She also never acquired the habit of over- reacting to the normal number of falls, scrapes, or accidents Sakiko might have in the course of play with the others. All feelings and emotions were controlled in the true stoic Japanese way.

Sakiko had been promised before she was conceived, therefore Seiichi and Haruko became her 'parents' when she was six months old. This period of time to reveal, if she was sickly or weak. Sakiko never felt like an only child, since most weekends and vacations were spent with the cousins, as more fun in numbers. In the summertime, the water storage pond from the family's factory was turned into a swimming pool, and the meals were more like a party. Her own parents were kept quite busy with their factory and could not spend much active time with her. Neither set of parents talked about the military's action in China or Asia openly in front of the children, for as long as it did not affect them or their business directly, it was none of their concern - *"shikata ganai."*

Sakiko carried an aura for hiding a secret, so became closed in and private. This reticence made the other children of her junior and high school years more taunting of her. Guarding what she felt was an embarrassment, and made her a vulnerable victim of the common and accepted practices of the bullies (it was thought to make the child stronger). She wanted to show 'them' all, those in her mind, who looked down on her, or ridiculed her transplanted roots.

"I'll show them all! Someday, I'll be a woman of distinction, rank and someday a lady of style." While the taunting and rejection may have made others weak, in her it did create a burning goal. "I'll rise above them, I'll find a way, whatever paths are necessary to not only survive, but succeed!" Her dream was that *'they'* would someday envy her, whom they had once put down. There was no charming softness or demure behavior to this young girl, she was sharpening a steel-hardened soul, which would make any famous Japanese sword- maker proud.

* * * * * *

The Japanese government tried to cushion the shock of the deprivation and hardships brought on by the war - a series of wars actually, which started in 1894, flared again in the late 1920s and went full-blown in 1937 - by assuring their people that they were part of something historic, and pledging them a lot of 'pie-in-the-sky' success. They were told that, "Standing between the past and the future, they were the custodians of a great tradition, a great trust." The unquestioning belief of this conservative populace in filial piety was used by the government to manipulate the people into doing what they wanted. Then even proclaimed this was a way of discharging their traditional debt to their ancestors, by building a greater Japan to hand on to posterity, and their children would then revere them. It could only be done through blood, sacrifice, and loyalty. Everyone must give their all, and to die for the Emperor was the most honorable thing of all.

Nagoya people, like most of Japan, were not in a position to judge anything with the lack of information, or international media. They only had Japanese newspapers and radio to tell them about Pearl Harbor, so they did not know all the details, or why it had happened. When an American ship was sunk, it was built up into this great, glorious, "Aren't we doing well?" thing. If a Japanese ship was sunk, if mentioned, it was as insignificant as possible. Many Japanese were quite shocked about taking on America, while they had accepted the invasions in Asia. The majority were taken in by the radio, as they listened and cheered it. Those Japanese who were opposed to the war with America could not say anything because if they did they would be arrested, or punished in some other way by the government.

In Nagoya, there were some people who had put out some newsletters against the war, but the government quickly put a stop to it. Everybody had confused feelings, there were those who knew about the anti-war propaganda, but would look the other way, and those who desperately wanted to speak out, but they feared for themselves and family to do so. Generally, everybody was quite confused, wanting to believe that the Emperor was leading them correctly.

No age was exempt form the war effort, as students began to raise vegetables on their campuses, or were sent to help farmers in the fields for weeks at a time. Others had to collect scrap materials, others used tea leaves to feed the army horses, visit the wounded in hospitals and make utility kits for the fighting soldiers. The sacrifices increased as the war situation worsened. By this time, Sakiko was seventeen and the annual school field trip for seniors had been canceled. Of course disappointing, but not to be complained about for many students had it far worse than her, having to work in factories. Sakiko had done well in her business courses, so was able to get a minor bookkeeping job at the *Meietsu* Railway Company headquarters in Nagoya.

She liked it was a clean job, where she could wear nice clothes and not get her hands dirty, or sweat alongside others on noisy machinery. These things were important to Sakiko. She was zealous in her diligence to keep the tedious, minutely detailed job, for she never wanted to be classified with other, common Japanese. She knew she was different, and would be even more unique as time would come. She was surely determined about that, as it was her one fixed goal. In a country, probably more homogeneous and controlled than any other so exposed to Western ideas, ideals and products, she wanted to stand out. She might not be able tot change her basic Japanese looks, but she could change just about everything else, and planned to do so.

By October, 1943, the government requisitioned home radiators, chandeliers, gallery rails, and any steel objects from the schools for military purposes. People, particularly women, had to spend long hours in queues for food and other household necessities. They had few pans left to cook in or with, as their homes had been stripped of any metal objects. Sakiko would not waste time worrying about these household things, they were her mother's concern and all mostly contained within the house and family. What frustrated her was not having enough of the right makeup, clothes and especially shoes to present the perfect picture that she had painted for herself, and the image she created for other people. She needed them to notice her, and most of all, too envy her. Others had so little, but she still needed to have more, and have it show.

In the following months, all high school graduating classes were required to work full time at the military factories. within six months the next younger group, until eventually all high school students had to do factory work and struggle side by side with the older, stronger men and women. By late 1944, the government ordered all schools, which by that time were cut down to only a fraction of their attendance size, to make available to the Army and Navy all unused buildings and equipment. Particularly in Nagoya, all sorts of munitions factories making parts, ammunition or whatever necessary, were moved into campus buildings.

The government had many older people, or those not directly involved in the war, do drills with bamboo spears in case the Americans actually invaded. They had various activities to raise morale and they created a kind of atmosphere where the people felt they would be able to bring down a plane with just their bamboo spears. They had these practices at school as well. The whole purpose of these exercises was, that they could at least feel positive about their defense, but it was soon all in vain.

The reality of the air raids began to destroy people's hopes, and see how foolish to think bamboo spears could stop the bombs, much less the planes. They had heard about the air raids in Tokyo and Osaka, but it was not until they began in Nagoya, they knew the fruitlessness and lost hope of it all. The people were quickly worn down, as the air raids were soon day and night. The sirens were a constant thing, and would say the direction of the on-coming planes. Some families would run and hide in makeshift air raid shelters, which were no more than dug-out holes in the ground. They had trained for this over a period of time, so they thought they were prepared, and knew what to do.

Sakiko clung onto her job with Meitetsu all through the war. When her parents' house and factory were bombed out in early May, 1945, they had to move in with the relatives in Yokkaichi. Daily, Sakiko then made the long, dangerous train trek into Nagoya. Haruko and Seiichi had lost everything - their home, factory, and all of their belongings. They were able to move into the old storage space above the factory of Seiichi's brother in

Yokkaichi. For Haruko, it was a tremendous blow to her ego, for she had always felt her in-laws were such country-bumpkins. Her husband had been much more successful than his younger brother, whose large family was his main asset.

Haruko felt disgraced at having to come to them once again for a handout, though this time it was for shelter, not a child. Seiichi, on the other hand, put his failure where it belonged - on the war - and did not hesitate to join his brother in his business, which had become short-handed with the circumstances. To her in-laws, Haruko presented condescending gratitude, excessive apologies for the inconvenience, and constant deferring to her husband in the most perfect way of the Japanese wife. Yet, in their quarters above the factory, the realties of the situation did not slow down Haruko's whining for things the way they had been, and griping about their fate. She had little appreciation for their survival and shelter, while eighty- nine percent of Nagoya was destroyed and tens of thousands of people were killed.

The family was startled awake at four-thirty in the morning, as the workers came in below and turned on the machinery for the day's work. Sakiko had thought it was an earthquake, but soon became accustomed to the horrendous noise that shook the little wooden building. They each had to learn to eat sweet potatoes at every meal, as more readily available than the precious rice, or other staples.

Rice became the country person's money, for it could be bartered for all of the other goods that were so scarce and needed for every day life. Haruko soon befriended the man in charge of her brother-in-lawn's rice mill, and gave him little trinkets she had rescued from their former home. In turn, he gave her the daily scrapings from the rice machine after he cleaned it. It was not enough for the three of them, but she would mix it with a sweet potato, or other vegetables - a meal prior to the war she would never have served.

Sakiko's 'cousin' had given her a new pair of *getas* - wooden clogs, the family had just gotten in trade for some rice. She felt since Sakiko went into work each day in Nagoya, she needed to have a more presentable pair to wear. When Sakiko's birth mother saw them on her feet, and knowing how she was about looking stylish disregarding the times, she accused her of stealing them out of the storage. It was a crushing blow to Sakiko's heart, as if she had been her niece and not truly her daughter. She could not have imagined the woman being so cold and hardhearted about such a basic item. The war had elevated the value of simple, common things to be hoarded. Sometimes, Sakiko could not block out the affects the war had on her.

On May 14, 1945, a strong psychological blow fell, as Nagoya Castle was bombed. This, according to the pilots who fly the planes, was a *mistake* (cultural assets were to be spared) as they were aiming for City Hall, less than a kilometer away. A partially, cloudy day and they had only been told it was a large building with tiled, Oriental- style roofs and golden decorations on top. The Japanese, on the other hand, were convinced the City Hall building was saved because it had already been designated as the headquarters for the new American government. The citizens not only had greater insight, but were truly giving their enemy more credit than they were due. No one in Washington, nor the Pacific, had any idea the war would end in three, short months. The Allies had predicted December or January, at the very earliest. They had no idea how stripped and drained of everything Japan had become, especially metal, fuel and food. The Japanese people were also just worn-out from over ten years of constant deprivation for military efforts on the various fronts in which they were fighting.

Meitetsu decided to move their offices to Narumi, a suburb south of Nagoya, as that area had so far not been a target for the B-29s. This almost doubled Sakiko's train travel, for she now had to go forty-five minutes into Nagoya Station, then transfer for another twenty minute ride to Narumi. As the summer progressed, the American bombing expanded to more during the day, as little anti-aircraft fire to prevent them from completing their assigned mission.

The initial psychological affect was perhaps as great as the physical results, for many of the Japanese were paralyzed in not knowing what to do. In their home, they could run to the neighborhood shelters, but at their jobs there were few air raid shelters large enough for the numbers of people crowding in to escape from the devastation. Nagoya had not yet built their underground subways, the usual protector of city dwellers. As most people lived outside of the city, it had not been a concern to the city fathers.

For others caught in their cars, trucks, or electric trolleys, more people were injured from veering off, or jumping out to avoid the bombs, than from the actual bombs themselves. But, the most vulnerable, trapped, and frozen in place, were the passengers on the trains. The commuter trains moved too fast to jump from, yet worse their method of movement tied them to a set path. Day after day, Sakiko took fate in her hands, as she challenged the odds of her train becoming the target of some B-29 pilot. It really was a crap-shoot for those sporting, as the choice of the support fighter-pilots who strafed the passengers commuting in the mornings, for they knew the difference between military troop-carriers and ammunition freight train. Granted, the tracks were also targets of the bombs, simply because of what they were used for. Yet, the Allies were well aware millions of civilian Japanese traveled on trains to their jobs.

More than once, Sakiko tenaciously took her seat and rode out to vulnerability, never considering what some would construe as Russian roulette. The repeated pattern of destruction seemed to systematically move toward her and the tracks, as she would watch the nightmarish bombings, burnings, and resultant massive destruction of the numerous ammunition and airplane factories. Despite already having to frantically throw herself on the floor of the train once, she kept riding it each day. It was more than just the pitiful money her job paid, it had become a test of her destiny and will to be the one to survive the game with machine guns.

Sakiko kept her eyes glued to the window for the fast, fighter planes that flew with the bombers and created so much havoc with their quick, vast sprays of death. She watched one swoop down, as if the trains's movement had just caught his eye, and she dove to the floor to avoid the onslaught of flying glass resulting from the bullets. Sakiko's kismet held, as she had just a few spatters of blood on her clothes from minor cuts she incurred. Thankfully, in the restroom, they easily washed out with cold water.

"I can still be presentable for work," a more important point to her. She pulled and tucked at her dress to hide its frayed edges, and situated her pinned-on hanky to cover the torn spot. Basically, Sakiko ignored the shapely body and quite pretty face, concentrating on the clothes which covered it. She took a deep breath before hurrying on to work. Her little white socks were still damp and carried a pink-tinge from the recently washed-out blood. Others on the train had not been so quick, or so fortuitous as *their fate* was fulfilled. Survival was a game she played well, and she never bothered to look back, as the rescue workers frantically moved the injured and dead people through the station. She had a job to get to, and people to impress with her success of surviving once again.

Nagoya: War Ends - Military Occupation Begins

The anti-air raid guns were like cannons near the sea, since the planes would usually come from that direction. But, their range was only within ten thousand feet, and the bullets did not usually reach them, as the B-29s flew higher than that. An accurate aim was also a difficult thing, as the planes flew fast and could change their direction quicker than the ammunition could reach them.

There were only two cases where they were able to shoot down the planes. In the one case, the plane was totally destroyed, and in the other the pilot parachuted out safely, but was killed by the people on the ground. There should have been more, as the crew of the B-29 was between five and seven men. Another American B-29 pilot, whose plane went down somewhere in Japanese held South East Asia, revealed when questioned he had bombed Nagoya, so he was given to the army in Nagoya and killed there.

There were few situations of war crimes in Nagoya, but the most famous one was about the American military pilot who had been shot down and survived the crash, only to be beaten to death by the locals. If it had stopped there, it would have been understandable to the Allieds, as the same thing had happened many times in Germany. But the body was then staked out on the wing of the plane for a week or more, with adults encouraged to stab it with sharpened bamboo poles, and children urged to urinate on it. Since it happened in late spring with the war going badly, some involved began to feel they would later be found out, so they burned the body.

Once the Occupation troops did arrive, and whispers of the mutilation revealed to the American military, an investigation was set up. An elaborate cover-up was developed with photos of a respectful funeral -

sorrowful attendants and all - saying they had honored him like one of their own heroes, and even a fake grave produced. After the body was dug up, more confessions poured in, for in the Japanese judicial system, once a confession was given and regret shown, almost all was forgiven. This was not understood by the Occupation Forces, so they continued to probe by interrogating numerous children. Finally, in typical Japanese fashion, the man who was thought to have been the instigator committed suicide, and the case was closed. There were no Prisoners of War, or any other people kept in prison for long periods of time in Nagoya, except for the usual Communists, who had spoken out against the military.

October 2, 1945, two hundred advance troops came to Nagoya from Kyoto, but it was a complicated procedure. The 6th Army returned to the States, and the 8th Army then came. In the City Hall and Prefectural building, the civil administration was set up, as the Japanese had expected. At the very beginning, the advance soldiers were mainly engineers and interpreters. First, the Occupation troops tore down whatever remained of Sumitomo metal facilities and Aichi ship building, along with the Mitsubishi Zero-plane facilities. Then any others which had been part of any war production. Disarmament was the main thing, though they kept quite a detailed list of all machinery which could still be used, for any manufacturing plants in good condition.

The wrecked and sunken ships in Ise Bay, delayed the landing plan of the Occupation Forces. They had to wait in the Wakayama area, while others were coming from Okazaki by train - 2,844 of them. The 25th Infantry was moved by boat. The Allied group had the intention of publicizing in the newspaper the route and arrival of the troops, so there would be peaceful acceptance, no shocks or surprises by the citizens at having the troops suddenly appear. Many families moved their young, single women out to the countryside, for fear of them being raped, as a usual side-effect of losing a war. The local policemen were used along the passage way to ensure no problems in the situation, as the main group of troops were over twenty thousand in number that came into Nagoya Port.

The 5th Air Force was between Osaka and Tokyo. Later, as the Occupation was waning, the Korean War had begun and Nagoya was a convenient point for the bombing of Korea, so it became a main base. The United States military had two installations in Komaki and in Moriyama. (The facilities are still used by Japan's Security Defense Force - their legal version of a military.)

The Occupation Army guided the new Japanese government, which was in place, and set the direction in how and which things would be done. When they received a report that the crops were not good that year, they actually drove by jeep to inspect and see if it was true. The censorship of the general Japanese population was carried out by inspecting a random sampling of the correspondence between them. A local Japanese staff actually opened the mail and read it, thinking to observe what ordinary people thought of the Imperial system and other things.

Many Japanese interpreters/translators were employed to carry out this censorship. So it was quite well known to all the people their personal correspondence was read and inspected by the Occupation Army. The information collected by this censorship was then reported to Tokyo, to let them know the actual thinking of the private citizen. These translators were not considered traitors, since it was a very well paid job, and they were only doing what had to be done. Of course, most personally never spoke of the work specifics, as they did not feel good about it themselves. The Occupation Army devised many ways to collect information about how the Japanese felt about many things. Most Japanese transferred their same previous feelings about the Japanese government or military, and thought there was no way to do anything about the Americans - *Shogen'nai.*

The American forces-personnel were encouraged to

pay a very good salary to their housekeepers. And, if the American boss was good, it was a very good job for the Japanese, but there were many bad bosses. The problems between them sometimes involved the third person who had arranged the employment. There were still obvious racial problems between the black soldiers and the officers. If the Japanese workers repeated a nasty remark, they had heard the other white soldiers say - knowingly or not - about their color, there were problems all the way around.

Private houses were confiscated as residences for the higher ranking officers, and in some cases the homes were almost destroyed, as the Americans did not want to change their Western habits. They would tear out the *tatami* - rice straw mats, and paint over the natural, polished wood. Most disgusting to the Japanese was the inappropriate placement of the newly installed Western toilets, (Japanese used 'squatty-potties). They were sometimes put in the tatami rooms or even worse, in the *tokonoma* - an alcove designed for seasonal art work. Many military felt they occupied the country and could do whatever they wanted. Among the Japanese, it would be a discussion if the American despised their culture, or perhaps it was simply stupidity and ignorance of the culture.

The American Village, which was later made into Shirokawa Park, was built for petty officers and the Old Kanko Hotel was where the commander of the 5th Air Force stayed. Tsurumai Park was basically used for the general troop soldiers, and the second story of the government building was remodeled to hold a basketball court. There was barbed wire surrounding the park, so Japanese people could not enter at all, or even take a shortcut through the park.

The main building had a large hall, which the military would allow the Japanese to use from time to time for concerts or meetings or such. These were the only times they are allowed into the park and must carry their special passes. Yet, the Americans did not accommodate the locals with the courtesy of actual private use, as they continued to have their own basketball game while the Japanese tried to listen to a concert below. The ponderous running and thumping were particularly disturbing at violin concerts.

The shortage of food was so extensive, the school grounds were used for various cultivation fields. At the request of the Prefectural government, the Occupation government gave out K-

Rations, but later the bill came to the government - it was not a free gift. For school children, a huge amount of dried milk was given free. Most of the children did not like it, but it was nutritional and very welcomed even if it tasted bad. Without the milk, more would have died because of their weakened condition. Many people who had works of art, or beautiful kimonos sold them to the military people, as they would pay more for them than the black market did.

* * * * * *

Sakiko stayed with Meitetsu for a year after the war. The office moved back to Nagoya station area, now flattened and burned black, while her parents had returned to their bombed out property. They only rebuilt the factory with some living space, as they had no extra money for a new home. Desolation was more profound than ruin. Straggling soldiers, men who had risked and lost everything, suffered beyond endurance and now returned to a broken land occupied by their former enemy. These were not the same men who had marched away, but transformed to the ultimate degradation to which war destroys the spirit, and the soul. They came home to nothing, with nothing after years of nothing, but suffering and deprivation. The basic character of the people would never be the same again.

In some ways, the rebuilding, restoring, remodeling,

refurbishing, gave every Japanese a belief of starting again. Feelings ran high with excitement of the challenge of change for some. Something they accepted best when it came from the outside, and was put upon them with a little force, they could not refuse. All Japanese had done without so much for so long, that though the black market was prohibitive, they needed to have something new, more than just food. The quickest, legal source of income to buy those things was to work for the Occupation Forces - the money people.

The Americans - there were few other Allied troops in Nagoya

- had finally landed October 28th, with just about everything they needed from food to equipment. A dozen or so American-made automobiles and trucks of 1938 and 1939 vintage were already present in Nagoya. But some of the GIs had to wrestle with the unfamiliar, smelly complexities of charcoal-powered engines, wartime Japan's gas-savers. Once the Japanese saw the actual workings of the powerful Caterpillar tractors moving earth and debris, which would have taken dozens of men, hundreds of hours to do, they quickly realized why they had lost the war.

The Japanese war-machine had been almost all heart and spirit, with little science and technology beyond the sources for the all powerful military. Within only six months, an additional twenty thousand troops had arrived in Nagoya, making its contingency second only to Tokyo. Just as it had been a military center during the war, it now had troops instead of factory workers creating the regimented atmosphere. Ultimately, each ammunition or military oriented factory would be turned into a park, therefore making Nagoya the 'greenest' city of its size in the nation.

It did not take Sakiko long to figure what she had to do for the quickest and certainly most profitable solution to her success - she needed 'their' language for few could speak hers. In between learning dress and suit making in the evening, Sakiko studied English from the few archaic texts available that she could afford. She perfected the former before the latter, but figured the language would come from usage if she circulated in the right crowds - those who spoke English. With a quickly growing grasp of English, Sakiko recruited referral assistance from almost everyone she knew to make the right connections. Since her work record and ambition were exemplary and well known, none hesitated when she asked. Introductions were (and still are) the backbone of Japanese loyalty in business, as it put the responsibility on both people. If the one doing the job failed for any reason, fault also fell on the person who introduced the worker to the job. The Occupation Forces soon learned the reliability and obligation of this custom, which they came to depend on for military business and their personal lives.

Quickly, establishing her talents with Japanese clothing clients, Sakiko's first American job was the head of the 5th Air Force's Military Police. Going on past knowledge, she hesitated, for she feared if she made any mistakes, because of her lack of language, her life might be in danger. Her friends assured her, it took very little vocabulary to express herself with a measuring tape, and the American Military Police were nothing like the hated, former Japanese *Kemeitai.*

Sakiko was then given a dormitory room in the same building as several maids and house boys, who worked for the various officers and their families. Seeking them out for introductions to expand her clientele and repertoire, she boldly asked everyone she met. Not ungrateful, or lacking in tradition, for those who assisted in a good referral, she whipped up something stylish that not even the black market would have had. Day and night she created and sewed whatever her customers, or the Military Police needed or desired - clothes, drapes, lamp shades, chair and sofa covers, etc. It seemed like it could not get any better than this, for she was housed, fed and paid. Just as before with Meitetsu, Sakiko hustled to succeed, for the war over, the good life could not be far behind, if she kept digging for it. Unlike her mother Haruko and her whining, Sakiko could clearly see the two worlds she lived in: one Japanese - filled with poverty, starvation, and living in the street; the other American - overflowing with food, large houses, and unlimited money to buy anything they might have wanted. Japan treasures, hoarded for so many years, were now sold quickly to the moneyed-people, and American goods arrived day in and day out on the big ships. Like everything Sakiko had accomplished, she persistently devised a strategy to make it happen - leaving nothing to chance anymore.

Striving so hard on her seamstress work and for what she

thought was the key element - English - Sakiko forgot to appreciate what she saw in the mirror. She enhanced her natural beauty however she could, but more for its presentation than personal delight. For if she had to make the choice between cosmetics, or accessories to embellish her style and food, the former came first, without question. Not that a lot, or vast variety of beauty products were available other than on the black market. Sakiko, like many poised Japanese women, protected her skin from the sun with a parasol or hat, so its alabaster quality had only the slightest ecru tone. Her thick, glorious black hair was kept in a fashionable long pageboy, that accented her beauty perfectly in matching East to West. The bold, dark eyes denied any fragility to her diminutive shape.

Determined to project femininity when necessary, on the job she had strength and endurance beyond her size or weight. Her feelings emulated actions. No matter how strong her smile was portrayed to clients or those she tried to impress, there was an emptiness to her gestures, with politeness as a reenactment, and almost a chill following her words, as if chiseled out and memorized. Even her trendy habit of smoking could be used to display her subjective stance, or personify an emotion and its luxury status.

Surrounded by literally thousands of American military men, she could pick and choose with whom she spent her limited free time. Sakiko's dating was two-fold, as it not only brought her many useful gifts, like cigarettes and stockings, but excellent English practice. Few Americans were intreated in learning more than the limited Japanese requisites for courteous interaction. She dated many more than she had a passing interest in, for one was stupid, she felt, to pass up the gifts. Yet, she knew only an officer could give her the status, as well comforts she had seen so blatantly spread before her. She felt she deserved them, if not having earned them, with all her creative efforts for the military.

Also her natural response, for she still remembered how she'd been raised, never wanting for anything until the war. And, more so, Haruko had instilled in Sakiko her own assumption of entitlement to a better life. She had lost the ability to succumb to passion, since keeping her emotions at bay for so long. Hers was a heart that beat and functioned, but for all practical purposes had been sealed off, or cauterized from any emotions that were usually attached to that organ. The United States military had taken so much away from them, and she would get it all back … maybe more if she was clever.

In less than two years, Sakiko opened her own shop and had enough business to hire several workers. Through her previous contacts she concentrated on more designer dresses for the officers' wives and the female military personnel. Her attention to every detail, along with adapting the newest trends from the American fashion magazines, given to her by customers, made her business soar. She never turned down a patron or an order, even if it meant working late into the night, or standing up a date. Still, she dreamed of attending the dances and balls that she made so many of the dresses for her clients. Constantly selecting and touching the beautiful, though limited materials procured via her connections, Sakiko's desire for them grew with each one she finished. Her mental chant was full of resentment: "That should be *me* in this dress, *me* going to the party … and *me* getting the attention for looking so beautiful." And, she truly was a beautiful woman, on the outside.

Sakiko made a rule not to date married men, but the number of unmarried officers was quite limited. Clearly, the officers had the best dances and their women wore the finest gowns. Sakiko was unfaltering in her determination to wear, not just create, one of her beautiful dresses to the elite weekly events. Expanding her network and diversity of clients could bring her the latest news of eligible officers. She was definitely more than the naive kid outside the candy store. She could be the deferring, fawning servant who had to nightly return to the ghetto life of her parents, while presenting a grateful, benign smile to her clients she catered to. She also developed a rare, synchronized ability to switch from the Japanese to American culture, not only in language, but the appropriate mannerisms.

To the shop employees, she worked relentlessly and constantly pushed them to produce more quality items quickly. To the Americans, and the few Japanese who could afford her designed clothes, she could not have been more polite. It was a punctilious society, where ingratiating the customer with obsequious actions was expected. Though Americans were embarrassed by the extensiveness of the polite mannerisms, it fed their ego with a white superiority, and in some way made up for the inconveniences the Occupation had put upon them. Since much of the staff personnel came from small-town America, the impression of her courteous refinement was indelible, and went to feed Sakiko's reputation more. They liked someone, who they thought, knew her place of serving them.

To the offense of most traditional Japanese, Sakiko emulated her customers in more ways than just language, for she laughed too loudly and joked too much in a carefree way, untypical of the expected demure, Japanese single-female decorum. Flaunting a Buddhist taboo, she now wore leather shoes rather than the wooden getas. Her outfits pinched in her tiny waist, and her necklines flirted décolleté. A Japanese man would not have felt comfortable with her on so much as a date, and she would have quickly been rejected by his family. She'd also become too financially independent for the average-income Japanese man, he could not have afforded her expectations of spending on her self-indulgences.

On the other hand, Sakiko knew her own limitations, for she was not a college graduate, nor descended from a family with name distinction. Her success with the Americans had boxed her in regarding marriage prospects, with literally no opportunities to marry a rich Japanese. Sakiko did not dwell on her situation, nor consider the passing time a dilemma, for she believed the gods of fate had always seen her through more difficult problems.

At last, expectations were fulfilled when an officer's wife told Sakiko about a 'most kind Captain,' who had just arrived and was *single*. With anticipation overflowing not to mention the preparations she'd put into their first meeting, Sakiko couldn't hide the disappointment revealed, in spite of her plastered-on facade. He was not tall, nor handsome, or generous - he had brought only a paltry, small bouquet - but he was single and he definitely was kind.

On the other hand, for Frank Williams, it was love at first sight, and regardless of him being a staunch conservative, she swept him off his feet. To Frank, Sakiko culminated and epitomized all the exotic beauty and elusiveness of the Orient of his dreams. Crestfallen and disenchanted by the dull image he projected, she paid little attention to his reaction to her, so she had no idea he would have instantly succumbed to her every whim. From that fatal moment, he would forever be a pawn for her to manipulate as she chose.

Also, unlike most of her dates, Frank spoke Japanese. Though their conversations were mainly in English, he always carried a Japanese newspaper and frequently asked her to explain the meaning of some kanji, too difficult for him to fully comprehend. His reading and writing were quire superior to his spoken skills, so Frank often sent Sakiko notes in Japanese. He was a born observer of the outside world, noting every uncharted sight, smell or noise that came within his space.

To Sakiko, he was too curiously-odd to be boring, figuring him out could be a challenging game. And, her dates with him were anything but typical, for he did not take her to the usual dives that Japanese girls were taken to, but where she was sometimes *the only* Japanese woman present. This would be hotel restaurants, or more stylish nightclubs with sedate dancing music, or private parties of his American friends. Frank never hid that he dated a Japanese woman, or felt there should be any stigma attached to it. An exalted Sakiko felt like a lady, especially when treated as an equal in a country where anything but separation of races was presumptuous. He indicated little derision from his cohorts, while she constantly received it from the Japanese, and especially her mother Haruko.

Frank's talking to Sakiko was limited, as most of his interest in ancient Japanese culture, history and customs, so not a real conversationalist. "I was wondering if I might ask you about the Golden Temple in Kyoto and the Shrine in Ise? One is so elaborate, while the other so plain." While not having participated in the war from an active or negative standpoint, he had no embarrassment or guilt showing real interest in her country. And, still questioning about this or that kanji, "I can understand what this kanji is, but when it is together with this one, it has a totally unrelated meaning. Can you tell me why that is?" But, most perplexing of all, Frank often took her to the Catholic church, only a few blocks from her shop. "Could you possibly help me translate the sermon, so I can memorize it and then compare it to the English-Latin version?" After repeated visits to the church, despite being a typical Buddhist/Shinto Japanese, the intriguing Christianity began to seep into Sakiko while clarifying Frank's understanding.

Sakiko continued to date other men, frequently stood Frank up for their more basic dates, and openly ignored his attention. Yet, he would not go away. When he would show up at her shop, she would relent and go to church with him or out for coffee, but she was dissatisfied by his lack of generosity in gifts. The dinners or dances though, she never hesitated to accept, of course. That was the whole point of being with an officer. She became more upset, when he finally told her of his being raised an orphan, for it meant he had no inheritance back in America. But, the final blow came when he realized she expected gifts every time he took her out. "I'm limited in spending money on impractical things, since I feel it's important to send money back to America to support my twins, whom I adopted."

Sakiko at first, almost as insulted as she was flabbergasted. It was worse than having a wife, she thought! How could he think she'd be interested in raising two gaijin children in Japan? Then she questioned his honesty, "I can't believe a man would keep two adopted children on his own!" Frank took the opportunity to show her his newest photos of broad smiling Paula and Peter. She stared closely, there was no denying their appeal. Slowly, he dug out the old wrinkled photo of Charlotte with him and the twins at tree months old. His pure sincerity touched the jaded Sakiko, and she quietly apologized to him. "I am sorry, I can see your honest affection for them." Frank Williams was a most curious man, and too tender-hearted.

Sakiko needed time to think, as she remembered too well her own taunted childhood. Several days later, riding the trolley home after working late one night, out the window she saw Frank. He was patiently standing against a building reading his newspaper, and reliable kanji book in hand. She was supposed to have met him there two hours before, for one of their church trips. Her first thought was he was such a fool to have waited so long. When this happened a second time, she got off the streetcar, walked back and apologized. He gave her an honest grin and never uttered an angry word. It finally dawned on her how much she meant to him, and how unconventional he was from the other supercilious Americans she dated. The fact to be considered also, the Occupation had been going on for several years. How much longer would there be Americans available for her to choose from for dating, much less marrying?

Sakiko's workaholic-ethic had not lent itself to conjecture about the choice of having her own children or not, for in Japan it was simply expected of women to produce them. The idea of children already started, so to speak, beyond that messy infant stage might be fun. Besides, she would not have the concern of pregnancy ruining her shapely body. Reconsidering the photos Frank so proudly showed her of the darling blonde, curly-headed girl and sweet, dark doe-eyed boy, she thought just like cute dolls, only more animated. She'd known the secret pains of being adopted, but with her as their mother, obviously it would not be a secret.

The basic fact still remained, Frank could give her what she had always wanted - status. No one could look down on her married to an officer, or the American children - adopted or not. She also loved the reversal of this situation. It certainly would make her noticed, as it was usually the gaijin couple adopting the orphaned Japanese, or unwanted bi-racial children. The uniqueness of it would give her an appearance of martyrdom, in bravely doing what no one else had done. The more cosmopolitan Japanese would perhaps admire her act. Needless to say, the common ones had never been a concern to her.

Frank surprised Sakiko, when he did not want to

plan the marriage immediately. He asked her to convert to Catholicism, and she'd become interested enough to do some studying, as she had to finish her catechism training before she could take the vows in the church. Frank went with her several nights a week to her lessons, and it became clear this was all very important to him. As Frank knelt there quietly on the tatami mats, practicing his Japanese by listening to the priest, his pride and love for Sakiko grew deeper.

The priest helped them both confront the culture clash and Sakiko's lack of experience with children. She'd rarely held one, much less taken care of any. Sakiko honestly questioned her temperament for raising the children, "My life has not been easy, so I am not always a sweet and gentle woman." Yet, Frank misconstrued her business success to his own tenacity in accomplishing goals, which did not tolerate spoiling children, for he believed that made them weak. He truly believed the hardships of the orphanage had made him into a strong man.

The hurdles behind them were minuscule when compared to those thrown ahead by Sakiko's family. She tried to break the news to her parents first, before either ever met Frank. Haruko was adamantly against it, for she could not begin to envision the loss of face by having a gaijin, even an American, for a son-in-law. Seiichi was surprisingly more open, for he'd gotten many contracts for his rebuilt factory from the Occupation Forces, and learned they were not such a bad lot. Besides, their money was good, most available, and generous. Haruko felt she might be losing ground, so for the first time she turned to her in-laws for support to stop the marriage. Haruko's excuse was with something so life-changing, they too, deserved to be part of the decision. She'd been quite positive the more rigid, country relatives would staunchly agree with her in this anti-traditional marriage.

Rather than face them all on her own, Sakiko decided Frank should join her to meet and discuss the decision with the whole family. Perhaps his knowledge of Japanese, fascination with the culture and history would be a positive influence. In many ways, the couple was the fulfilled yin and yang, if not a match, then a balance. His quietness, kindness, and reticent manner stood out when next to her. Sakiko had honestly contemplated she might never be capable of falling in love with any man, as her life had always revolved around herself only. Remembering how ordinary Frank had seemed at first, he had grown on her when she realized what a rare, sensitive man of action he was. Whether it was love or not, this man, whom she had not been sure of entirely wanting, became desirous. Sakiko was now determined to have Frank. She did not like being told 'no.'

Putting Frank into the picture almost convinced them, for her birth father reiterated what her father said, " … times were changing and Americans were not such bad people." The fathers agreed, the Japanese military would never have been as generous, had they won the war, and they saw Frank as a part of that. "So, if he and what he was connected to was what and who Sakiko wanted, then she could make the decision." Though the photos of the doll-like children made everyone swoon, it was not enough for Haruko. She managed to get Sakiko's birth mother to collaborate with her in saying the couple had no destiny together, because of the culture and racial clash. The mothers refused to accept the marriage, or give their blessings, until the fortune teller said it was a good match. Frank was totally taken aback that his future life was to depend on the reading of a few tea leaves and star crossings, but Sakiko never questioned the propriety of the suggestion of her future destiny.

Haruko, of course, had her own favorite soothsayer, who was quite prominent, so said she would make the appointment for them to visit him. She took in the birth dates of the intended, and then proceeded to bribe the mystic, so he would tell them they were a total mismatch. She went so far as to request he say Sakiko was destined to marry a good, wealthy Japanese man. The appointed time cam several days later and the four parents filed in with Sakiko and Frank. The fortune teller went into his chants, trances, and rituals before he started the details of their match and relationship. Though he often caught the powerful, furious and domineering eye of Haruko, the sanctity of his profession, and the pride of his discovered revelation forbade him to lie. He finally said, "Yes, they had been star-crossed, and although it would not be an easy match, sometimes turbulent, Sakiko and Frank had a destiny together."

The bride's and bridesmaids' dresses were made by Sakiko herself, as she had Frank order some of the nylon tulle from the States, as not available in Japan, much less Nagoya. It was the most elaborate, formal wedding of mixed gaijin and Japanese at the reception that had ever been held at the new Kanko Hotel. Many of Frank's military associates attended simply to see "Mr. Kanji," as he was called for his persistent studying, married to the well known and beautiful Sakiko. It was a match most could not believe ever possible, yet others saw they were both getting exactly what they *thought* they wanted. Before their vows were taken, the plans were finalized for the house Frank would have built for Sakiko, her parents, and the twins on the old, burned-out property of her parents. Haruko was given full control over the design and furnishings, while Frank picked up the cost. Money was the fastest way for him to become more acceptable to the denizens of the family.

The transfer up to Tachikawa base, outside of Tokyo for a year or so, was also Frank's idea. Sakiko could adjust more quickly to military life, and having more gaijin families around would probably make the adjustment for Paula and Peter a little easier, too. Frank had been in Nagoya for a little over a year, and finally a month and a half after his wedding, he returned to America to retrieve his twins. He settled Sakiko into base housing, with several comforting friends to assist her, before he flew out. He also gave her a generous budget to do the redecorating of their new home, and whatever other wardrobe expansion she wanted. Freedom at the commissar would keep Sakiko satisfied for some time. The task that lay before him was more challenging than anything he could have perceived. His children were to meet their third mother, a Japanese. It was less than five years after the war that had made enemies of all of the ancestors whose blood ran through the veins of his expanded family - American, German, and Japanese. Maybe their success could be a paradigm for guiding others who felt such trusting was possible.

Paula and Peter were four years old, with her dolls, and his toy guns they watched the new television, or played outside with friends. They had some vague remembrance of their kind father, but to his distress, both twins were visibly upset at leaving their grandparents, Elsie and Cliff. The years with then had been formative and healing since they could sink into and get lost in all of that physical comforting from such caring people. The food had been country-good and basic, with lots of creamy mashed potatoes, fresh whole milk and sweet, ripe fruit. Things their child minds would remember, but would not see again for years.

On the plane, Frank kept saying, "You're going to meet your new Mommy," and "Be sure you call her Mommy." Sakiko feared their rejection because she was Japanese and would look so different from them, so he knew he had to program the twins to respond to her correctly. He'd already, direly learned how upset she'd get when things did not appear proper or run smoothly. Frank kept combing Paula's curly hair as they flew back over in the air force plane. Peter was distracted, as well as entertained by looking out the window and at the plane's surroundings. He would only repeat his lines to his father when the latter's voice would raise, after the second or third time. In spite of studying his kanji, Frank's nerves would not calm down as the hours passed and he prepared his children for what would be an auspicious meeting.

Dutifully, at the military airport, the children ran to Sakiko calling out, "Mommy, Mommy." Peter followed Paula's lead, knowing she would always do the right thing and never betray him. It seemed they played their parts well, yet the responsive reception had not been what they had expected. Sakiko put a hand on each of their backs and kissed them on the foreheads. She smiled and tried to act like she knew how to greet them, yet she was not capable of throwing her arms around them, and smothering them with the kisses they had so recently been given on departure. She had neither the comforting girth, nor the intention to display such affection in public, or in private for that matter. It simply was not the Japanese way, and it made her feel awkward to try to show any display of affection. In so many things, she'd been able to aptly Westernize, but regarding this, she was grateful Frank was not a demonstrative American.

Sakiko held the twins at arm's length to see how much they looked like their photos. She pointedly straightened Peter's suit, took out her comb and carefully removed the tangles from the back of Paula's head. After she felt they were presentable enough to accommodate her, she took a hand of each and walked out for her first proud display. Frank was struggling with all the luggage until they reached the staff car, where the driver then quickly helped him put them in the trunk. Immediately, Sakiko told him he should have had the man come into the airport to help.

She felt people had stared at her presumptuously, as if she were the maid or nanny, rather than their mother. She was wholly unprepared for the emotional complexity, as well as inadvertent chaos, these children simply would create or attract to them, or those around them. Not a concept Frank had thought of either, but one he would constantly have to plan ahead to prevent. A Japanese married to an officer created obstacles simply because of the lack of precedence. While at the same time, she was their new mother, but never bothered to point out the unusual sights surrounding the twins, who had been gawking at the strangeness. In the military atmosphere, there were many different-looking people speaking something that was more like noise than words. It was a magical, mystery tour without a guide.

Life on the base did not seem so strange to the twins because they were together, just as they always had been. Inside the military, Westernized compound no strong cultural impact was made since they still spoke English to the American children they played and attended kindergarten with everyday. Days moved on and the memories of their Illinois life slipped away, as the adaptable minds fused to the new environment, while adjusting to the military community atmosphere. It was more fascinating than queer to have a Japanese mother, and fun learning new words of the language. Sakiko had personal problems because most men who were married to Japanese were younger, lived off base, and did not associate with the American families. Many of the neighbors had extended themselves to her through other associates and friends of Frank. If people outside their immediate area looked at Sakiko strangely, or made remarks that she took as denigrating, the children's only cognizance was her transferred brusqueness to them.

In many ways, on occasion she was fun to play with, for she was young, small and agile like themselves. One hot August day, the three of then were noisily cavorting in the swimming pool, which was restricted to Officers' families, when an older officer's wife walked past. She yelled sternly at Sakiko, "Keep those children under control before I report you to their mother!"

Only moments before, her mind had gone back to the happier days of her own childhood, and playing in the old tank-pool with her cousins. Sakiko slowly stood up out of the shallow water. She calmly, but strongly answered back, "They're only children having fun, and I am their mother!" The woman was too shocked and embarrassed to make a comeback or apologize, so she just marched off. After Sakiko rejoined the children in the wading area, the uncomfortable feeling so permeated them all, their pitch of enjoyment could not be recaptured. Perhaps if she had taken the time to say something to the twins, it may have been easily forgotten, but the obvious confusion that something was wrong, left them in an unsettled mood. The children naturally felt they had done something wrong, and once again had upset the defensive Sakiko.

If not for the other accouterments of an officer's life - staff car at their disposal, several servants, Post Exchange privileges, etc. - Sakiko might have complained even more. But the status indulgences made her an equal to any woman whose husband had the same rank, and superior to those below his. She could not be refused respect, or rejected because she was Japanese. The American Military, like her own society, had rigid rules and regulations that once learned, could be used to one's benefit. She always appreciated that to the military it wasn't who you were, but what your rank was.

So, rather than withdraw from the challenges of her right to do something or be somewhere, Sakiko made herself known from one end of the base to the other. She pushed the introverted Frank to not only attend parties, but to allow her to give them. There was a natural competition between the officer-wives entertaining anyway, so she jumped into it. She could bring an authentic Japanese flair to the occasion, that her neighbors merely imitated. Sakiko spent untold hours sewing clothes for herself and the twins, as well as constantly making or buy-ing new furnishings for the house. Never would someone see her, or them, or the house, in something old, worn, or out-of-style. She still might need to learn some language from the other officers' wives, but soon she was setting a pace in fashion they could not follow. Frank never said a word, for it was her time and talent with very little of his money. Experience was a good teacher for him, when she was happy, they all could be happier.

Frank would soon be finishing his two years in Japan and felt it was a good opportunity to return to the States, so the children and Sakiko would have the language and culture set well into their memory. He was able to get a transfer to Denver and though Sakiko was concerned about leaving her aging parents for that long, she relented when he told her of the mountains, open scenery, and their opportunity to travel around the country. He promised her they would return to Japan once his duty was over, and since he had paid for the house they built in Nagoya, she believed him. It had been difficult to redevelop the whole economy, but with the Korean War in 1950, everything jumped back to life. Nagoya once again became the industrial backbone and workhorse of the nation. Encouraged by the Occupation government, there was a more open labor movement improving the economy, so life was finally getting better for all in Japan. The children adjusted quickly to the new food and environment, though the base life could not really be called Japanese. Still, Frank felt it was an experience from which they had all benefited.

* * * * * *

Upon arriving in Seattle, Frank bought a new car and they set out on their forty-five day leave to travel all over the country. Immediately, he headed for the grandparents in Illinois, then to Pennsylvania and New Jersey for his relatives, to show them all how proud he was of his family. Sakiko and the children eagerly took in the vast scenery and expansiveness of the country, especially when compared to Japan. Surprisingly, they attracted very little attention to upset Sakiko, simply because she was speaking English and most people had no idea what she was, as simply Asian to most. Since she was always geared for the offense in Japan, she relaxed as it rarely appeared in the States.

Every relative marveled how well Sakiko had dressed and taken care of the twins. She included in their suitcase some Japanese outfits, so they could visit their cousins' school and speak Japanese for the other children. Their discipline and behavior were also exemplary, especially when they attended church, following the rituals of the Catholic Mass perfectly. Sakiko doted on Paula's appearance, with her curls done just so and her dresses more frilly than any of the other girls. She was careful to scold them only in Japanese, as was her habit when she expressed any unpleasantness to Frank.

Once they were settled onto the base in Denver, the children began to attend school full time, and the Japanese they had used between them dwindled down and then disappeared. Sakiko had to once again assert her position among the wives, but did not have nearly the problems or negative feelings as at Tachikawa, for she was the only Japanese on base. The adjustments came easier, but her sinuses flared out of control in the dry, thin air. It couldn't have been more opposite to Nagoya, and soon her skin reacted, too.

For the children it was another adventure and they settled in, depending as always on each other for their basic support. This time, Sakiko was just not drawn to do all she had back in Japan. These women were so ordinary, and most of them had not been over seas. She became quickly bored, and not keeping occupied, her physical ailments seemed to mushroom. Since she didn't drive, and the accommodation of a personal driver was not allowed Stateside, she had few excursions for shopping. She had absolutely no interests, or distractions, or even hobbies to fill in her time.

Ambitiously, Frank took several extra courses and soon was promoted to the Civilian Intelligence Division of the military. For all but Sakiko, the time flew by and was enjoyed. This time there was no domestic help, so she discovered the twins and house to be an encumbrance on her personal life. Her mind stayed occupied with her obligation to take care of her parents in their old age. She was filled with guilt, having left them for such a long time on their own. Truthfully, she missed her culture and society which made the two years overly long. There was no such thing as Japanese rice in Denver, and she begged Frank to get some brought in for her. With that and her *miso* - soybean paste mix for soup, Sakiko felt she kept her Japanese roots from drying up.

Playing at being a Westerner in Japan was much different than being a foreigner in America. She more than acknowledged the need for better English, and the minute miscellaneous details of the culture. She hated making mistakes and being misunderstood when speaking upset her greatly. At the same time, she had no excuse for not taking English classes, except not wanting to a admit to her lack with it. Needless to say, Frank and the twins alone reveled in the camping and fishing trips up into the mountains and the nature ares.

Just before finishing, Frank was offered a commander's post in the Civilian Intelligence. Sakiko had come to understand the danger and extensive travel connected with his job, and flatly said, "No, I don't wan to be a widow, - physically or psychologically - and raise the children by myself." The pouting wife was showing some venom. "I'm tired of the military, and the fact that they can move us just anywhere they want." She changed her stance and approach, as she lit another cigarette in response to Frank's silence. "I want to go back to Japan, be with my parents, and live in our new house that we have not even seen completed." With the Korean War dragging on, it was not easy, but Frank managed to extend enough time to take an early retirement. It was the first of his steps backwards, and giving over total control to Sakiko. He still could not handle confrontation, and his twins needed a mother to care for them.

In contemplation, Frank agreed with Sakiko, for he truly wanted more time to study and write about the

Japanese culture and history that still fascinated him. While he was finishing out his time, he applied to the newly sanctioned Catholic-based Nanzan University in Nagoya, so he could do graduate work in anthropology. Once the acceptance came through, their return was scheduled by ship. Frank thought sailing might be a fun way to return, since the ship stopped in Hawaii and Guam. It had full entertainment and activities for all the military children, including a swimming pool. Sakiko was again the only unhappy one, for the constant smell of the ship being painted and rocking caused such seasickness she rarely left her cabin.

The misery both on land and sea, made her doggedly determined to never leave her homeland again. Sakiko sealed the fate of the four of them without any consideration of their gaijin heritage. Frank may have been willing to embrace a Japanese lifestyle, but Paula and Peter would not so much, as having the knowledge and experience of another way to live or choose. But then, choice would not be something available to them in Japan anyway. These childhood memories would fade with time, but the power of America would only grow stronger, as its influence would always be there to remind them.

* * * * * *

Some Americans, waxed romantic over Japan without ever having been there, or lived there, but never learned enough Japanese to completely understand what was going on around them. The Japanese culture was covered by an opaque veil, on which they could project whatever romantic fantasies they wished. When the veil dissolved, disappointment invariably set in. Once the European-style newspapers were started in Japan, in their typically blunt fashion, they quickly "exposed the fact that in these isles of the blest, in which some foreigners supposed existed only innocence, gentleness, or good-mannered poverty, reeks every species of moral filth, abomination, crime and corruption." Shangri-La, even for the most diehard Lafcadio Hearn follower, could not be maintained for long.

* * * * * *

After the Occupation troops departed, the city government tore down, or sold and moved the special military housing in the American Village to make Shirakawa Park. The houses and buildings were given back to the original company or owners. Some of the big, private houses that had been occupied by the higher officers were totally remodeled and too Western, thus ruined by Japanese standards. If they had not liked the furniture or tatami mats, the Americans had thrown them out. Other troops stayed in the Nagoya vicinity after he Korean War and the Security Treaty had been signed between the United States and Japan. They were stationed mainly in the Moriyama area until the early 1960s. As Kobe was R & R - Rest and Recuperation - for the Korean and later Vietnam War troops, Nagoya was designated for processing of the dead bodies and casualties of the 5th Air Force.

Seemingly, as the numbers of foreigners continued to pour in or pass through, the exotic or at least mysterious Japan still fascinated many, while it relented on releasing any of its secrets that made it so curious. Those who knew the culture well, readily compared Japan to the various pungent smells of *shoyu* - soy sauce, the main cooking ingredient of almost every food, yet was processed into numerous different textures and tastes to give a specific flavor to a certain dish. The Japanese could be such an enigma, so similar in a stereotyped way, yet each one slightly different on their own, when you least expected it. Never, you learned, take them for granted.

Chapter 3 The Adaptable Daughter

Japan tends to be a closed society and is basically insecure, while at the same time tending to regard itself as superior and unique. While they can be generous and hospitable to strangers, this is almost off-putting or embarrassing to the point that it does keep them at arm's length, which may have been part of their intention. There is no way for one to ever integrate into their clan, though you are always welcomed as a temporary guest.

Bernard Krisher,
Japan As We Lived It

In Nagoya, Sakiko's family and relatives treated the twins like celebrities, cooing over them and saying repeatedly, *"KAWAII! KAWAII, desu-ne!!"* "How Cute! Cute, aren't they!" Receiving so much attention, Paula and Peter began to believe that they were very special. Sakiko was especially proud to be their mother, and being overly fastidious, she would always do Paula's hair in curls to make her look like a blonde Shirley Temple. She became more ambitious with fancy dresses for her to wear the moment she stepped out the door. Peter did not get the spotlight as often by Sakiko, since his dark hair was only wavy, and boys' clothes did not lend themselves to such frills. Besides, a boy was supposed to be more of a father's concern.

Kata - What it Is and What it Means to Life in Japan:

Foreigners have long presumed there was something mysterious about the Japanese, that made their character so extraordinarily different. In past days, some thought it was their diet with the way they ate so precisely with chopsticks. Then again, their *Zenish* spiritual beliefs and practices, combining unlimited 'gods,' karma, reincarnation, and once in a while a touch of Christianity, as if all existed in a a walking- meditation. Or, maybe it was their ability to perfect minute things, insinuating a 'compact culture.' In reality it was, and is, more the indelible education outside of any other traditional books of training and instruction - *Kata* - the Way things should be done.

These cultural molds shaped the Japanese to be extremely sensitive to any thought, manner, or action that did not conform perfectly to the appropriate kata. With the masses never seeing, much less experiencing, any *other way* of everyday life, the Japanese became acutely sensitive to any deviation from 'their' way of doing things. This factor contributed significantly to their developing especially strong beliefs of being unique in the world. Though it was technically the *Japanese Way*, it was also considered the *Best Way*. Thus, *Everyone* (in the world) *should know how to do it that way.*

Unfortunately, for the majority, particularly those born before 1950, these feelings persist and influence their personal behavior toward non-Japanese, business relations with foreign companies, and government policy in international affairs. It's also difficult for them to relate to Japanese who have broken some of these kata - molds, usually from spending extensive time abroad, which invariably tainted them. These blemished-Japanese were often treated, in varying degrees, as outcasts in their own society, making it difficult to work or continue with their lives.

The untouched credo of perceived nonpareils or peerlessness, was used to justify discrimination against both foreign nationals and their products, at every level of Japanese society. In sometimes not so subtle ways, this was supported and encouraged by the national trade policy. So, while the government talked loudly, and often, about *Internationalizing* the country, it thwarted any true support in bringing Japan into the world family, as an open, accepting member.

The formalized culture and systematized role-playing, which influences the deeper and most personal levels of the Japanese, were taught to all, in exactly the same manner. Or, at least accepted by the ones who want to fit into, and be welcomed in 'the group' - any group was important to them. This was not a magic wand, but the intricate step-by-step process of Japanese acculturation, systematically embedded from infancy to adulthood, or longer if necessary for those with an independent streak. More formally called *shi-kata*, or 'way of doing things.'

It's more than just the mechanical process of doing something, as it incorporates the hundreds of physical and spiritual laws of the cosmos. Most importantly, it teaches the way things were supposed to be done. The Japanese Way of form and order was a means of expressing and maintaining *wa* - 'harmony' in the society. Thus, the absence of *shikata* was virtually unthinkable to the Japanese, for it refers to an unreal world, without order or form. Much like the United States, where people do what they want most of the time, within a loose legal/moral framework.

Early in their history, the Japanese developed the axiom that form had a reality of its own, and it often took precedence over substance. They also believed anything could be accomplished, if the right 'kata' was mentally and physically practiced long enough. Since most of Japan's numerous kata have been well established for centuries, the average Japanese neither thinks, nor questions them.

Over the generations, the kata not only became institutionalized, they also became ritualized and sanctified. Doing things the *right way* was often more important than doing the *right things*. Eventually, the proper observance of kata was equated with morality - therefore doing something the wrong way was a 'sin' against society, which could be fatal. This linking the individual to society, meant if one did not follow the correct form, one was out of harmony with both his fellow man, and their perfect kata-Japanese world.

In formal, as well as most routine situations, every action was either right or wrong, natural or unnatural. There were no shades of gray to accommodate individualistic thought, preferences, or personal idiosyncrasies. Just as there was only one acceptable way to perform all the various actions of life in pre-industrial Japan, from using chopsticks to wrapping a package, there was naturally one right way of thinking - the 'Japanese' way. This was shown most often, so unconsciously, when they would speak: "We Japanese, ..." as if each individual had the ability, knowledge, and permission to speak for the other millions.

The shikata are responsible for making the Japanese formidable in peace or war, and began as mechanical processes designed to perform specific actions, or create specific products. Among the earliest and most pervasive were the 'the way of ...': wet- rice farming, court etiquette, writing kanji, tea ceremony, making of arts and crafts, the Samurai, use of the Japanese language, *honorifics* - hierarchical speaking with a strict cyclical etiquette based on a caste of seniority and sex. The Millennial generation and its extensive travel - particularly to the United States - has wreaked havoc on shikata, and why so many have chosen to live in the States or freer countries.

Starting even with the youngest children, something as simple as counting using one's hands and the bending of the fingers to increase the number over ten - simple, basic, but if not done - one had not been raised properly.

More simply, if one did not follow the prescribed kata, there was something wrong with the person, or they were simply stupid. Being a gaijin was sometimes excused, but most believed that *everyone in the world* had learned these things as they in Japan had. *One should just know them.*

On the other hand, this lifelong conditioning in this intricate, finely meshed web of rules and forms, made it second nature for the Japanese to expect every situation had its exact process and order. When confronted with a situation which did not have its own kata, they were either incapable of action, or would take action which was often the opposite of common sense - and many times violent.

This *inability* - as in never been taught - to make a decision based on deductive/cognitive thinking was the significant difference between the Japanese Way and the customs developed in most other, especially Western societies. Since the Japanese kata-ized their whole existence, practically nothing was left to chance or inclination, much less choice or personal decision. The kata factor was applied to everything - and the Japanese goal was not just the minimum acceptable standard of behavior, action, or work … it was *absolute* perfection. This also meant only the top boss could make a decision, and if not available, a consensus had to be made by those on the next level down. For modern business, there could be a lag in time for the group to come to a total consensus to take responsibility for a decision.

* * * * * *

When the twins were enrolled in the local Japanese grade school, the special family treatment turned from positive to negative. As the impact of their anomalous physiognomy penetrated their young minds, Paula and Peter would talk to each other about it, trying to understand why no one else really looked like them. Confusing since in America their mother's appearance had not been so different from everyone else, they had seen other than just white people. But now, they were the ones with such peculiar features in school. The innocence of this discussion one day was reacted to when their door happened to be open as Sakiko walked by, and took the curious questioning as criticism. She swept into the room almost yelling, "Well, if you don't like it here, you can just get out! Get Out! Go wherever you can find another home!"

Even after she controlled herself, she never consoled them, or apologized in any way, just simply left the twins in the mystified dark. Now fear was added to their disorientation, for they did not know how seriously she had meant it. Despite their tender age, they realized there was not much they could do to change their situation. The incident clearly set the tone for them to not go to Sakiko with their questions or problems, experiencing the cultural shock they were having. They feared she would defend anything Japanese, "What's wrong with that?! That's the Japanese way, the way you must do it." Shikata ganai. "Why can't you just learn to do it???!!"

In the same vein, Sakiko was not cognizant of those things she might forewarn the children of not doing, to make life easier for them. Nothing was explained until the mistake was made, or the twins were called stupid for not knowing the right way to do something. Justifiably, Sakiko was a victim of the educational system which had taught her all things Japanese were universal things and the way everyone did them, if *they* had any sense. The twins could only wonder what they had done wrong to receive such chastisement and rejection. The fall from the initial pedestal was disconcerting, and crushing at the same time. One moment they were fawned over and the next they were scolded, with no real comprehension of either.

Sakiko, though quite Westernized before, once she became an active member in her neighborhood, she began to follow the hallmark of Japan's kata-ized culture of the promotion and maintenance of wa - harmony, balance, social accord. Personal behavior, as well as all relationships, private and public, were based on strictly controlled harmony - consensus in the proper inferior/superior context of Japanese society. Or, for Sakiko, the need to maintain a facade of harmony/agreement in all things. This was done by many Japanese by the use of ambiguity in speech and nonverbal communication. They used ambiguity in the language to avoid commitments, disagreements, responsibility, and to help maintain the appearance of harmony/ concord. It became a vital part of their life outside the home. Other Japanese also used it to keep outsiders, competitors, and enemies uncertain, or at a disadvantage.

The ritual weekly trips to the department stores held both a fascination and fear. Peter and Paula had to deal with all the children and adults staring, pointing, and calling out "gaijin, gaijin." The twins would be holding onto their mother's skirt or hand, as the Japanese came right up to them and pointed in their faces. Some small Japanese children would stare with fear and start crying or screaming. Peter clung to Paula questioning, only with his eyes questioning what he must have done wrong to cause this kind of response. "What did we do?" Paula would ask her mother, and look up at her defending herself, "I didn't do anything!" These uncultivated people had obviously never seen foreign children, especially not with a Japanese mother. Despite their experience of the Occupation, many kept the leftover conviction old history had taught them to be always, intrinsically afraid of the unfamiliar.

Sakiko gave no reassurance to the children of their innocent actions, nor explained the homogeneousness of Japan, and its reaction to dealing with the unknown, especially foreigners. She too, was embarrassed by this negative attention, yet simply brushed the children off with brusque comments, to ignore their frightening reactions.

Sometimes she simply made the twins move out of direct sight of the disturbance they had caused. So hide the problem, do not talk about it was the lesson learned. The twins really needed at least verbal acceptance from her. Their tactile senses still had memories of being literally smothered with hugs and kisses by their first adopted mother's parents. As children, there was no explaining to them their deprived state or vacuum of feelings. Frank had already involved himself in his classes at Nanzan, and with every minute not studying, Sakiko had him teaching English at the house. Sakiko made sure the twins did not disturb him, especially in front of his paying students.

The twins came back from the States with only the simplest of Japanese remembered. In their Gokiso Grade School, they wandered around the classroom while everyone else studied. They were on their own, as the teacher did not want to bother with them, and just gave them paper, so they could draw pictures or whatever they wanted. After several days of attendance, the teachers relented, for it seemed the twins were not going away. They began to learn Japanese when the other children had gone home. Once some basics were practiced, following regular classes the twins attended the *juku* - cram school, to catch up to the other students' level of Japanese. In less than a year, Paula caught on enough to be able to take Japanese dance lessons, learn the abacus, and do most everything else the other Japanese children did.

The fundamental effect on the nature and use of the Japanese language itself, was imperative. Like almost no other language, it *was* the culture. Honorifics - the highly respectful subservient language, could be called a linguistic form of groveling. The expansive demands of non-confrontational 'wa' not only influenced the way the language was used, it also contributed to the appearance of new words and word-endings. Importantly as a child, at that time, one must have the language to exist and function in Japan. Paula strived to have it and use it, properly.

One also needed to know and understand the language itself tended to make less of the individual, and more of society or of the Nation/State. The numerous different levels between people were shown by the actual words and amount of honorifics. But, this usage comes to the adult-individual naturally, which indicates the extent to which gradations were taken for granted. There is no single word- equivalent for 'love' in Japanese. The closest they have are words which mean - duty, loyalty, honor, respect, and desire or simply like a lot. One might say the personality is clipped like a hedge, as self- sacrifice is made a universal obligation, and patience means to 'hold back emotions."

They can and do communicate clearly, candidly and bluntly to members of their own families, close friends and subordinates. But, automatically go into an ambiguous-mode when confronted by anyone else. This ambiguity maintains a surface harmony/kinship, and it keeps foreigners outside of their inner circle. To be obvious in one's speech was rude, revealing more than people wanted to know. Just like in the public bath, no one looks at the other's body.

The language problems for the twins were minor compared to the teasing and bullying. When it first started, Paula and Peter had no idea what was being said to them, but as they learned the language and slang, the words were understood, yet the meanings behind them were not. "You're an American, you don't belong here" "You get out of here." "You're our enemy." "You're an adopted child." Being an object of ridicule really hurt, and their names used with many references to the war was confusing. No rebuttals to these attacks could have been made or comprehended by either side, since the Japanese children had obviously been fed the information by their parents. Even with an ex-military father, their lives had no associations to war, per se.

Feeling these things were all the results of something they had done wrong, Paula told Peter to say nothing to their father or Sakiko. As if Paula feared more disapproval, or disparaging remarks, or reactions from them. The taunting rejections were held deeply inside and fed the certainty of not belonging, yet having nowhere else to go. Peter stayed lost, while Paula's keen sense of awareness for adapting, indicated it was strictly up to them to fit in, and become an integral part of the cultural scheme of things. Rarely would she be piqued by the unusual.

Since everyone else looked the same, it was like looking through a shut, glass door out into a world that sometimes seemed so tantalizing, because everyone else was having so much fun. But the door just would not open for her. To Paula, their life was a small, limited room, and they could only look out that glass, for the door opened from the outside only. Their sporadic forays allowed out with Sakiko were restrictive with definite conditions, limitations and barriers. She wondered if she ever truly made it out permanently, if these people would be curious to know how she felt about them, and how they had treated her. Disenfranchised people, like Paula, reach so far to find an opening in that glass door. The seeds were planted for the 'some day.' Then, the bigger decision to contend with, would be how she'd participate in that outside world.

She'd shown herself to be a feisty tomboy in Denver, so whatever the other kids said, she would yell something right back at them, or easily get into fights. Sensitive Peter, on the other hand, if someone did something to him, he'd come crying to her and she'd go fight for him. They soon developed their own 'kata' or role-plays for dealing with the bullies at school.

In the fourth grade, the old, wooden school building had student bathrooms that were not the flush kind. As with most older, or rural Japanese homes, the honey-dipper-man came early in the morning to empty out what was called 'night soil,' which he recycled to the farmers. Paula went into the bathroom, with its tile cracked floors and wooden doors with stiff sliding locks. Though she was familiar with it, for some reason, maybe standing too close to the hole in the floor or what, she fell right into it.

Calling for her friends, they could not get the door open because she'd locked it. Her arms stretched out on the floor, but with nothing to grab onto she couldn't get out, while from the waist down in the 'toilet' sewage. Finally, after much struggle, she pushed herself out of the hole. The teacher could not allow her to go back to class, because of the interruption it would cause, and told her to go home. Once she got there, her mother would not let her in, but made her strip outside in the back. Sakiko gave Paula a cold water bath before she'd let her into the house. From then on, the teacher said only she had permission to use the teachers' bathroom, a flush-type squatty-potty.

By fifth grade, there was still one menacing boy plaguing Paula, and during recess one day she got into another fight with him. This time, since he was bigger and stronger, she was losing, which made her more angry. She finally broke away and walked home, not returning to class. Her well-constrained frustration, that she had so little control over her own life, had slipped out with the barbarous child. The teacher sent a classmate to her house to say he wanted to talk to her, since he'd already spoken to the boy. Eventually, it worked out and the boy apologized to Paula, but she knew he did so under duress. The civility, not the sincerity, of apologies were an early-learned cultural lesson.

In most of Paula's elementary school pictures or classroom group photos, she was not smiling, but had a determined, serious look on her face. She eventually developed some good friends, as the harassment settled into an erratic flow from a mixed group. It went on until Junior High school, when it changed more than stopped. A reflection more of Paula's assertive personality, and the fact she fought back for both herself and Peter. She'd not let either of them become victims to the bullies, which she quickly learned was a normal phenomenon among the other Japanese children. Early on in grade school, a hierarchical system was established as to who was powerful enough to boss around the others, especially weaklings or more sensitive children. Also, not unusual to see some teachers supporting, encouraging or definitely not stopping the bullying.

The older boys specifically picked on Paula until she ran after them, and it soon developed into a game. Some of the negative attention was because of the way her mother dressed her, making so many clothes much fancier than the other children's. Sakiko continued to put her blonde hair in long curls, which the boys would always pull on. The teachers finally told her mother it had to be tied up or in braids. When a boy threw a rock at Paula, the next day she came in with a huge bandage on her head. Not really a bad cut, but she wanted the teacher to see it. She intuitively had learned to use the rules to her advantage, for the boy's bad action would bring embarrassment and chastisement to the teacher, for his inability to discipline.

After a while, Paul realized her character was too strong, conspicuously for a girl, and more particularly a Japanese girl. She began to lose some friends, because they did not want to play with a female who fought with boys. Her actions just were not done, and they could not associate with someone who did something not condoned in their society. Paula had to change her ways, be more Japanese and be nice to people, in spite of them doing nasty things to her. Once she saw her girlfriends playing with others, rather than with her, she knew they no longer wanted to be around her. In addition, the newness of her for them had worn off, as the intrigue of associating with her was long gone. Her English was as non-existent as theirs, and except for her clothes, she was as Japanese as they were. She'd lost her trendiness.

Along with this, Paula felt very self-conscious about her strange, very Western-style dresses with huge petticoats her mother sewed for her. None of the other girls at her school wore anything like them. Even in America, girls probably would not wear them to school, unless it was for some special party. But Sakiko would not listen, and made her wear them. Her step-daughter was her *living* Barbie Doll and had to be dressed the best. She felt it showed not only could they afford it, but she knew how to dress her daughter American-style, the most fashionable. The fact this style came from women's magazines did not matter.

Since people still commented on how cute Paula was - "You should put her into modeling, or children's show business" - and how beautifully she was dressed. This reaffirmed to Sakiko Paula's complaints were based on ignorance. The vicarious praise and attention Sakiko received was what she lived for, now that Frank was out of the military, for she had no attention-getting status of her own. Yet, the more Sakiko paraded Paula to the department stores, around town, or to visit friends and relatives, the more she became introverted. and no longer the gregarious child she'd been. The trips to the department stores had been a fun adventure and Sakiko would buy something for the children, which gave them great anticipation. But to Paula, being a constant showpiece in tow or on parade, became too much to cope with and no longer worth the trinkets.

* * * * * *

Frank, having grown up in an orphanage, lacked the experience, or ability, to physically express feelings to his siblings and other relatives. Sakiko, on the other hand, raised in the traditional, conservative Japanese way, had received limited physical expressions of love and feelings from her parents. Thus, they were both quite incapable of demonstrating affection. Restraint in all emotions was considered the more desired trait called, *jishuku*, or self-restraint, and sometimes called "the soul of Japan." Not just the individual controlling his behavior in a responsible way, but a form of behavioral repression enforced through societal pressures. In some ways, this was interpreted as "the less emotion one shows for something, the stronger and better person they are." Also, one reason Japanese men considered American men weak, as they openly practiced concern and kindness to their women.

Though the 'skin-ship' of any touching did not exist in the Williams family, Frank did display his love by playing and wrestling with the twins on the floor. And, the good night kiss upon the cheek or forehead was a ritual. At the same time, Sakiko believed her attention to their clothes, food and clean house proved her own sentiments of love. Yet, as slight or vague as these caring communications were, they too, became mute as the children grew.

Teenagers everywhere become difficult for parents to relate to, while in Japan, school and the sports or club activities were the replacement for any attention. Frank and Sakiko became functional parents - ones who simply and adequately maintained a household, performed the requirements, and duties implicitly expected of them by the society they lived in.

The twins developed an emotional starvation which made them look for any bit or piece of affection and favorable, personal attention. Just anything that could stave off the hunger and longing for what they had once known, and been so well fed on. Then, it was as if a confused shield came over the children, sort of an acceptance of, "This is all we're going to get, so we may as we'll accept it … but maybe if we try harder to please them, we'll get more."

* * * * * *

While Paula was Sakiko's showpiece, she complained of Peter's slowness with school work. She questioned Frank, but he denied there was anything wrong. He remembered too clearly how Charlotte rejected Peter once she found out his mental capacity was slightly limited. Although Frank was not the birth father, he attached some embarrassment to having adopted an imperfect son. He refused to let Sakiko have Peter's mental abilities examined thoroughly. Frank feared Sakiko followed the strong Japanese tradition of believing any physical or mental disability was a curse, and thus, brought shame unto the family.

Sakiko could only hope that since most of her friends and neighbors had so little contact with gaijin, they would not notice Peter's deficiencies. It was easy to attribute his diminished abilities in school to his being foreign born, while Paula excelled, it was ignored since she was only a girl. In reality, if Frank had relented, Peter would have been stigmatized still more, because in Japan there was a rigid separation of those with any disability. A real black and white world, where if one was a little different, it meant un-acceptance and subsequent rejection.

The school system was only interested in mass education, with students from one end of the country to the other, being taught identical material from a justified point of equality. It did not matter if one's teacher was better qualified or not, in the public schools exact texts were taught, even down to the same pages on the same days, all across the nation. There was no individuality, or input or response, just learn the material, be tested and move on to the next. No one dared to question the rote learning, the texts, or how successful the program. It'd been prepared for them by the government, and that was all there was to it. *Shikata ganai*

* * * * * *

Peter was more than a son to Frank, he was an extension of his manhood. Perhaps, Frank felt inadequate for being sterile, and he lived for the idea that in Peter, he would see his name carried on. He protected Peter more from the carping and derision of his mother and mother-in-law by trying to spend what little time he had with the family during the week with him. Peter prized his time with his father and from early on he physically responded with an excellent talent for baseball. It also was his way of getting the attention he so desperately needed, and in his mind, made up for his studies lacking in success.

No one had to tell Peter he was 'different' or 'slow,' it was too painfully clear to him from an early age. Just one more thing to feed his growing insecurity, which started his self-destructiveness steps. He saw his penchant for, and ability in baseball as the escape from it all. He might not have had the agility and fine tuned timing for other sports, but he related to a bat and ball with finesse. He also had the good fortune to have a stronger, gaijin body, with more game-stamina Busy from early morning to late at night, Frank combined his graduate studies at Nanzan University with teaching English at various schools. Those evenings he was home, he squirreled away teaching their private, little English school in the upstairs of the house. He depended on the reports from Sakiko on how the children were doing and their day-to-day activities. She, of course, as the dutiful Japanese wife, only informed him of those things that reflected on her being a good mother.

A time-honored tête-à-tête, Sakiko thought all wives did for their husbands, so they would not be burdened by the trifles of family life. The man's job was to earn the money, the more he could bring in, the better man he was for bringing pride to this family, as well as status in the neighborhood. The latter was the key to any happy existence in Japan, especially atavistic Nagoya. One's financial rank gave prominence which overlooked any flaw, even one of being a gaijin, and then gratuitously extended to the Japanese woman who married him.

The twins were put to bed early, with the only exceptions being for extra time spent on homework, when necessary. Chastisement was incurred if homework was due to lack of attention, or ability in the classroom. There were little family interactions, as everyone had their restive duties and responsibilities to perform. Frivolity was channeled mainly to the available time on the weekends, and Frank's need to get away from the city. The usual excursions included a hike, picnic, and competition to gather chestnuts for roasting, or other things to learn about in nature. Frank may have been thought of as stalwart and earnest, but he was not dull or lacking in humor. His own insecure childhood might have been compensated by regimenting his life along military principles, yet he relished the spontaneity of his children, particularly when it was only the three of them out together sharing treats and laughs.

There was also the required visits to Sakiko's relatives with their numerous children in Yokkaichi, and hour or so away from Nagoya. Trips to the zoo and parks were set aside for the nicer weather, while shopping was done at any time, like an avocation or diversion for Sakiko. The many local shopping areas were arcades with covered walkways to protect their goods from the rain, that fell in and out of season. So, exploring for new items while socializing was more of making an appearance, than the need to purchase something. These neighborhood shops were significantly welcoming, as compared to the big department stores, as they eventually accepted Frank and the twins into the area. The children were easily entertained at the cooking stalls or penny games.

Walking the market streets was like giving the nose an exercise program. Some orders reached so deep, as if to fill the throat with the memory of its taste. Others, simply challenged the sense to recognize the ingredient, and how it had been ingested or used. For those scents not recognizable, it could seem one had something new to look forward to when dining. For those who enjoyed the experience of it, a visual could be brought to mind. The pungent permeation of green tea roasting in the large metal barrel, that tossed the leaves around like a giant clothes dryer, also fascinated and educated them. Varied flavors of soy sauce from hight, sweet and salty to syrupy *soyu,* to the dark t*onkatsu* sauce and even the paste of *miso,* whether used for soup or thickening, had become now so familiar.

Volumes could be written on the unlimited soy bean - considering its diversity and high protein content, volumes could be written on the unlimited soy bean - so much more of a food foundation than the sacred steamed rice. Once in a while, Frank would treat the children from the numerous noodle stands and they would sit and laugh about the long-life noodles, as he teased them. "Could they truly extend one's life, if eaten diligently, and belief was given to their power?" These moments all three of them cherished, never mentioning Sakiko's absence.

Frank happily quelled their questions, when they passed the various neighborhood Buddhist temples or Shinto shrines. The wafting-out of incense burning piqued their curiosity, as well as the giant, frightening statues that stood 'protecting' the old buildings. Simply in studying the language history, the national religion of Shintoism, and the Samurai beliefs from Buddhism, gave him a lot more detail and knowledge than he realized, until he began to share it with the children. He made sure, at the same time they did attend the Catholic Church, reassuring them this was the better way for them to believe. Though, he often did remark how the Buddhist honored and remembered their dead in set anniversaries of the death, and special ceremonies the Catholics did not have.

The malleable Paula no longer wanted to be paraded out in public, for what to her was humiliation. She blushed so easily through her light skin, she soon earned the nickname of 'boiled octopus,' because it turned red when cooked. Sakiko still ordained what Paula wore out of the house, as if she were a possession that had to be presented in its best light. The presumptive Sakiko chose the most flashy materials, and the brightest colors, especially red. The styles she meticulously created were for an adult woman attending a party, not a high school student in the conservative city of Nagoya.

In response, Paula wanted darker colors, navy blues, grays or black. The more she was pushed out and shown off, the more she pulled back and wanted to hide, or at least blend into the crowds. She was not just more introverted, she simply never got used to the continuous and explicit pointing and staring by the Japanese on the crowded streets. Especially on weekends, the surrounding country people, mostly rice farmers, made their excursions into Nagoya. For them, the searching out and finding of gaijin to point and laugh at was a game to them.

In a calculated response, Paula requested to attend an all girls school for her remaining junior high years and three years of senior high school, so she could wear a uniform. She preferred a simple, plaid-pleated skirt, white blouse and penny loafers in her free time. Again, trying to regain a personal life on weekends, she feigned preference for staying at home with her grandmother, Haruko. For fear of angering her mother, by the lack of her public appearances, Paula offered to do chores she knew Sakiko detested, like cleaning out cabinets or closet shelves.

Though Haruko kept a tight rein on how Sakiko raised the children in the traditional Japanese ways, she showed great leniency toward them herself. She could share with them a love on a different level, as grandchildren usually received universally. She could spoil both of them without having to be responsible for its influence, yet this never stopped her from telling Sakiko to be stricter with them. Haruko encouraged Paula to go out and have a good time with her friends, once she felt sufficient cleaning had been done.

And, sometimes she even gave her money to spend as she liked. Paula soon learned to love the symmetry and simple rewards of cleaning, without developing the obsessive-compulsive needs of Sakiko. She had a sense of accomplishment and success Sakiko could not criticize or find fault with, for it was one thing she had no interest in perfecting in herself. She wanted it clean, she just did not want to do it herself.

Though Haruko spoke no English, she did understood some of it, and knew when Frank and Sakiko were arguing about her. She thus used Paula to inform her as to what they had been arguing about, which Paula revealed quite openly, without realizing the consequences.

She did not understand why they would not want her grandmother to know what was the matter, as if she might help. It did not take Sakiko long to figure out the source of Haruko's information.

She strongly jumped on Paula for her naiveté with the woman, and her ignorance of family power plays.

Paula was caught in the middle, as her mother instructed her to say she knew nothing, while her grandmother insisted it was her right to know. The loyalty was tinged snd tainted by both fear of retribution, coupled with rejection. Likewise, Sakiko demanded to know what criticizing things her mother said about her and Frank. It could be said, neither woman was an edifying character or role model for Paula, as they mirrored each other's bad side.

In spite of this, Sakiko and Haruko were very close, although there was a competitive struggle for direct and indirect power. Still, no matter how much Sakiko wanted it, honor and obeisance to her parents rose above her personal ambition to dominate them all. She had to acquiesce to them for being the controlling, decision making power, commanding each member of the family to do what was expected or indicated to them. It had from the first, been assumed Frank's understood position in the family was simply of the provider of funds. Not the same significance as breadwinner, for he had little input into any family decisions, or any power.

If he had been the Japanese son of the house, other than the son-in-law, the power would have been his by inheritance. But, he was the outsider, taken in by their graciousness, and allowed to contribute to the finances for this privilege. Frank loved Sakiko, not only for her beauty, but because he felt she was good for him in her authoritative, disciplined ways. He believe once he was able to emulate more of her ways, it might make him more acceptable to his in-laws. Unfortunately for Frank, this never came to pass. The fact Frank had paid for the house was a moot point. Haruko had always insinuated it was a dowry of sorts, as if he had purchased Sakiko with it, and it was their generosity to allow them to live there with the twins.

Once Sakiko's father, Seiichi, had his stroke and was bedridden, Frank relented what little resistance he had about this mother-in-law's reins over the family. He was concerned the bickering might make Seiichi worse, but he also had the misguided belief once the grandfather was gone, he, Frank could assume his rightful place as the head of his family. To his personal disappointment and eventual perception of reality, Frank saw his mother-in-law's powerful authority and demand for respect become more dominant in every aspect of their lives. Then Seiichi lingered, confined, as much psychologically as physically to his bed, for the next thirteen years, expecting to be waited on, yet losing any rights of command.

Each of them had a new chore added to their list, as Seiichi's care at first became preeminent, and then just another duty as the days, months and years crept by. He had to be specially cooked for, though he could somewhat feed himself, moved in and out of his wheelchair for those short times he was able to sit up, and bathed, at least every other day, if not daily in the summer. Nagoya was known not so much for a blistering heat, but a dripping, humid one. In late afternoon, the humidity hung over the city like a thick murky, visible foam. With houses so close together, and shade trees a real luxury, the few breezes were looked upon as blessings. Even the use of electric fans was limited, because of the prohibitive cost of the power.

* * * * * *

Peter's junior and senior high school years were spent at an all-boys school known for its sports program, but this did not make his life any easier. Simply knowing the basics of the language, or his designated place in the culture, did not make him totally accepted. Being separated from Paula took away a lot of his emotional support. His goal had been to become the first gaijin, professional baseball player in Japan. His chances looked good, if for nothing else but the drawing power his uniqueness would've had. Yet, he truly was talented for the game. Then fate pulled one of its cruel tricks. He had a motorcycle accident just before going into high school and the seriousness of his injuries kept him hospitalized for over four months. For Peter, it turned out to be the end of a dream and the beginning of a misplaced life.

Peter never regained the full use of his right arm and leg, which had been so badly damaged. *The irony of the identical physical impairment or fated connection was lost, for none of his immediate family had known the extensive injuries of his birth father, Terry.* So, his dream of baseball was lost, and nothing else seemed of any importance. After missing so much school while hospitalized, the studies became a pit he could see no way of digging himself out of. He did not have Paula's tenacity, and avoidance took over as he began to skip classes, then whole days. The struggle with his studies, never easy, seemed impossible with little encouragement. The energy he did put into them was dashed, when the school refused to keep him back a grade, so he might catch up. In typical Japanese fashion, the school felt it would be a bad reflection on them and their teaching ability, rather than his needs. Sakiko, of course, totally agreed with the school, as she didn't want the embarrassment of a failed son. Peter never had a chance to speak to his father about it all.

The charade started out in the morning with Peter and Paula, both in uniform, leaving the house together with lunch and book bag in hand. Paula went on to school by the trolly car, while Peter jumped on his bicycle and detoured to the park where he spent the day. Sometimes he went on to the classroom, only to be chided by the teacher, instead of counseled. Over the months, after calls from school and confrontations with both parents, Peter was finally allowed to drop out. He could not stay around at home, so he started to work.

The atmosphere of the factory job was in some ways more welcoming, as he was once again treated in a more celebrity status. As a gaijin, who was fluent in Japanese, he had an unprecedented appeal and the new friends wanted to show him off. Soon, he was joining the older workers after the job to drink, play *pachinko* - a mindless kind of pinball game, or other things which were definitely a negative influence on a teenager. Peter was not lazy, he never hesitated to do the same job as those around him, however hard or dirty. As before, soon his uniqueness wore-off and others stopped picking up his bar tabs, so he would leave his gaijin identification card, saying he'd be back to pay the bill. Eventually, Sakiko had strangers knocking on the door wanting to collect payment, presenting his card, or a signed note.

The admonitions grew to vitriolic proportions, as Sakiko felt the embarrassment of having a son who was not fulfilling his role of duty and honor to the family. "We haven taken you in, and supported you in a good home with fine clothes and food." She paced the floor wailing, as if in the presence of a criminal. "And, in return you bring shame to this house and my family." Haruko and Paula listened intently from the other room feeling his pain. "Paula does not do these things … she goes to school, does her lessons, and obeys her family." Sakiko swung around to confront the frightened Peter. "Have you no pride in who we are, and in the job I got for you?"

There were no questions as to why Peter had gone drinking, or much less empathy to his emotions in not being able to refuse to participate. No longer just critical comparisons to Paula, but deep- cutting remarks to make him feel guilty for having brought shame to the family with his actions. These secondhand-compliments to Paula, at Peter's disgrace, were the few she ever received from Sakiko. Almost in retaliation for her brother's shame, Sakiko then questioned Paula's grades and how they could be improved, or higher. "Are you trying or not? Do you also, purposely want to embarrass me?"

This was not hate, as Sakiko was merely following the Japanese belief that children will become egotistical if lauded, and not live up to their potential. Frank could not question her, since he'd been raised in a similar environment. His Catholic nuns felt fault-finding was a benefit to the child, in making them want to overcome any slight short-coming they had. But, it was much more personal for Sakiko, because a Japanese mother's standing was judged by her children's academic success, or lack thereof. In her mind, Paula must now shine more to make up for Peter's failure as a successful son. The insistence was equally verbal and tacit.

With Frank's absence from the home so common, as he was now teaching full time at a university in Osaka, Peter sometimes found solace with his in-firmed grandfather. At other times, when the verbal battles with his mother escalated beyond his mental capacity to deal with them, he simply ran away. Sakiko actually encouraged most of these escapes, as she yelled the same phrases at him as when they were children. "If you don't like living here, go find somewhere else to live!" At first, Peter would only be gone days at a time, when he would stay with friends, or go to Yokkaichi to visit with relatives.

But once they stretched to weeks, Sakiko, out of fear and worry, lost face and went to the police to report him missing. Several times they found him living at Nagoya rail station, with the alcoholics or mentally ill hungry, in filthy clothes and dirty from head to toe, having not bathed. There were few public facilities, and no public shelters or government assistance for people. Families were expected to take care of any problems with its members. Peter obviously being so emotionally distraught, had not planned these flights of freedom in advance. He never had finances saved up to fall back on, to successfully break away from Sakiko's grasp. Alcohol soon became a friend which would help him deal with her, or process temporary illusions of retreat from the reality of his sabotaged life.

* * * * * *

Besides Japanese dancing and *soroban* - abacus study - Paula took gymnastics and table tennis in high school. She really wanted to take swimming, for it was one of the few sports her gaijin-size and strength favored success. She competed in grade school, and looked forward to continuing it in her junior and senior classes. The school had a pool when she first started, but after the first year they closed it, without any explanation, except it was not used enough and was quite old. Paula wanted something on her own she could excel at, but was not based on her gaijin looks or a team effort.

Paula wore her long, blonde curly hair braided or in pigtails, anything to keep it out of the way, and attracting too much attention. In desperation, sometimes she ironed her hair, almost burning her skin in the process, and pulled on it to make it straight. She wanted so desperately to have straight, dark hair like all of the rest of the girls. Fitting into the group, universally was important to any teenager, but in Japan the group was survival. Ostracism was deadly, which the soaring, teen suicide rate showed. To many Japanese, it weeded out the weak, as they owed it to the Emperor to have strong people, who could do whatever was necessary for the country. Paula did not have an alternate group to hang-out with, as she was the only outsider. Yet, her mannerisms, speech and decorum were all pure, traditional Japanese.

The solution she saw was to adapt, adjust, try to please, accommodate, comply, and above all harmonize with the rules and regulations. One did not make waves, for waves caused problems that might create the need for change, and above all else, change destroyed harmony, or made it necessary for new harmonic patterns to be set up. This, then meant decisions, and decisions required group consensus and total agreement, even when one's own feelings had to be buried via coercion and pressure. Conform, fit-in, and be the same, for 'the peg that sticks up, must be pounded down,' one of the oldest proverbs - practiced religiously.

The rigidness of the society gave many people, particularly the older ones, a sense of order, security, and tradition - "This is the way it is done, the way it has always been done." *Shikata ganai*. Even when change would be an improvement, it was rejected until the government, or some other empowered group said it was good. At first, modern electrical conveniences, appliances, especially those useful for the household and women, were frowned upon as frivolous. Women who had such things were considered self-indulgent and lazy, or felt themselves superior to their ancestors, who had done without such things. Then, the new struggling government, in boosting the economy, encouraged the purchasing of such new revelations as a *national benefit*. Many of the radical changes brought in by the Occupation were slowly being erased, unless the government, or enough of the society accepted them.

Dating, an uncomfortable quest for all teens, was a real challenge to Paula, and of course, to the brave boy who would go against the grain, to be seen with her. In a Western country, Frank would probably have had to beat the boys off, but in Japan, she had to depend on those she'd known in the neighborhood from grade school. Inviting a boy to her school festival was a risky step, because she knew more eyes would be on them than anything else. It was quite impossible to have any serious friendship with a Japanese boy, unless his family had known hers. In the eleventh grade, Paula happily dated a family friend. And although, the evidence of Sakiko's manipulation showed, she enjoyed the attention for the few months it went on.

* * * * * *

The word 'internationalism' was beginning to be commonly used, for the new economic Japan pushed to expand into American and other foreign markets. This trendy term, and its vague practice of having the government encourage 'experiencing' foreign things, was a long way from the conservative, but wealthy, Nagoya society. The industrialists had done well, very well with their economy, as it doubled and tripled year after year, following first with the Korean and then later the Viet Nam War - as it was first called - which jump-started its fledgling electronics industry. It looked like their prosperity could not, or would not be stopped.

No Japanese worked harder than the Nagoyans, for it was beyond their paychecks. Their pride was in the quality products they guaranteed, when they signed their individual names on the work slips. No one could lose face by producing an inferior product, for it was not just their job, but their life. Suicide, arcane as it seemed, was still considered the ultimate solution to failure in not doing their part in the group-team project. It still, unfortunately, had an honor attached to it, left-over from the military doing so, rather than surrendering.

* * * * * *

Sakiko's plotting of Paula's future then gathered strength, as she investigated every contact, especially those involved with international business. In this way, Paula being a gaijin and speaking English would be a big *sales point*. As any good Japanese mother, she had to plan for her old age, which meant securing a son-in-law to support and take care of her. Peter was forgotten, even if he could get a Japanese girl to marry him, how worthy would she be? Obviously, she would not be the dependable type, who would wait on her mother-in-law, in the fashion in which Sakiko felt she deserved. That left finding a suitable second or third son for Paula, as the first son inherited his family's estate, but also had to live with them. MacArthur changed the inheritance laws for daughters to inherit equally, but only the greedy ones broke the time-honored tradition of filial piety to sons.

In that vein, of *joining* the wealthy Nagoyan society, Sakiko devoted and dedicated herself to honing and shaping Paula into the traditional Japanese wife, obedient to her wealthy husband. He would have to be chosen well by Sakiko, as one who would live with her family, but most of all, take care of the mother who had sacrificed her all for Paula. All the embarrassments, the apologies, the loss of face would be made up for time and again, if Sakiko got Paula married well. Sakiko would know too, her own future and old age were secure. It had not been easy to keep Paula away from the few other gaijin in town, especially when she was as excited as a Japanese, when she saw one on the street. "Oh, mother, look! A gaijin is across the street! Can I talk to her?" Paula would almost jump up and down in excitement.

"Don't be ridiculous with how you act, you're a gaijin, too!" But since many of the gaijin were important people, Sakiko did not hesitate to investigate who they were, for she still enjoyed associating with people of status, reminiscent of when Frank had been an officer. Yet, when Paula became friends with the daughter of the United States Consul, Sakiko hesitated in having her spend too much time with them, as they went to the international school. The holidays - Halloween, Christmas, Easter and other special parties were a world away for Paula. The few times she did get to go, the international students seemed to have so much more fun, got to eat hot dogs, which she had not even seen before, and did so many more activities while interacting in an open way which mesmerized Paula. Besides, they did not have to wear uniforms, but real clothes and not showy ones like Sakiko made her wear. The teenager liked what she saw, and became enticed about the foreign country of her heritage - America.

Once they had returned to Japan from Denver in the 1950s, they had not been back for any visits. So, over ten years before, and Paula clung to the few veiled memories her visits to the international school parties brought back. The more Sakiko pulled her back and pushed her into tea ceremonies, flower arranging, Japanese dance, or other traditional cultural practices, the more Paula began hoarding whatever little American things she could collect, made in the U.S.A, or symbolic of America. She delved into reading everything she could and practiced her English with a new fervor. The obsession grew as she felt she was being drawn to the distant, unfamiliar roots of both her fathers. Her mind was made up, somehow, someway she was going to live there. Any door could be opened, if she found the right key. She'd make these more than just pipe-dreams, which were so common in Japan. The details would make them real, and bring her such satisfaction, if she planned it all out.

Yet, Paula knew on the surface, she must continue to be cooperative with whatever Sakiko wanted, for if she rebelled, there was no way to realize her dream on her own. The irony of it, Paula could share her dreams with her Japanese girlfriends, for they, too, wanted to live in America, and be what they thought was an American. Sometimes, they'd go shopping and buy American makeup. They were not allowed to wear it to school, and Sakiko would never have allowed it either. They kept the makeup hidden, only to look at it or open and smell it, as they believed it represented the smell of an American girl. It was teenage escapism feeding a dream, and made them feel there was hope of another life, without restraints. Paula's quandary was universal for her age. The crux of the curious difficulty lay in the fact that conscious views of what life ought to be seldom corresponded to what life really was. Whether or not, the full impact of this was accepted by her, or any young adult was rare. It was better for the ego to whitewash, or rationalize the chances of improvement, by making a plan of sorts.

Soon the time of high school graduation was approaching. There had been few talks between Paula and her parents regarding her future, as to what school she would go on to, or what career, or job would be best for her. By the late 1960s, it had become popular for Japanese girls to go on to a junior college, mainly because it was an acceptable higher education which made them more 'salable' through *omiai* - the marriage-arrangement process. This way the girl would not be too much smarter than the man, who would be a university graduate. She also would not be too career minded, as to actually think of having a real job, and just have one to occupy her time before she got married, then stayed at home preparing for her future family to arrive.

* * * * * *

The most common option for the educated, Japanese female was to become an *O.L.* - Office Lady. In Japan they were the ubiquitous, uniformed female servant of the office. Her extensive, demanding duties included the serving of green tea to customers, visitors, and the men of the office. Then, there was the strenuous, mind-boggling making of photo copies, answering the push-button telephone, cleaning the desks of the men, and other requested functions that obviously required little use of any intelligence. Possibly, they may be given the opportunity to do a little bookkeeping, but it depended on the size of the office. One would not want to tax their brains, as the slightest competition with the men would be considered offensive.

They were hired for their good looks, figure, and congeniality of putting up with verbal and physical sexual affronts. It was a male- dominated society, and one did not question his needs, wants, or desires, even if it included harassment, molestation or rape. The Japanese female had been taught to never say 'no,' nor speak of any indiscretions, as the *man* might lose face.

The OLs, Office Ladies or Office Flowers - were of particular importance to travel on business trips with one's boss for the sole purpose of opening his doors, following behind him to show his importance, and any other catering to his needs, sexual or otherwise. In return, the Office Flowers, in their identical uniforms, were applauded for their decorating of a room without intruding into its function of business. It was a work world in which the accepting woman clearly knew her place.

As for those few who actually wanted more, they truly had to be made out of the strongest quality of tempered, Samurai-style sword steel. They could never marry, for no Japanese man would want a woman who put her job before waiting on him hand and foot, as well as his parents. It was not a question if she might earn more than him, for women were rarely paid more than a survival income. It was expected, the decent woman continued to live at home with her parents. She had no family to support, therefore she had no need for additional pay. The company set and controlled the pay scale, which depended on this practice for them to be more competitive in the world market - thus, the companies had full government support on perpetuating inequality of the sexes. These were the options most Japanese girls had after finishing junior college, and it would change little in the next twenty years.

* * * * * *

Once Paula had the chance to tell her father she wanted to go to school in America, he could feel her need, and became cognizant of his neglect in helping her experience its culture. Without a definite course indicated from Paula, Frank decided he would contact his brothers in New Jersey and Pennsylvania to see just what was available for someone like her. Naturally, she would stay with his family, and in some ways he felt it would make them all closer. The brochures of several business schools were soon received, and Paula got to make most of the decision. She'd attend a business college where she could become a legal secretary.

Still, freedom eluded Paula, for Sakiko overruled her immediate departure for the States after graduating. The Japanese school year ran from April to March and though some part-time class did start, Paula might have too much free time on her hands. Sakiko insisted it be used more wisely in Tokyo at a dressmaking school. Again, the skill of a refined-wife must come before those of any career prospects that might deflect a good Japanese marriage partner. Paula was to live with her aunt, while she attended the school in Tokyo. Sakiko then had more time to secretly fine-tune her directions through the maze of 'internationalized,' willing Japanese men for Paula. Her dressmaking training finished at a Nagoya school, for nine months was an impressive enough time for living in Tokyo. Sakiko was concerned about the expense, so the local school would suffice until Paula left, now a year later for New Jersey in June. She was building a resume for marriage and it could not be too expansive in time, money, or expenses to threaten the would-be son-in-law, or his protective mother.

While modeling some of her own designed clothes at a fashion show, Paula was asked to represent a food company doing a six-week tour of Japan under the promotion of "Snow White and the Seven Dwarfs." Sakiko managed to get involved by making Paula pretend she could not speak Japanese. In this way, Sakiko could be her interpreter, take charge of the situation, and most importantly, ride around everywhere in a Mercedes Benz. But, old habits are hard to break and on the trip to Kyoto, one of the promoters overheard Paula and Sakiko arguing in Japanese. She was soon sent packing as Paula was, of course, easier and cheaper to deal with on her own. Sakiko got several weeks out of it, so she did not mind too much

The money was good, the travel fun, but most of all, for the first time in her life - with the Snow White wig -

Paula would have long, almost straight, black hair. Her gullible innocence could not have backfired more, for even with a perfect wig, and perfect fluency in Japanese, Paula was still a gaijin, no matter how she covered it up, or tried to fit in. The smile her mother made her practice from such a young age was now useful, but it had nothing to do with happiness. Sakiko even chided her, "Do not make the smile too wide or tight, so it appears false. It must be as real-looking as possible." Unfortunately, when not on show or display for something, a natural, easy smile rarely crossed Paula's face.

There was little in this life to be happy about, and she just grew tired of pretending. Once she finished the tour, she was almost bitter about the excessive attention she had received, because it had concentrated on her freak status - a Japanese-speaking gaijin. Ironically, Paula never realized she was not just play-acting, Snow White was her life (minus the dwarfs, but definitely with the jealous step-mother), and so in need of a Prince Charming to kiss her into happiness and independence.

Paula more than ever looked forward to leaving Japan and having the three months before school started in September to adjust to the American customs. Gratefully, she had several cousins her age who would teach her what was happening in America, a place she had only wisps of memories. Aunt Marge had five children, so she would be easy to get along with. Paula only had old pictures of them, but they, of course, knew Paula from her high school graduation photo. All the way over on the plane she cried, for it was not only the start of a new opportunity of living on her own, but the first time without Peter. She knew only the Japanese way of things and though Sakiko told her Aunt Marge was a more relaxed person, Paula must not do anything that would embarrass, or bring shame to her family in Japan.

It was a rare revelation to Frank, to acknowledge how hard it had been to say good-bye to his daughter. His reputation was for writing only Christmas cards, but he had foreseen Paula's anxiety and wrote her a letter. His only analogy and guide was his first Army trip to Panama, so he tried to give her confidence in her first steps into a new adult life. In the months that followed, Paula began to see her father in a different light, for through his letters he could verbalize all the little feelings and sentiments he had never spoken. The secret treasures would buoy and support her during some raging rough waters, as the future was waiting to rain down on her. There were no great sage-sayings regarding success or failure, much less anything about boys or romance, for he still thought of her as his little girl.

Paula was once again to be a 'stranger in a strange land,' but as more of an adult, rather than the previous trusting child with no fear of the unknown. Now she had great fear, for there was little of American life that she knew. The only 3-D America she'd seen was in the movies, the rest of it was quite one-dimensional from magazines or books. Her broken English was slightly peppered from pop music, and more movies where the sub-titles in Japanese told her what was being said, as they smiled and all looked so happy.

She was without glass slippers, and would not have known what to do if her hero had come charging up on his white horse. Still, there was the mystery of that yet, possible magical kiss and being carried away to Disneyland, to live happily ever after. Yet, with all of her fears, there was a determination to find out what her American heritage was, and who she could have been if she had been raised in the land of her fathers. Perhaps destiny had played some cruel trick on her, and it was now about to be rectified.

Part II: From Vietnam and Japan to America

Chapter 4 Home Town Boy Makes Good

... my greatest disappointment in Japan or with the Japanese was their treatment of the Vietnamese ... when the Vietnam War ended, and when all the boat people were looking around for a haven elsewhere, and countries as small as Switzerland ... took in Vietnamese. ... and other people so distant and so culturally and racially apart from the Vietnamese, all opened their doors to the refugees, I suddenly realized how selfish the Japanese could be. ... The refugees couldn't come into Japan. Not only Japanese boats, but also foreign boats couldn't land in Japan if they had Vietnamese refugees on them. The Japanese authorities wouldn't let these people off the boat. ... You could really detect their xenophobia, that they'd never been part of the world.

Bernard Krisher,   *Japan As We Lived It*

A Red-Blooded American Boy:

James Robert MacAllen never liked being called 'Jimmy.' Once he entered high school there were enough other 'James' and 'Roberts,' so he got his friends to start calling him 'Mac.' It sounded so much more adult, and manly ... what he thought he was, or at least, would be, once he was given the chance to prove it. Great success was his destiny, he knew that. He would just have to wait for the right opportunity and once it knocked, hesitation was not in his game plan. Neither was he afraid of risk. He knew 'winners risk,' not like some people around him. He definitely wanted more than the East Coast, blue-collar, middle class life he'd been raised in. Working for General Motors' factory like his father and living in the same house all his life had no appeal, no matter how much security it appeared to give. *"There's more to life than this"* he figured, *"and I'm going to find it even if it means leaving America."*

Mac realized knowing a foreign language would give him chances his friends wouldn't be considered for, or probably desire. In seventh grade, after his aptitude test showed an ability for learning a foreign language, he was given permission to jump into both French and Spanish. He was lucky his suburb had new schools with the latest equipment, but they lacked the capacity to handle the baby-boomer group. By high school, he and his peers did not have full day classes, since their numbers had busted out of the ill-planned accommodations. Mac hoped these increased numbers would not dampen his dreams of a scholarship, or exchange program to study in Europe and learn the languages in a real life setting. He definitely had dreams of a different nature than the children of most of the other blue-collar workers.

Unbeknownst to Mac, there could not have been a better time in American history for a young, clever, ambitious mind to flow into, and make the move from one social level of society to another. The "apple pie-Chevrolet-conservatism" of the Eisenhower administration had ended, civil rights in full swing, as well an anti-establishment movement which was breaking all barriers. Added to this was the shock-inducing reality of assassinations, and later the Vietnam War being served nightly on the dinner-time news. These things infiltrated Mac's goal plan and changed his formula for success, from a university education to the appeal of a hands-on, experiential participation. Experimenting was what the '60s were all about. One did not have to be on the West Coast to get into the attitude change.

Following graduation, Mac took an interim job when he could not decide what he wanted to study at the university. He did not want to make a mistake with his course direction, and something was just telling him a bigger, better opportunity would be coming his way.

"Hey," he thought with prideful satisfaction, *"it's a clean, more white- collar job, at least."* As a lab technician for DuPont, he was using his wits, instead of being a stock-factory-slug doing the repetitive mind- bender. Admittedly, the swing-swift was less prestigious, as he could not spend time with his buddies. Yet, he justified it in which his skills were remarkably expanded in math and chemistry.

On the downside, he also lost his "2-A" deferment as a college student and would be prime in the ranking for the military draft. *"I'll deal with that bridge, ..."* he thought confidently, as he got the first full taste of independence when the paychecks started to roll in, while he still happily lived at home with his parents. The big step came with a new car - its payment, and finally feeling he was making many of his own decisions in life. Summer was good, life was fun, and the girls enjoyed his sense of humor.

Not too far down the line, Uncle Sam's "welcome to the war" letter came as a rude interruption. Once the shock wore off, Mac saw clearly to use his brain. *"I'll get into some special school and training, so I become something other than cannon fodder."* As a veteran of World War II, his father criticized him for not going to college when he had the chance, yet he also saw his son was quite savvy about taking a situation and making the best of it. Before Mac knew it, he returned from boot camp and his father's support was priceless, as he became disheartened over the promises not kept by the military.

Nothing seemed to turn out the way he had expected it. This was a real-world lesson that gave him a quantum leap in maturity. The pressures for Vietnam messed up special training programs and no one cared about his choices. Mac had lost most of his rights working for Uncle Sam, and had few decisions he could make on his own. Just before succumbing to an inevitable fate, he saw a poster in the mess hall by the door he had not seen before. Once he found out his name was at the top of the list to be sent out as infantry to Vietnam, Mac jumped instead to enlist in the Army Airborne. Being a real paratrooper had style, he thought, *"and it's the only school the military can't deny me."*

Somehow there was an enticing appeal to parachuting into Vietnam, rather than slogging his way through the rice paddies and jungles. The elitist allure did not escape his desire, for again, Mac did not want to be one of the ordinary ground pack. In the highly competitive Airborne school there was a vast difference in the men surrounding him, the over-achievers - like himself, and a number of various misfits. He observed carefully all the extremes as an education: from the 'goody-two-shoes' college or high school honor roll boys and super-jocks who were trying to prove themselves, to the Chicanos from East Los Angeles and Blacks from Chicago escaping jail terms. Most had gone for the extreme macho, 'do or die' program. Few were accepted in, and even fewer would make it out.

Only the SEALs had a more rigid training, and water had never really been Mac's thing. Any stereotypes and prejudices he may have had about different groups or people were quickly broken-down. It all came down to one's survival through camaraderie and superior ability to do the expected job. That, and that alone, leveled them all out as equals. It was not muscle and brawn either, it was agility and brain. Those who could not make the grade, no matter what their background, were dropped. He learned more than any civil rights pronouncements or Psychology 101 classes could have convinced him. Mac took pride and relish in adapting to making friends without reservations as to who they were, or where they had come from. *"If my friends could see me now!"* He learned the true meaning of 'melting pot' as he moved through it and stirred it up a bit, too. More than once he mediated between the factions any high stress and pressure situation would lay on them, while their bodies and minds were being exhausted. Little of his foreign language ability came into play, though he believed it put him on a higher rung of cultural exposure to other G.I.-Joes. But most importantly, he felt he had found his gift of getting along with just about anyone, even under the most dire circumstances. This was not something he would have been exposed to at the local university. It was a valuable talent that would play an even greater role later in his life, beyond Vietnam.

Being an exclusive member of the 82nd Airborne Division did not change the scenario or remove Mac from Vietnam. In some ways, he raised his mortality risk factor, for all paratroopers were going to Vietnam, the time frame merely needed a scheduled place. To their surprise, they were given a bit of a preview when dispatched to Detroit to quell the riots in 1967. The convulsions of his confused country were thrown right up into his face. There were more real racial issues erupting than just the harassing dissenters of the Vietnam war. Fear, intolerance, and animosity of the National Guard's white majority soldiers had fanned the flames, and hundreds of people had died.

Solemnly, with a keen eye on every movement, Mac along with the other armed paratroopers, rode back to back on the fire trucks to protect the firemen, who were just trying to do their duty. Racially balanced and trained for interdependence, the Airborne gave professionalism with authority rarely tested. Killing their own country men was not something they had been trained for, or chose to do, but eliminating the 'enemy,' no matter who, was a preliminary watershed learning opportunity. Vietnam would test their decision making skills of life and death, like no other war.

Before his seasoning in Detroit, Mac had known some of the dissension and strife of the minorities, but to see it in the living and dying color of blood, was almost too close to assimilate on command. Still, it was more of a loyalty tester to the minorities in the unit, for the bonds of their squads became stronger, than the blood that might have once connected them to those on the outside rioting. Perhaps it was a noble thing, as simple as a belief in country, or maybe these men from the minorities had learned there were other ways to accomplish and change the system than by trying to destroy it. These paratrooper became more than any drill sergeant could have dreamed of, for they had solidified, moved as one, and believed as one instantly-responding body. For many, this practice test saved their life later in combat.

Eventually back to their base, the 82nd Airborne Division was combined with those of the 101st Airborne, who had not already been to Vietnam. In December, 1967, it was move-out time and the biggest military airlift in history under General Westmoreland. He promised the President, the Vietnam War would be over in six months, because of these men and their ability. *"No small proclamation to live up to,"* Mac thought, as he and each man around him gave his best impetus.

They were no discredit to each other, for Westmoreland used the Airborne skillfully, attaching them to all of the major units from the 1st Infantry, to the 4th, the 25th, and the 9th Infantry. They worked the De-Militarized Zone - DMA - with Marines in the North, and into the crucial Tet Offensive. It was one of the biggest battles they won, while beginning to realize they might lose the war. History would tell of the politics, and the miscalculations of not knowing their enemy, while the telltale signs were beginning to pop-up on the front.

Mac was there through it all with more than two hundred air- drops, supporting and believing in Westmoreland, not knowing how his hands were tied by the politics. It was the height of the war with more than half-million Americans fighting on Vietnam soil. Most still trusted their government, believing they fought in the name of Democracy. In these battles were the earlier professional soldiers, who were not so tainted by the drugs, frustrated by the monotony of fighting and dying, or questioned the rationale of their being there. With time, Mac felt the new soldiers who came in lacked something basic his Airborne fellows had, maybe as corny as an 'esprit de corps,' or the deeper understanding of each other man as family. This was proven when the life and death of the heavy fighting put all to the test.

With one drop-zone after another, Mac's questioning had not been of his American Military presence, but of the Vietnamese he had day-by-day contact with: the interpreters, the trackers, or military officers who fought side-by-side with the Americans. He wanted to know about the Vietnamese people, and what their true ambitions were concerning the Communist government versus their freedom.

Mac was assured the majority of the these Vietnamese, especially those in the South who were Catholic - from the one hundred years of French control - knew from experience the Communists would simply kill them for their religious and capitalistic beliefs. They certainly did not want the French back, but they knew these freedoms they'd had were repressed in China and the Soviet Union. It was easier to discern what they did not want, rather than what they truly wanted. Not having had the power to govern themselves for so long, the intangible glow of freedom was the only guiding light.

Mac developed a high respect for these Vietnamese, not only the ones he fought with, but those he encountered within the villages.

He had seen many signs in English of their support, and wanting the Americans to back their fighting. This advocacy encouraged them, maybe because he and his cohorts had not become jaded, they were a different breed of soldier. He saw little abuse of these Vietnamese, for there was no resentment of them by these men. He also found the Vietnamese he was involved with to be happy, honest, and trustworthy, a trait he transferred over to Asians in general. When he came in out of the field, his fascination grew with listening to the captivating sounds of eerie music from China. It rang of a tenseness, like a pulse radiating from the center of Asia, which China was to Mac.

R & R - Rest and Recuperation - for the troops was determined by a point system, and a soldier being available to take the dates allocated to the destination he wanted. These safe-havens of escape were quite diversified from the exotic Sri Lanka, Bangkok, Kuala Lumpur and Kobe, Japan to a more westernized Australia, or even Hawaii. The number of days varied from four or five to several weeks, depending on one's time the field, rank and duty under fire. It did not take long for the troops to learn the benefits and drawbacks of the various locations. Many of the minority soldiers, though perhaps accepted in their own platoons, preferred the non-English speaking countries of color, rather than the rumored highly, racially-prejudiced Australia.

This was especially true of the blacks, who had come from the northern sectors of the States, where they had more relatively accepted lifestyles, than those from the

South. It was an acknowledgment of reality in the world outside Vietnam where they fought and died together, equally. These were a few of the distasteful things that could not be known vicariously through television, or informed of, unless one was unlucky enough to actually have a loved one there. Mac took it all in, considering what the men said and their reasoning behind it.

When his turn came up for R & R, he was anxious to get out, so off to his choice of Taipei, Taiwan with a black friend. In between the usual drinking and extensive carousing, he went to a Chinese opera and a comedy. He did not understand a word, but somehow he did not have to with the intricacies of their movements and facial responses. Though he had no resounding affinity being piqued in the women, or music, it did expand his ideas on Asians. With eyes wide open, Mac tried not to miss a thing, filling his olfactory, as well as his taste buds. Unlike his friends, he had learned not to ask what it was he was eating. The smells and tastes were only out-done by the visible appeal of color combinations, stimulating their tired sights of gooey black mud and jungle green foliage. Along with the clean sheets, his skin became sensitive to the previous unknown sensuous feel of silk. A full sensory overload was in the works. He may have been just passing through Taiwan, but the bigger world out there, beyond the United States, was definitely calling.

One night by himself, Mac did some serious drinking in Taipei with several career Australian soldiers, known to be brave fighters in Vietnam. He was quite impressed with their gregariousness, generosity in buying drinks, and pioneering spirit that reminded him of an older, bygone era of America. It was an essence he had felt from the John Wayne Western movies, or actually some Texan and Wyoming soldiers who had talked to him about their wide-open states. Yet, he could not help being taken aback by their prejudice and pride in being a 'white' only fighting force. They never picked-up that he did not join in their agreement, yet he was wise enough not to turn it into an age-old political argument.

With Mac's return to Vietnam, and the dog-days of war became the grind, he sadly saw the deterioration of the military leadership, and then the men. Politics had dragged their fight down into an ugly, cruel killing ground that no longer seemed to have a cause, or reason for what they were doing. He wanted to be proud of his survival skills, leadership, and timing in knowing how to be at the right place, at the right time. As a sergeant, Mac, along with most non-commissioned officers, went through a lot of 'hand-holding' of the green-lieutenants who came and went so quickly. Many only Reserve Officers Training Corps - ROTC, were usually more concerned about being addressed, and dressed correctly, than the battle game. Consistently, he'd seen the bullheadedness of these young lieutenants get themselves shot, sick or disqualified for battle in some way. A few he'd worked with well, as they trusted Mac's experience to let him lead the platoon, or make the decisions on how some details should be planned. These few had seen the respect Mac garnered from his men. It was something earned, and could not be demanded, or expected because of rank.

As the battles became repetitive, useless, and wasteful of good men, at least the calendar was changing, and his release from hell could not have come too soon. The highly decorated Mac was surprised when he was approached while still in Vietnam, with his military release papers imminent, to be a 'professional' soldier for several oil companies. This meant riding the pipelines in Saudi Arabia and Africa. The offer included his training of these mercenaries, at money his own government only paid generals. Yet, Mac had enough living on the edge. His ego might have become a little inflated at his own accomplishments, and there was no denying he still had a cavalier spirit, so the decision was not a quick one. As much as he had considered the desire to live abroad, this opportunity to be a soldier of fortune was just a little too far away from his blue collar roots. He could see how the addiction of the money and pushing the law of averages was more than a typical job challenge. It was not the destiny Mac's big picture had.

Deep in his soul, Mac also knew it was time to get back in touch with 'real' people, not the 'soldier/animals' of the jungle, they had all turned into for survival. He had reached his limit of adapting to become one with the cruelties of war, and ready to let his protective shield of defense be dropped. Unfortunately, Mac had lost too many comrades, who either slipped into a lax state, or metamorphosed into a headless, killing creature. There were only so many tenuous threads which allowed the veteran to be re-acculturated for acceptance back into the hearth and home. If too many of those thin threads were severed, he was lost.

At worst, he could become a warmonger, returning to battle, seeking death and destruction of all, including himself. They were the ones who reenlisted for another tour of duty. Yet, other soldiers and friends were lost because they could never find peace, for the memories of their war would not fade away. For many the war had only bound them by its isolation and the privileges of sacrifice. For others they would never be able to accept why they had lived, when so many they deemed more worthy than themselves had died. It was a survivors guilt complex like no other.

Mac had no way of knowing how long Vietnam and its killing of fifty-five thousand American soldiers would continue. Or, the fact another one hundred thousand would die through suicide and self- destruction within the decade following the dragged out conclusion of the cruel war.

Untold numbers would not be able to cope with the aftermath-life, though among friends or family who wanted to love them. Mac knew he needed his family, their open touch, support and understanding. He wanted to be a man of success, not a victim of war. He knew time would regain who he was, before he tackled who he wanted to be.

At last the waiting and paperwork was complete, so Mac took off from Vietnam on December 31, then landed in Japan as January 1st rolled in. They only had a few hours layover for refueling, but he took the opportunity in the airport to join in drinking to *"O Shou gatsu"* - the Japanese New Year. It had never occurred to him that the Japanese celebrated their New Year on the same date as the Westerners, since the Chinese followed a lunar calendar.

Back on the plane, the men crossed the international dateline and when they landed in Anchorage, Alaska, and they got to celebrate New Year's Eve again. Once they hit their final destination of San Francisco, Mac and several buddies, who had been with him since his first paratrooper training, were looking forward to making it a New Year's holiday to remember. Since they had waited for five days for their flights back, there was a lot of pent-up energy. Numerous men kissed the ground, once they had descended the steps from the plane They were all surprised at the big welcome-back steak dinner the military prepared for them at Travis Air Force Base. But with nightfall, the men were anxious to be processed out, put into regular uniforms and turned loose on the city to celebrate the New Year. Finally, the men were allowed to load into buses for processing, Mac and several others noticed the wire mesh covering all of the bus windows. It was too eerie a reminder of the local Vietnam security transportation they had seen for so long, and he was curious why it would be necessary in the States. The cruel answer bombarded them, as the bus excited the base gates into a crowd of protesters screaming foul profanities, chants of anti-war protest, and throwing various items at them.

Mac's heart sank, along with most of the soldiers. They had heard news about some of the anti-war protests going on, but had never imagined it would be directed at those who had risked life and limb for their county. They naively thought the protesters only attacked the draft boards or inductee centers. Silence followed the shock, for these people were the general public - those they thought they had fought to protect from Communism. A lasting and haunting vile impression descended on the men - *These people had chosen to take their time to protest at these veterans, rather than go out and celebrate the New Year?* It put a definite damper on Mac's own thoughts about being happy to be back. The heroic medals he had so bravely earned, would never have the same meaning, or luster again.

With the early morning light starting to creep up to the horizon, Mac's only concerns now turned to getting back to the East Coast and his family. There'd been at least ten plane loads of men, so the processing and red tape had taken much longer than anyone had expected. Once they'd gotten into San Francisco from Oakland, most of the men were only interested in a few drinks and a couple of laughs. It'd all been too strange watching the civilians partying away - were the ex-soldiers the aliens, or had they been dropped off in an alien nation? They said little to anyone outside their groups, for most were self-conscious about what the uniform said they were, and from where they had recently returned. Not the blow-out bash they had all imagined, and yet no longer wanted. Barely one or two drinks later, sufficient to say good-bye to old friends, was all most shared. Just get out of there and get home, was the basic thought.

At the airport Mac tried to pay for a ticket, because he was afraid if he depended on his military stand-by discount he would not get a seat. The flight attendant guaranteed him few people flew on New Year's Day, and there'd be no problem, so he could save his money. Waiting hours for his flight, Mac was too wired to sleep and tried to assimilate whatever he could from the movement of people around him. *"I must have been gone more than a year,"* he felt, dazed that everything seemed so foreign. *"They don't act like they even know the country's at war."* His mind puzzled, *"Was it truly that far away from them to even care about?"*

Mac happily boarded the plane, praying it would take him to more familiar ground. Amazingly, there were perhaps two dozen people on board. Just before the plane took off, the same flight attendant came and tapped Mac and a sailor across from him on the shoulder. He had a moment of fear, he was going to be thrown off or something, before he understood what the man was saying to him. "Gentlemen, would you come with me please." He moved them into the first class section and reassured them, "With compliments of United Airlines, welcome home!" Mac looked at the sailor across the aisle from him, and they both shook their heads. Perhaps he had also been reeling from the vast contradiction of feelings - first being rejected and then welcomed. The adjustment back became a series of dichotomies.

Mac knew deep down Darwin did not mean 'survival of the fittest' coming from who had the bigger or more powerful weapon. Killing one's competitor is not survival, it is murder, under the guise of war, or any other excuse. What most 'winners' forgot was, present dominance does not guarantee future superiority. As H.G.Wells wrote: "In the case of every other predominant animal the world has ever seen, the hour of its complete ascendancy has been the eve of its entire overthrow." In other words, no one is naturally superior, or will always be so. Enjoy one's basking in the sun, but don't presume it will last. While the Chiefs may bask in whatever glory the winners had, still the warriors were who dealt with the physical and mental ravages of war.

Mac was home almost a month before he was ready to leave the solitude of his home, especially his bedroom. The anger boiled inside against any authority, yet, the latent animal was not quite ready to be put to rest. The world had been so much simpler when it only depended on the program directive of kill or be killed. It was equality in its purest extent - no politics, no racial barriers, no political restrictions. Survival of the fittest animal - go out and do your thing and if you survived, you got to go out and do it again. No thinking right, wrong, good, bad, of if. Just do it, and you lived or died. He had never realized how complicated civilization was. He was so bitter, *he actually missed the simpler life of trying to stay alive in Vietnam.*

Yet, there was no really getting away from Vietnam, as the fighting was on the news every night, and the turmoil on the campuses continued almost daily. Mac wanted more education, but he was not ready to go back to school full time and be surrounded by those, who he believed hated him. He'd lost his self-perception, so turned to what was familiar - General Motors. He worked full time during the day, so he'd be an evening student with other veterans. Mac did not want to recognize he was doing what he said he never would - assembly-line work, just like his father and uncles had always done. But his mind needed mending, and the repetitive work was the best thing for it. Few decisions to make and the physical, methodical movements brought a healing flow into his emotional body.

The family melded change in the usual time honored fashion - his brother and several cousins got married, the males continued to play the backyard sports of baseball and football, while the women decorated, cooked and planned for new babies. On the surface, they were all normal, average American families, with picnics, barbecues, and reunions of distant relatives. Even as Mac's high school buddies also returned from the war, there was little talk about Vietnam, unless it seeped out through the alcohol. Eyes may meet and lock, but none wanted to know of the other's experience, or how far along they had gotten with processing and burying the memories. It was support, without all of the embarrassing ugliness of divulging one's own atrocities or personal knowledge of war. Each truly believing, "… if we don't talk about it, then it will slowly go away."

The months changed with Mac's college classes having as little, or as much influence on his thinking as anything else. By their finish in June, he did not feel any closer to making the significant life decisions than he had upon his first return. This floating with little resolve gave an insulation, a healing of not doing the wrong thing in situations that were still uncomfortable. Yet, many of his quick reactive nuances to noise, or peripheral movements became more relaxed as his darting eyes calmed down. The warmer weather did bring opportunity for him to go 'crabbing' with his uncle in the bay.

The New Jersey dawn on the water brought a satisfaction to both of the factory men, rejuvenating the elder and gave hope to the younger. It became one weekend activity Mac began to look forward to.

One warm Saturday, after a banner catch of over one-hundred- fifty crabs, Mac and his uncle retuned joyously home before noon. His aunt, seeing the bushels of crabs had to be cooked and eaten quickly, so got on the telephone to the many relatives and neighbors for a spur-of-the-moment picnic. When the call came for a couple of the cousins, they were across the street visiting other friends. Once they were reached, they naturally asked if they could bring these friends along, particularly their friends' cousin, who had come over from Japan. The response was positive on all sides, as the neighbors and relatives poured into the backyard, bringing their own food and drink contributions for the 'crab fest.'

Paula had great hesitation about going to a picnic so unplanned, and also when she knew only her cousins and their friends, having met them a mere few weeks before. She paused at the gate of the large backyard to take a deep breath to prepare herself, as her cousins walked in before her. It was heightened further, when she saw the dozen or so other strangers already there laughing, talking and eating heartily. Yet, they all looked just so relaxed and unpretentious in their actions, like her 'new' relatives.

Obviously, they were very comfortable with each other, and their lifestyle. It all could not have been more totally opposite to her life in Japan. What attracted Paula most was the casualness of touching, hugging and kissing each other. One would think they'd been separated for years, not several days or weeks. The closeness of this extended family appeared like an exclusive club she may one day learn how to join, as they did welcome her. In the meantime, Paula became the momentary center of attention, as the cousins' friends introduced the 'new friend' from Japan.

Mac looked up from his large plate of food, a crab piece still in his hand, but his chewing quickly stopped. "She certainly doesn't look like any of the Asian beauties I saw!" He mumbled more audibly than he realized, and several people around turned to glance at him. Not just the curly, blonde hair, or saucer, blue eyes that took Mac by surprise. But the bright pink blouse and skirt covering the curvaceous body so nicely. Though the skirt was loose fitting, the blouse could not help but be snug over her non-Japanese, ample breasts. She'd sometimes tug at the buttons trying to make them cover what no Japanese designer had to be concerned in covering.

Mac's piercing hazel-green eyes were still deeply staring when they were met by Paula's, with the introduction by her cousins. She instantly blushed-bright, from the subliminal recognition of the meaning of how and where he was looking. Definitely not accustomed to the gaze of men, as she'd learned in Japan it was usually when inebriated, they fixated on her blossoming mounds. Since most Japanese men only drank after work hours, not going out at night eliminated the basic problem for her. The long pause was obvious enough, his uncle chuckled, and several others looked over again at Mac, to take note of the silence. He finally mumbled, "Hello," grabbed his beer and chug-a-lugged, to distract from whatever attention he had received. It had certainly been a long time since any of his desires were so instantly and deeply stirred.

Paula took a seat at the far picnic table with her cousins, and delved into the food with more gusto than Japanese female decorum would have allowed. She also appreciated the distraction from the attention. Still, she could not control her eyes from wandering in Mac's direction, since his unusual dress and appearance intrigued her. He was wearing a woolly seaman's cap over his long, reddish-brown hair, and the Army fatigue shirt was open over the T-shirt and jeans. Not really skinny, but sinewy with his taut, tight muscles showing below the rolled up sleeves. He certainly did not look like anyone she'd ever seen in Japan. She could not help but wonder if he was a 'hippie,' a new category of personage her parents warned her about.

With each stolen glance, Paula would either see him looking, or almost on cue, turn to meet her gaze, as her face burned each time and her internal temperature rose. The minutes and hours of the sunny afternoon slipped by, being pushed along with talk and laughter. Only a time-lapse camera could have recorded the various movements of people, and how Mac gradually finagled around to position himself sitting, so nonchalantly across from Paula. Others who noticed smiled, but said nothing of the providential meeting. In the time honored Japanese tradition, honed into her so tediously, she sat smiling demurely. If she giggled or laughed, her hand immediately covered her mouth. With few questions, she intently listened to every word he said, as if they had been gems dug out and polished just for her. His baritone voice, solid and strong, she had rarely heard before, especially not in this supportive way, as if she were being spoken to as an equal.

Mac was enraptured, as he should be, for Paula's image embodied what many Western men dreamed of: the compliant, acquiescent Oriental female behavior in the preferred American body. There was obviously no Japanese blood in her, but how much she had infused from osmosis, or induced training was apparent to his American eyes that had seen many Asian women. She was, one could say, a good specimen for the biologist-anthropologist argument of environment versus hereditary. What had not been spun and coded in her DNA strands, had been pounded into her by discipline. There was a definite template guiding her movements, actions and reactions.

Mac had not tried dating after he'd returned from Vietnam. It had been made quite clear to him, he belonged to a shunned-category of men. They - the Vietnam vets - were disgusting, and despised for where they had been, and what they supposedly had done. He was neither up to defending himself nor his honor, for it all dwelled within things he did not want to talk about. It hadn't seemed possible to him that his country could have changed so drastically, in the relatively short time he'd been overseas. What he had thought of as pride in serving his country was now considered selling out, or being too stupid to avoid. In Paula, there were no barriers to overcome, for she'd not been tainted by American opinions. Also, many Japanese looked at Vietnam in a positive light, as it brought much business and industry to the affluent-hungry corporations, wanting growth from anywhere.

Finally, the gentle, stretched-out summer dusk dissolved, as the friends and relatives began to bid each other good night, with languid hugs, kisses, and added on conversations while strolling out to their cars. The cousins had held back leaving to see if Mac would offer, or ask Paula to join him somewhere for coffee or something. They knew he'd been withdrawn over the past year, yet everyone had whispered how he'd opened up to the cute blonde, curly-headed Paula. At last, without any invitation being proffered by Mac, the cousins said they should be going. Paula quickly gathered up her things, bit her lip tightly and smiled, "Thank you … for … delicious crab. I enjoy … it and talk … to you." Mac rose to walk her to their car, and noticed the nervous Paula was half-bowing, as she was saying thank you and good night to everyone.

She held her sweater and purse close to her body, while several people tried to give her a hug good-bye. It was an odd sight, like she did not know how to respond, rather than a rejection of the affection. Mac found himself kind of stuck toward the rear of the small group gathered around the girls, and it was not until they started out the gate, Paula turned to find his face and called out, "Bye-bye. Thank you again." The slight smile crossed her glowing face once again, but was quickly covered with her hand in pure, female Japanese style. She dissolved as the street lights came on, then his aunt called him to help gather up the garbage, to take to the trash cans. Mac responded with a slow agreement, as he stared after the mirage, and pondered how very different Paula was. Timidity was on the surface, yet great substance filling her lovely body. He knew distinctly, she had no idea how sexually appealing she was, most obviously to him.

A little more than week later, Mac's mother gingerly queried him at the dinner table. "Remember the pretty girl from Japan … who you met at Aunt Betty's the other day … when we were all eating the crabs?" Somewhat hesitant to push him, afraid he would quickly retract back into his solid, protective shell.

"Yeah, Mom, I remember the girl." Though she had not left his mind, he was not sure if he was ready yet to risk being rejected. A girl like her, could probably get any guy she wanted. He picked at his food as he'd had numerous conversations with himself, as to the pros and cons of going out on a limb for some girl, who *seemed* nice to him.

His mother was not one to let go of what she felt could be a good thing for her son. "Well, you know, I think your Aunt Betty said she's going to be here for quite a while. I think she's going to go to school." She knew to nudge and not prod, as she tried to let him know the details of Paula's stay. The family had all been talking about her, and hoped she would open him up and bring back the fun-loving boy they'd all known.

"So, what are you getting at Mom?" Mac became slightly defensive, as he'd felt his mind had been read. "You want me to take her out, or something?" He began to stab at his food with his fork, since he wanted it to be his own idea, but knew he was afraid. "What, I can't pick my own girlfriends, you're going to start picking them now

… you don't think I know how?" They both knew he'd not had any girlfriends since his return, but that was beside the point.

"No, I'm not … But she did seem awfully nice and sweet. You don't see that very often in such a pretty girl." She paused momentarily to pick another strategy. "She doesn't know very many people, her cousins and yours."

She finally dropped the conversation, hoping at least she'd put some kind of bug into him to react. Over the summer, Mac's parents saw Paula several times when she was visiting with her cousins's friends, their relatives. If she could not get Mac to act on his own, his mother decided to approach Paula directly. "You should call Mac sometime and go out together. He's usually at home, and I'm sure you'll have a good time together." Though Paula nodded and smiled, there was no way her Japanese-bred etiquette could allow her to ever call him first. The American girls might have grown more forward in recent years, but in no way could Paula imagine ever speaking first to a young man.

One Saturday night, a month later Mac had some of his buddies over to the house for a game of poker. They all laughed, joked, and carried on in the typical style of young men trying to portray their independence and manliness, like the semi-jocks they were. But, that night it was not working for Mac, and as the evening wore on his run of luck at cards kept scraping the bottom.

He dropped out of the next hand, since he felt so fruitlessly inept at what he was doing. Even if it was a game, he still hated losing so badly. A little confused with what to do, he first wandered into the kitchen, then paced the front porch, and finally walked straight into the living room. There, like the next logical step, he picked up the telephone and called Paula. He could not recollect when he'd memorized her number, or say exactly why he decided to call, but it suddenly seemed the thing to do - as if she were awaiting it. And, she was.

It did not take more than ten minutes on the phone with Paula, and Mac's crabby-feeling of being a loser was gone. The visuals of her danced merrily in his head, and he was laughing once again. She'd raised his spirit so effortlessly, he could not have said when he had last felt so good. While the boys played on in the other room, Mac found a new world that gave enervation to his existence, and added vibrations to his latent dreams. In the background, the big talk and regurgitated- reminiscing felt imitated, and its appeal for his participation was lost.

Paula's simple talk and quiet listening invigorated Mac to risk exposing his emotions and chancing rejection. He suddenly decided he had to see her face to face. Though it was after ten, her uncle said he could come over for a few minutes. He called out to the others his excuse of going for a drive to pick up more cigarettes and beer, as he walked out of his parents' house leaving his buddies behind. Reticent Paula and chatty Mac sat on the front porch for almost an hour, before her uncle said it was time for her to come in the house. When the skittish Mac felt the moment slipping away, he quickly asked the unassuming Paula for a date. He was ready to express emotions, no longer laden by fear. He was sure she cared too, and wanted to see him again. Paula was more than open and non-judgmental, the fresh honesty exuded like a safety net.

* * * * * *

Timid Paula was not without her own apprehensions and feeling of inadequacies, along with those fed to her by Sakiko. Quickly, she'd seen how different her behavior and speech were from her cousins. They were like most people in groups familiar with each other, and a natural urge to stay in sync, like favorite melodies. The constant smiling and easy laughter really threw her off. She did not remember from her own few years in America, that it was an encouraged idea to show how happy she was. Yet, completely counter to Japan, since smiling was considered frivolous, and one would not be taken seriously if it was shown. Embarrassingly, her vocabulary seemed childish, and she felt hopeless figuring out any of the slang or idioms spoken so fast and casually.

It made her self-conscious to continually ask her cousins to explain their meaning, and then her strange syntax became the center for joking and slight teasing. Paula's aunt and uncle would patiently answer to explain things, while her cousins were out with their boyfriends on the weekends.

The visual surroundings also impacted on Paula, barely realizing the common greenery - particularly the freshly mown lawn - could smell so vivid and different. There was little that reminded her of the trips to the parks of Nagoya. While numerous, they were all surrounded by streets - cars, buses, exhaust fumes, and constant noises of every of sort, in all directions. One really had to learn how to filter it out, or just add to it by trying to speak above it. Even the largest parks never achieved this quiet, or these fresh smells.

Everything, absolutely all of the sites and environment around her, was so much more than she had planned on or expected. She truly needed the time alone, or with her supportive Aunt and Uncle to absorb it all. As much as the suburbs had felt like country to Paula when she first arrived, she quickly acclimated to someone driving her everywhere. Yet, later with no available public transportation, even a walk to a store for anything was out of the question. Still, her biggest benefit were her cousins' introductions to their friends. This new lifestyle was what she had dreamed about, and the experiences opened up more of the outside world.

There had been few distractions by the young men in her English classes at the junior college, and Paula felt more comfortable talking with the other Asian students. She was never self-conscious about her English with them, and most would not have presumed to date her, because she was Caucasian to them. A Thai student, with whom she went to a school dance, was barely taller than her, yet she felt he was too forceful in his attention. Paula was too shy for any public display of affection, even hand-holding. So, when he put his arm around her to kiss her, she quickly pulled away, "No, no, no! We not do that in Japan!" She was more embarrassed when he stepped back and laughed at her. The indoctrination from her mother and grandmother had been indelible about what 'good girls' should and should not do, and the castigation if done.

* * * * * *

On their first date, Mac saw some hesitation in Paula, as he asked her questions about herself and life in Japan. After reiterating the basics, as she had so often recently, Paula kept looking down, while biting her lower lip, or putting her hand over her mouth. "So, uh … what else do you do in your spare time there?" Mac could only think pretty Paula was shy, and he wanted her to know he was as interested in her life, as she'd been in listening to him and his.

Paula looked up into his eyes and mumbled, "It is hard to explain … everything. I … I don't know what to say. It is … very different … not like here." Mac was stunned when he realized there was fear around her eyes. He could not imagine what things she'd experienced in Japan or her family.

"Hey, what's wrong? … Uh, it's cool if you don't want to talk about it. I mean … I was just asking out of curiosity." He looked away, because those big, blue eyes drilled such holes in him, he lost control of his concentration. She was so pretty, it was actually distracting.

Paula pulled in her bottom lip again, and took a deep breath to talk. She'd been so excited to be with him, she'd hardly touched her sandwich. She believed she could trust Mac and he would not laugh at her bad English. "I have … problem … sometime my English. I don't

… know right word … or how you say something … right way." He turned back to see little pools of water around those saucer blue eyes, and became afraid she was going to cry.

"Hey, that's cool with me. I mean I'm no William Buckley, ya know. I'm just a guy who works on the assembly line … but I am going to college, ya know." At a loss for words himself, and not sure how to say what he should to reassure her. "You sound just fine to me. I mean if we were talking about rocket science stuff, or something, I'd be as lost as you." He smiled really big at her, and was relieved none of that water had gathered into tears. "I think you talk just fine … but if you've got any questions about something, ask me … I'll be happy to explain anything … or tell you the right word." Mac was quite proud now, as he felt he had assumed the role of teacher and protector for Paula. In return, a shy grin began to spread slowly across her face. It was certainly different having a girl who not only considered him worthy to date, but also one who he could teach and help understand things. A soft, warm feeling began to fill him.

Paula saw in Mac the kindness and patience she had loved so dearly in her father. Unfortunately, with his constant teaching schedule, he had so little time to share much of it with her and Peter. She pulled in her lower lip further, put her hand once again over her mouth, took a deep breath, dropped her hand and slowly began to tell Mac her story. She sometimes felt, it was a maze without an end. Her eyes would switch from her fidgeting hands, up to his puppy dog eyes. Yet, Paula could only look at them, until she felt a blush rising. She'd met few gaijin men in Japan, but from the magazines she'd seen, Mac definitely fell into the 'cute' category, even with the long hair, that seemed so bizarre to her, but was actually fascinating.

More than anything, he was giving her attention for herself, for he was truly intently listening, never uttering a word of criticism, but often encouragement. These positive, invisible strokes were absorbed into her body and mind, like a healing cream, massaging every little past hurt or wound. They were two lost souls finding more meaning in life, by giving support to each other. Paula's naiveté overcame Mac's fear, as the protective bond of trust was built.

When Paula talked of the numerous things Sakiko had done to parade and publicize her and Peter, Mac could not comprehend her true humiliation. He only thought it'd be fun to be on television, photographed for newspaper articles, or the focus of so much fawning attention. Paula's '*Japaneseness*,' which gave an exotic aura to Mac, was exactly what repulsed her about her past. "I do not deny I love Japan, I … just hate … be … " She was moving her lilting hands in a continuous open gesture trying to grab the right word.

"Displayed," he filled-in for her as she nodded, for she knew the words when she heard them, she just could not get them out in a quick or correct order. "Like a circus-freak performer," he continued caught up in her emotions. She looked at him questioningly, and he thought it too harsh, then she shook her head vigorously in agreement, as she finally understood what he had said. The translation process was suddenly funny and they both began to laugh. There was a sense of accomplishment for them both.

Speaking to him was a safe way to reconnect with all of the feelings and experiences she'd shoved deep down inside of herself - all the painful little hurts, despicable little remarks, disdainful little gestures. They'd added up over the years to become rather mammoth in proportion to her heart and soul. They simply had to come out to make room for real love, possibly even, unconditional love. Something not in any figment of her imagination.

She slowly looked back up to his face and it revealed nothing but consolation, in trying to understand her repressed anger. This relaxed Paula's defenses in knowing, she did not have to convince him of any wrongs done to her. There were times in the past she'd enjoyed and not felt so awkward about. "I often dance … in kimono and my father," she became animated with her hands, magically filling-in the words with her fingers describing. Mac's eyes, mesmerized, followed every gliding twist and turn, appreciating the soft, Asian femininity of her. "He dress in … *hakama* - male, traditional-dress - play … *shamisen* - a thee-string … *in-strulment*."

The mispronunciation, caught Mac's attention, and he re- pronounced the word carefully, as she listened and repeated it. "Instrument," and then continued her story not frustrated at all. "In high school," Paula proudly said, "I refuse … it fake and … uncomfortable I did not want to do … any more." He gave an empathic smile, maybe not comprehending her reasoning, but supporting her independence. She may never understand his bravery in Vietnam, and he'd only later realize how much strength it had taken for Paula to commit one refusal to Sakiko.

Bringing back up those memories was all part of the healing process for them both. To reclaim the essence of being, to be able to let go of the negative feelings, so she might discover how life could be lived, in what should have been her culture. In Japan she was good at telling people what they wanted to hear, or even more so, what she thought they may want to hear, other than that she'd been almost voiceless. Paula had never quite felt strong enough to say what was really, truly inside her until meeting Mac.

They were a balancing act, for if Paula was a safety net for Mac, he was a vehicle for her entrance and understanding, of the society she wanted so much to join. Her body had crossed borders geographically, but daily her mind struggled with the psychological between history and myth, to find identity as an American. Paula needed to belong, to secure herself a niche to create the comfort of community, and identify herself as a true participant in the abiding American story. This longing to discover what it meant to be American, was a sort of a rite of passage into the cultural foundation of independence from family.

A good six months before Paula finally readjusted to no one staring at her, or noticing she might be different, for she no longer was. She relaxed with the realization she also did not have to justify her existence or place in society, as she had in Japan. America lacked the numerous innuendoes that presented one's class distinction, and constant appearance to protect a family from losing face for any reason. Paula would not have been prepared for the fun, if not confusing challenges of so many decisions - what to wear, what to eat, buy, or do. In a true, free market of the States, there were no government restrictions on competition or selection, as in Japan. But most of all was the laughing, really laughing out loud, since no longer necessary for her to cover her mouth for correct Japanese feminine decorum. In the relaxed American atmosphere, people's responses were individualized, with few set expressed patterns for over politeness.

The friendships naturally grew as the summer fell into autumn, and Paula became more comfortable with the familiarity of her aunt and uncle's family, as well as Mac's. Once Paula's business classes actually started, she had a curfew during the week and with return to his classes also, their time together was mainly on the weekends. By the holidays, she'd been received in as another member among the numerous relatives, with hugs and kisses at almost every entrance and exit. A more confident, Paula developed an eager acceptance of the level of touching within the family, becoming a regular part of her daily life. It rekindled warm memories of times with her grandparents. New words were as active a part of her vocabulary, as they were of her life - she was cozy, sheltered, snuggled, and most of all loved as she was, her new self.

She did not want to be separate from steadfast Mac, or any of these new-found feelings. He'd drive her home from a date, only to sit in her uncle's driveway for another two hours talking. Neither one wanted to be the first to leave the other. The intensity of her listening to him and he likewise to her, gave significance and meaning to their feelings, neither had felt before. It was not unusual for them both to have goose bumps, and really understand where the rush was coming from. Their talks also kept them warm in the winter, as their love incubated and grew.

Mac awakened a personal emptiness, and spawned an unknown tactic sensitivity Paula soon depended on to want fulfilled. Being simply held and kissed, created a soothing protectiveness she had never enjoyed before. Paula had been the protector of Peter, and rarely had her father sufficed against Sakiko's wrath on her. If Mac did not call her, she was back to sitting at home bored with her aunt and uncle. She'd get quite angry, if she turned down doing something with her cousins, and then disappointed when Mac did not all. Without her knowing it, he was controller of the world she wanted to be a part of. So, it seemed once again, Paula looked at it all through glass, rather than living in it. There was no way she'd understand his need to balance his time with friends and activities. Mac had also fallen in love, he just was not needy or desperate to be enveloped by it, since his life basically always included family love in it.

Mac, of course, had more options in his life, not only because he had a car, but the roots of a lifetime of connections to people and various things to do. His abundant physical energy found an outlet in coaching basketball to junior high boys in his parish, while still

144

maintaining activities with his circle of single friends. He did not want to have total dependence on Paula as his world, for if she left, which he feared she would, he'd be even more lonely than before. Yet, the more time spent with her, the more she filled his life like nothing else.

It did not matter what he suggested to do, she agreed, whether it was watching his basketball practice, or just visiting with his parents or relatives. Mac assumed Paula enjoyed these things, for he did not fully understand acquiescence, as the foundation of the Japanese female in public. She'd have preferred going out dancing or to the movies, but Mac was not comfortable with either. He could handle the openness of the drive-in, but the enclosed theater with its crowds was still difficult for him to relax in. With little bits and pieces of information Paula gleaned from Mac, his parents and relatives, she began to understand these avoidances were not normal, or usual before Vietnam, when he was quite gregarious.

These inferences to Vietnam seemed bizarre to Paula. As much as she'd seen it talked about on the television news, she had no direct cognizance of its reality, or Mac's military experience connected to it. Personally, Vietnam only came up briefly for her family in Japan, as when Peter was called to the American Yokosuka Base for his military physical examination. When the clerk handed him a paper cup and told Peter to "go piss in it," he simply stood there looking at him and waiting. Peter could only connect a cup with someone giving him something to drink. His English was more limited than Paula's, and neither had a context of slang or cuss words. Peter was quickly rejected and sent back home to Nagoya. His Vietnam experience was finished before it ever started.

Frank never sat either of them down to talk about the political, or military consequences of Vietnam, for he was only slightly more versed about it. He'd virtually no contact with any military associates once the Occupation

Forces left Japan. Years later, there'd been many demonstrations by Japanese university students who feared they, too, would be pulled into Vietnam because of the United States' power over Japan. Still, Frank, not wanting to show his ignorance, said nothing, which gave a tacit dismissal to the subject's importance.

In many ways then, Mac's family and friends placed much of their hope for his return to 'normalcy' on Paula. War never ends for those subjected to it - one did not have to be a solider or injured victim of some battle to be a casualty. The inflicted pain, whether physical or mental, might be buried deep within or covered over without, but it never truly went away. The little things people said or did, could make the reality of those exposed to humanity's capacity for brutality and evil remembered.

As a studious observer, there were no alarm bells set off by any actions Mac did around Paula. Though he drank regularly with his friends and brothers, he never was the falling down drunk, like the common nightly sight of the Japanese man. As the conversations and talks about Vietnam became more frequent between Mac and his friends, Paula thought of them as merely stories, and not revelations of actually witnessing or participating in the events. To confuse her even further, the emotions they expressed ran the gamut from unapologetic to total futility of the human endeavor. Yet, taking place in the past, Paula thought these feelings were unconnected to their current lives. With expectations colored by the typical Japanese man, who disregarded a woman's opinion in every sense, she made few remarks or asked few questions of them.

Paula kept a continual flow of letters to her family, letting them know all of her experiences and her happiness with her relatives. After she and Mac were dating on a regular basis, she wrote about how she liked him, and the simple things they did together. Since many of their 'dates' had included her spending the evening sewing or crocheting with his mother, while he watched sports on television with his father or friends. With this information, there was no backlash from Sakiko. While no definite timetable had been set for Paula to return to Japan, she had assumed she'd finish the two-year college and get her degree. By the time summer rolled around again, the seriousness of their relationship grew to where both Paula and Mac began talking about a future together. Paula got a part-time job, so they both started saving extra money.

Mac had often expressed his dream of living in another country, so Paula did not hesitate to be honest and tell him, "My family expect me live Japan … it my responsibility take care parents

… they go old." With more knowledge of Japan's inheritance tradition, Mac would have questioned why this responsibility was not Peter's instead of Paula's, but he took her at her word. Still, it was no surprise to Mac's family when he gave Paula an engagement ring.

Yet, Mac was concerned about doing the proper thing for her family, as if some Japanese protocol was not met with her parents, he would be rejected. Paula talked so often about their rigidness in exact following Japanese customs, so Mac was rather hyper about the approach. Paula reassured him, "Just write long letter … about you, what you do, and you … future plans, and you come Japan." She still pulled in her lip, and bit it nervously. "I sure it be all right. My father military man before … he understand."

While Paula had not revealed all of the details in her letters, or her true feelings regarding Mac, Sakiko likewise shared none of her plans or expectations with anyone. It was her game to manipulate and play, with a false belief Paula was both her pawn and ace in the hole. It was barely a week later, when the telephone call came for Paula after eleven o'clock at night. Working her shift as an order-bagger for Avon Cosmetics, she did not get home until twelve. Sakiko called again by seven the next morning. Paula did not have a chance for a full "Hello," before Sakiko started in on her indecency for being out so late at night. Since their conversations were always in Japanese, relatives in the kitchen could not know how surprised Sakiko was, when Paula bravely interrupted in English, "I working, not out ... date."

There was a brief silence, but Sakiko was still not happy at the situation and started a rapid fire of questioning what Paula's intentions were with Mac, as to how serious was she about him. Then the bombshell dropped, before she could even respond. "We need to talk this over together, you have no right in doing anything on your own. This is not your decision to make. There are other people here who are interested in marrying you ... and they come from very good ... reliable Japanese families ... who don't mind that you are a gaijin.." Paula was dumbfounded, as she had never thought her mother would try to arrange a marriage for her.

All those times Sakiko had dressed-up Paula and dragged her to the International Ladies Club, was nothing more than putting her on the sale-block for marriage. Many wealthy Japanese women, whose only connection to "International" was that their Japanese husbands did business overseas, joined the club for its status symbol. For years, Sakiko had been wheeling and dealing with them to find just the right Japanese husband for Paula. Now, she had clinched a great arrangement with the wife of a large pharmaceutical executive, whose son was cooperating on the basis of having only seen a photo of Paula. Sakiko had kept them in touch with Paula's progress in school, schedule of return, and her activities, minus Mac, of course. It was all too clear, Sakiko was planning for her own secured-future by finding a wealthy husband for Paula.

The return letter Mac received, at about the same time was more shocking. There was definitely no military camaraderie from Frank. Though he'd never met Mac, he considered him, "no good, and had simply taken advantage of a naive girl who had never dated, or knew any men before." As Paula read the letter, written in her father's own hand, she knew too clearly the words had come from her mother and grandmother. To Mac, also, the language and meaning was bizarre, "What does he mean, Paula, that our 'Union is a mixed- marriage?'" Mac contained his anger toward Paula, for he could see how embarrassed and hurt she was, not being able to speak a single word in her father's defense.

The comment blatantly told Mac, Frank looked at Paula as a Japanese daughter, just as Sakiko did. "I really like this part where he is damning the American East coast area as, 'not being fitting to raise a family in!'" Mac started laughing thinking Frank was not dealing with full mental capacity, or simply so completely controlled by Sakiko. The locale had been Frank's own birthplace, and where most of his siblings lived and raised their families? "Who does he think he's fooling?" Mac stalked out onto the front porch to try to cool off in the night air. Since meeting Paula, he'd become so positive of himself and rarely felt he did not belong, or was not accepted. Even the nightly news on Vietnam hardly dampened his spirits anymore.

The rejection drew them closer together to strengthen their relationship rather than pull them apart. Paula was no longer that girl her father had described, just as counter to Japanese ways, she no longer denied or discounted compliments given to her. She had been in America more than a year, and it was more than a cultural change she had learned. It was love, and not just Mac's, but his family and both sets of their relatives. Also, an understanding of one's own life choices, to make one's own decisions, even if they may not be the best. And as

149

well, their right to do so. Obviously, a different kind of freedom than Paula ever had in Japan. But most importantly, now that she had experienced it, going back and losing it would be difficult. Sure, Paula still had insecurities about herself, but her confidence grew daily from the praise and acceptance she received from all areas of her new life.

Paula suddenly knew beyond a shadow of a doubt, one of the reasons she'd come to America was her fated-meeting with Mac. He was more than a great part of her learning a new life. He looked at her with those endearing eyes, and without words between them, they committed themselves to each other. There was a bond, as if they had spent years in courtship, or been born under the same divine star. Neither could have explained the realization that rushed through their minds and bodies, yet there was no doubt, no question, nor a moment of wanting to turn back. The two became greater than the circle which had brought them together. In her mind they were bonded, but if it would be strong enough to see them through the turbulence she felt coming, she did not know. She only knew this was a strength she'd never known before.

For days Mac could not let it go, as he was so totally unprepared for the discrediting and dismissal, while Paula had to deal with more phone calls. She'd never seen him so angry and upset. He ranted and raved, "I just don't understand their unfair judgment!" He grabbed for words to express the disdain he had received. "That's ah

... such insularity! ME ... being unacceptable, solely because they didn't choose me!" He paced around the kitchen table like a proud Siberian tiger building his determination. "I'll show them, I'll make a good husband for you." She rose from her chair to join him, and soothe the ego which had not been so ravaged, since she'd come into his life. "I'll be someone that you can be proud of, and most of all accepted into their restricted Japanese crowd."

He had no idea how little it all meant to Paula anymore, yet she gave him her nod of agreement. "I promise … some day I'll make you real proud of me … and being married to me." He kissed her with more passion than either of them thought possible. But more than just passion, it was a commitment of enduring love.

The ominous phone calls continued every few days to Paula, but she stayed steadfast. There was no backing down to her parents, or recanting her love and intention to marry Mac. When Sakiko then threatened to withhold Paula's money for school, she responded by saying she did not need to go anymore. She knew she could get a full-time job without the degree.

Finally, Sakiko pulled another ploy, and pretended to relent about the marriage. The only catch was that Paula had to return to Japan immediately, so they could plan the wedding Japanese style. When she told Mac, he had now figured out how manipulative Sakiko was, and refused. "I don't care if we go together to Japan after, but if you go without marrying me first, forget it. I just don't trust her that we'd get married. We must get married here first. You have to decide, it's your decision." It was the gamble of his life, so Mac only hoped that Paula's love and trust could stand the challenge of her mother.

Paula had dated Mac for more than a year, yet, it was more than just choice between twenty years loyalty to her parents and the man she loved. Ironically, she wondered who was capable of the bigger temper - her mother or Mac? It was for her herself, and the right to make her own life decisions. Her embedded *"Japaneseness"* in so many ways made her easily slip, and instantly fit back into the kata-mold when she spoke to her mother. Still, she'd found something more powerful everyday with Mac's support.

When the next phone call came, there was little of the previous respective-nodding to the telephone, which represented her mother. Paula stood tall as she told her mother "No," she'd not be returning to Japan until she married Mac. "We marry first here, and ceremony Japan." Paula had thought making the offer for a second ceremony might suffice, as her mother could still put on a showy-celebration. But her mother's refusal came without any hesitation, and with the threat of being disowned attached. Mac was right, she had no intentions of letting her marry him - there or in Japan. She was told to pack and come home immediately. Before Paula could respond, her mother again slammed down the receiver in her ear. Sakiko was stealing their time, moment by moment.

Paula was shattered as she heard the words, as if her mother had killed Mac, and the balance of her life suddenly shifted. She had to steady herself by grabbing onto the counter. She and Mac had become interwoven, the creators of each other's universe. She'd often noticed they were only in each other's presence for a short time, and their breathing patterns were matched. Paula knew there was no way her mother could understand their interconnectedness, for Sakiko had always been a stand-alone person.

She felt herself slipping down the counter, and each knob of the drawers painfully catching her elbow. Paula finally landed on the floor, with one leg under her and the other splayed out. When Aunt Marge came into the kitchen responding to the noise, Paula still had her hand gripping the metal edge of the counter above her head. It was the dead silence of the young woman that frightened Marge, as she kept calling out. "Paula, talk to me! What happened? Are you all right?" The phone was sitting innocently on the counter above. Marge picked it up and listened. There was only a dial tone.

Consciously, or subconsciously, desperate lovers have been known to be driven to risky, hopeless, and irretrievable extremes to keep their love together, when circumstances go against them. Paula seemed almost amazed, yet gratified, when later in the month she discovered she was pregnant. Surely, her mother would take a more compassionate resignation to the situation and relent.

Paula could not contain her joy from slipping out, when they were once again on the telephone. Sakiko was more stunned at her stupidity, than shocked at the incident. She became resigned, but not as Paula had hoped. "I can get that taken care of here very easily. Just get on the plane as soon as possible, and don't tell anyone about your condition ..." Abortion was a common birth control method in Japan, since it had no religious or governmental repercussions. Besides, birth- control pills were not easily available and most Japanese men refused to wear a condom.

The picture suddenly cleared for Paula. Her mother had no interest in her happiness, Sakiko was totally determined for her to marry the Japanese man she had chosen, simply to guarantee her own future. The fact she had been with another man, and even carried his child, did not matter. It could all be hidden, or would disappear, if they did not talk about it, and no one ever knew. Paula slowly pulled in her lower lip, took a deep breath - at that moment she had no idea how her mannerisms, expressions and life were a reflection of her birth mother, with the same plight more than twenty years before in Germany - and slowly, but sternly cut her mother off from the instructions. "No, Mother! I'm going to marry Mac and have his child, if I have your blessings or not. And you ..."

"You have no right to make those decisions on your own ... to do those thing without us. If you do that, we will consider we do not have a daughter and never did. What you're doing is wrong, completely wrong ... you go ask a priest, he will tell you ...You MUST obey your parents. You want to do things on your own, then everything you do is on your own. All of your things will be thrown out, and nothing will remain to remind us that we ever had such a disrespectful daughter." The receiver was once again slammed down, and Paula had not even had a chance to speak to her father. The pain hurt like never before, and she sobbed. Sakiko was squeezing the life out of Paula's life, by trying so hard to control it.

Duty to family - the one you were born or raised in, not the one you married into - was the constant Japanese force, the underlying foundation of who you were, and why you did the things you did. One would never question one's loyalty to family, or the prerogatives that made it so. Part of that duty was to support the family by obeying whatever might be requested/required, and therefore never bring disgrace or loss of face.

With the mention of a priest, Paula suddenly felt indecisive, and afraid maybe what she was doing was wrong. Mac knew it was just another way of her mother trying to dominate her, but still arranged for them to go and talk to their priest. Paula had continued to attend church with her aunt and uncle the whole time she'd stayed with them, so the priest knew her well. Though the precepts of the Catholic church may be the same universally, their interpretations may be given leeways to follow by the respective cultures internationally.

Shintoism, along with Confucianism, in Japan more than supported the parental restrictions over the child. Even after marriage, their honoring of parents went beyond the Biblical requirements. But, this was the States, and the priest gently reminded Paula, who was now twenty- one, she certainly was not a child. Therefore, she was thoroughly capable of making her own decisions. Besides, abortion was a greater sin than disobeying a parent ever would be, for the church saw it as taking a life. Sakiko was again presumptive of her command of the situation, while still trying to play by whatever set of rules worked best to her advantage.

The wedding date was set, with all of Mac's and Paula's relatives and friends behind them, as they started their new life together. Paula was most appreciative of having her aunt and uncle's encouragement of her marriage, for she realized they had been caught in the middle with her parents. Sakiko and Frank chastised them for not protecting Paula better, or restricting her from becoming so involved with Mac. Still, her aunt and uncle had defended him, for they knew he was a good man and loved Paula very deeply.

Her uncle tried to tell his brother the hours Mac had spent in their home talking to them. Frank truly did sympathize and tolerate his brother's position in the situation. But, Sakiko continued to place a significant amount of blame for the 'fiasco' on her brother-in-law's incompetence, in guarding Paula's virtue. Frank was more confused than ever, for he also had not fathomed Sakiko's marriage scheme, or the years she'd spent creating it. As well, he was the one who had to live with Sakiko and her mother Haruko, as peacefully as possible, which meant agreeing with everything they said.

Part III: Living As *'Gaijin'* in Japan

A Different Cultural Perspective

Chapter 5 Trials and Tribulations

For the mythological hero is the champion not of things become, but of things becoming: the dragon to be slain by him is precisely the monster of the status quo: Holdfast, the keeper of the past. From obscurity the hero emerges, but the enemy is great and conspicuous in the seat of power; he is enemy, dragon, tyrant because he turns to his own advantage the authority of his position. He is Holdfast not because he keeps the past but because he keeps.

Joseph Campbell,
The Hero With A Thousand Faces

The Outsider's Eternal Struggle:

Paula never had any misgivings about her marriage decision, yet there were frequent drawbacks from too much 'family' in their family life. Financially, the options were limited, and at first it was fun living with her in-laws, as she loved them all. For Mac, little changed in his life, so he changed little in how he lived it. He still went to work at General Motors everyday on the first shift and spent his time with his family, friends and college classes.

Paula was like an added attraction to be enjoyed and shared, without having to leave the house. She could handle all the togetherness during the week, but Paula definitely wanted some alone time with Mac on the weekend. He'd become more ordinary and run-of-the-mill than he'd have dreamed possible. Though a plebeian-lifestyle may have at one time been attractive to Paula, she never would have thought she'd get too much coziness. But, it did all have its limitations of enjoyment. One of the things she loved from the first about America, was the privacy and individual space. She could not actually cook for her new husband in her mother-in-law's kitchen. And, there were so many other ways than sex, she wanted to spend private time with him. Mac's seeming need to have his friends and family around all the time, made her feel she was not enough to fill his life for even a small part of their day.

Paula continued to work until just before John was born, and then it was helpful to have the support of the family. She had an easy, uncomplicated pregnancy and delivery, so she went into motherhood with great expectations of being so sure she could manage it all. To her surprise, and the family's, the commotion caused by the small addition of John was more than any of them could handle. John's schedule would not fit into anyone else's, so Paula was up all the time trying to take care of him and not disturb the others.

Within a few weeks, it all came apart at the seams from lack of sleep and the impossible frustration of pacification. To everyone's shock, the accommodating, and acquiescing Paula walked out with John. There were vague references of where she was going, as she simply said, "I can't take it anymore." Once put to the test, Mac showed he could make the necessary changes, while Paula stayed at a little motel refusing to return. Within a week, he purchased a small mobile home, and found a space for its set up.

There had been no contact from Japan until just a week before John was born. It was a simple letter stating Paula's grandfather had finally died. Then, a few days after his son's birth, Mac saw a promotional, commemorative plaque in the liquor store for "Old Granddad" whisky. He ordered it and sent it off to Frank within the beautiful bottle. Paula felt it was an opening, and she wanted Mac, as the man of the house, to call and tell her parents about John. Paula worked on the timing, and it was perfect, for Sakiko and her mother, Haruko, were out shopping. Happily, Mac and Paula were able to speak freely to her father, undisturbed. It was not a long conversation, since Frank was a basically shy person. And, also reticent about *being caught talking* with them, as it might cause a confrontation with his wife and mother-in-law. To Mac's surprise and Paula's delight, a few weeks later traditional baby gifts, and wedding presents came flooding in from Japan.

Paula had hopes all was forgiven and forgotten, as she began writing to her parents, and telling them of her new, happy life. The struggles she'd keep to herself, but she did take great joy in their simple life. Mac worked hard at General Motors and took pride in his promotions along with his growing son. A great father, he spent hours playing with John and taking him out to show him off to his friends, entertaining him with their sports activities. For now, settling into a routine was an acceptable thing. In only a few short years, he'd gone from a lost and lonely Vietnam vet to a father and husband. Mac's dreams were definitely not gone, they are merely put on hold, while he adjusted to his new life and its responsibilities.

Almost four years since coming to the States, Paula wanted to return to Japan to visit and show her parents their grandchild. Mac felt it would be better if just Paula and baby John made the trip. He was an active elven-month old, when Paul boarded the plane to Tokyo. Too, she carried, the news of her next pregnancy. Her parents met and took them back to Nagoya. Paula was so happy, as they welcomed her back in a formal manner, she knew it meant they still loved her. It was a two-month stay, and John delighted everyone with his cute looks, bright smile, and hazel eyes. He was a big, happy child and his bouncy, dark curls attracted attention.

Sakiko had already been making plans as to how Paula could stay, and just have Mac join her. She may not have gotten the husband she wanted for Paula, but he could be made into a very useful contributor to the family. The Arab Oil Shock was on, and once Sakiko learned from Paula Mac's hours had been cut at GM, she began promoting how English was becoming an attractive paying job in Japan, especially for gaijin. Qualifications were not strictly regulated then about a degree required, so she suggested another option could be Mac go to school to study Japanese, but still teach English part-time.

Sakiko could see the little school Frank ran part-time, when not teaching at the university, expanded into a big money-maker with Paula and Mac working there. She quickly offered reassurances to Paula, that she and Frank would help support them in whatever they needed. The unspoken law, as usual, would be that Sakiko was in charge of everything and made all the decisions, including the money distribution. In just a few short weeks, Sakiko had confidently gotten Paula back into her viselike grip. She convinced Paula to go to a doctor there, and arrange to have the new baby. She insinuated *someone* - not her - would take care of it, while Paula, of course, taught English. She only needed to return to the States, pick up Mac, and comeback to their new, secure life in Japan.

It took very few conversations for Mac to realize Sakiko already re-established her control of Paula. The manipulated entrapment was easy without him there to balance the thrust of her encroachment on their lives. Mac was not so gullible as to jump at Sakiko's simplified answers, or solutions to what he felt was a temporary job problem.

He paused to choose his words carefully, not to offend his mother-in-law in Paula's eyes, then explained to her his mind was stuck. He needed to look at both sides, as he was not into believing unflinchingly, as he did not wear blinders. With no immediate response from Paula, he then realized she had not understood what he meant. Before she got upset not understanding, he just told her to come home as planned and they'd discuss it, as he was open to change. Paula returned as scheduled to Mac and discussed his answer. Sakiko was furious.

With investigation on his own, as Mac expected, there were not any independent, good-paying jobs without a bachelor's degree, and he'd not finished his. He had no intention of being tied down to his in- laws English school and their financial support. With diligence, and Mac's amicable character, he had finally built up a communicative rapport with Frank through their letters, and respect had grown on both sides. Frank may not have any influence in the family, but he was capable of reliable, *truthful* information. Mac did have a sincere interest in becoming a teacher, so he asked Frank to inquire about some university programs that fit into Mac's degree schedule. They would go to Japan, but it would be on Mac's time schedule, with his plan to best benefit him and his family.

By the time Jane was born, Mac had already applied to Nanzan University's newly expanded program of Japanese Studies. With his acceptance, they began to sell everything they owned to leave for Japan, so he could start school in September. This time the separation from his family and her relatives was felt by both Mac and Paula. All their support had been the life-blood of the new marriage and their happiness together. Mac qualified on his own to the university, quite proud and confident of being able to study a language again.

Not as if he was going off to Vietnam or something, he naively thought, *"How difficult could Japan be?"* At least he was correct in assuming, no one would be shooting at him. The ambushes would be more psychological, but not any less dangerous. It was Sakiko's turf, and she'd been manipulating everyone within it, to dance to her directions for over twenty years. The game was on, and he truly had no idea how brilliant, but unfairly she played. They'd be gone a year, he'd planned, as that was the limit of the language program. He did happily acknowledge it was the start of a major life change, again. Finally, he felt, he was on his way.

In a great show of welcome, Frank and Sakiko again traveled to Haneda Airport in Tokyo to meet them, then rode the *Shinkansen* - Bullet train, down to Nagoya in comfort. Once the women and children were settled, Frank took Mac to the buffet car. Alone, together over a beer, Frank studied Mac's face, as he watched the landscape whirl by. He questioned if it reminded him of Vietnam. Mac reassured him there was little similarity, with all the industry in Japan, and he definitely had no negative transference. Mac was duly impressed with the train's technology, but the compact housing along the tracks, made him slightly claustrophobic. the cramped housing could only be related to an inner-city situation. While it did not look trashy, there was an obvious grime of pollution that hung, rain-steamed on the buildings, or just about everything else that sat out in it. The hundreds of bicycles and motor scooters at every train station or shopping plaza, caught Mac's attention, while the Tonka toy-sized vans and pick-up trucks almost made him laugh. Regarding his own six-foot frame, their miniature sizes for the diminutive people, he fully realized how he would stick out..

After seeing many particularly stylized, glitzy buildings, with numerous flashing neon lights, and extremely large parking lots in both country and city settings, Mac questioned Frank what they were. Rather distractedly, Frank drolly replied, "Pachinko parlors. It's a monotonous, pointless pinball game." He glanced out the window, at another procession of them not far from the fast-moving train. "Something for the mindless to do."

Pachinko - Another Gift from the Allied Occupation:

Nagoya's other claim to fame - besides manufacturing and the most ostentations weddings in Japan - was Pachinko. There were many stories, but the most common said, during the Occupation, some Japanese had found an old warehouse full of American recreational equipment. The military had confiscated and stored it away in the 1930s, as too decadent for the new regime. Since the horizontal pinball machines took up too much space, a clever Japanese engineer converted them to work vertically.

The actual creator and creation was not patented then, as most likely it was put together from parts of partially destroyed pinball machines. To some, this sort of vertical pinball machine was an embarrassment, as it had not existed in the ordered, controlled serious- minded prewar Japan.To most, it was too puerile, frivolous, and especially pointless. Which was exactly what made it so popular after the war-defeat, and continued to make it grow in numbers in modernized Japan as a distraction.

Before any great reconstruction plans sprung from the ruined city of Nagoya, pachinko parlors appeared, as if by magic. They were inexpensive places of pleasure, or more honestly, escapism from the poverty-stricken environment. The interiors may have been spartan and tawdry, but the noise alone of the clacking, falling, metal balls could put anyone into a zombie state. Therefore, the player did not have to deal with the total loss of identity, as to who they were, or had become with the annihilation of their country.

In the group society, where no one must stand out or speak out, pachinko served the purpose of being the sole recreation, which could be played alone. One may go with a friend, but was not expected to leave, if the other lost all his money, nor wait around if the other was winning. It also required zero talent, education or mental input - anyone could play and did. With the insertion of a coin, a certain number of metal balls were released - usually twenty-five. They aimlessly fell on their own with little physical assistance, such as 'body-English' in pinball, for the machines were not to be abused.

There were no flashing lights to add excitement to a high score being racked up, and there was no competitive scoring per se. One's only reward was more balls, which could be exchanged for cheap goods, and then those exchanged for money. This was not a socializing situation, as each person sat quietly, maybe smoking, in front of their machine, elbow to elbow. The only supplied amenities were a toilet, wash basin, pay telephone and cashier's booth. There was no drinking or eating in the pachinko parlor, and the background music was loud and abrasive, like at a race track, or following the war, military marches. This was not related to slot machines, of Las Vegas - as no entertainment or pleasurable enticements.

At first, the patrons may have been the jobless, and later the hopeless, forlorn repatriated military, so rejected by those who had once cheered them, when they had faith in success. To some, the droning cacophony was like meditation chants or prayer wheels. This could take them away from their mundane existence, or battle with survival. A wordless communion could be built up between the man and the machine, to such an extent, this respite could actually result in feeling refreshed. The lines formed at the doors long before opening, since the faithful must get to his 'own' or 'personal' machine, in which a connection or rapport had been built. Perhaps it had a positive side, in that it was not destructive to the body like alcohol or drugs. Though, the addiction was the same, so any claims to mind damage could not be ignored. Of course, such escapism and addiction did not go unnoticed, and soon the pachinko came under the *protection*, if not control of the *Yakuza* - the Japanese mafia - in one way or another. *(As of 2000, almost thirty million people played regularly, and the eighteen thousand or so pachinko parlors take in over $200 billion a year, or seven times that of the auto industry. Escapism still seems to be the national past time, if not the obsession.)*

* * * * * *

Frank, in many ways, was no surprise to Mac, as he had been much what he expected. Though, his now stooping posture and extreme Japanese mannerisms were a bit surprising. Few native people would ever take notice of the slightly built man, maybe five-foot, eight inches. So Japanese in his demeanor, he seemed to be one of them. But Mac's assessment of Sakiko stunned him almost speechless. Even in middle age, it was no doubt she'd been a real, striking beauty, as she still was a beautiful woman.

Yet, he could see how those looks had deceived many before him. She smiled broadly, in a very Western style, perfected with her whole face exquisitely made-up, and raven hair in a stylish of coiffure, requiring no expertise to recognize.

She exemplified a fashion model, except for the pitch-black eyes. They remained cold and piercing, almost separated or independent on their own. They constantly examined every inch of Mac inside and out. Sakiko just could not seem to get past his strong, reddish-brown, curly hair. Even though it was short now, the superstitions about red hair were so very wary to the Japanese. She took it as a warning to be aware. He could not control the unbearable chill, streaking down his spine, as his body gave a slight shudder of caution. There was definitely power within this woman, but it was an unresolved power, which gave a slight quality of imbalance about her demeanor. As if, she had the capacity of so much more, but it was being held back. Once he met her mother, of course, the puzzle was solved - Haruko was where the real power was.

To Mac, quite disconcerting, even when mildly questioned, Sakiko responded by not looking directly at his face. This did not seem to be a physical defect, or an ignorance of Western culture, but one calculated to throw the inquisitor off balance. It quickly became evident to him, every movement, word or deed had a motive. There was no spontaneity within this woman. As a result, Mac and Paula, though more secure with him beside her, could not relax around Sakiko. Mac constantly felt scrutinized, as if she were looking for his Achilles heel, in order to exert her power over him, also.

He could only step back in amazement, as he observed her ability to ignite defensive responses in the people around her. While she covered each ploy with guilt, etiquette, or role requirement. Sakiko had mastered a passive-aggressive power-play of give-and-take keeping them all dancing on eggshells. This way, no one ever knew when she might not be satisfied with their action and response. Mac knew it would take some time for him to figure out how to play her, but with patience and determination he could. Yet, he also knew Paula was rarely able to challenge Sakiko, unless *her family* was at stake.

Nanzan had grown in stature and size since Frank had attended the first Japanese language course, so many years before. Now considered the premier, private university in the central area of Japan. The program was also quite international, and Mac felt proud to be part of it. So far, on the surface, Paula's parents were treating him like a royal guest, with a hot bath waiting, and a *yukata* - robe, laid out for his use.

The comfortable feeling Mac sensed, was the atavistic Eisenhower-era-type sensation, of the atmosphere around him - strange, yet familiar at the same time. So many things, sort of Western, yet then the 'alienness' of himself, by some Japanese staring or his surroundings, would shake him back to a resentful reality of gaijin nonacceptance. Within two months, Sakiko had gotten them a little apartment only a few blocks from their house, and she helped furnish it with what *she felt* the four of them needed. In response to their expected gratitude, she presented Paula and Mac with a schedule for them to work classes at her school. Grudgingly, she also paid them a small amount of cash, to cover their expenses and nothing more. Mac expected the pay back charge, he just wasn't prepared for Sakiko to be so blatantly-usurious in collecting.

The grind of school and work began, so Paula and Mac had little time for themselves, much less their children. Like most foreigners coming to Japan, Mac had long presumed there was something mysterious about the Japanese, which made their character so extraordinarily different. Now, in his Nanzan class, Mac learned the indirectness of the Japanese people was clearly seen through the language. He slowly absorbed its circuitous function for avoiding prompt decisions or direct answers. Previous curiosity over the years, regarding Paula's behavior, he began to understand as he learned the intimate details of 'kata,' and the culture it controlled. It created basic procedures required to disseminate words which *implied*, not spoke intentions of desire or preference.

Conversations were made more ambiguous for no reason than it was usual - the Japanese way. Needless to say, with Americans being so bluntly-outspoken, Mac made countless errors which Paula would diligently try to explain. What amazed him most often, was how Paula had quickly slipped back unconsciously to the common saying: "We Japanese …" As if, not only one of them, but like them, had the ability, knowledge, and permission to speak for the other millions of Japanese. So, not easy to bite his independently-prone, American tongue.

Another exacting, personal example of kata for Mac, was the kanji system of writing. Like so many other Japanese, cultural things, it had been directly imported from China, and then *Japan-nized*. And again, it required years of concentrated effort to master the kanji. This alone, had a fundamental effect on the physical and psychological development of all educated Japanese. The process ingrained in them patience and diligent, enhanced manual dexterity well beyond the norm, and prepared them for a lifestyle in which a step-process, and order of all things were paramount. Learning how to draw the thousands of kanji characters, also imbued the Japanese with a highly developed sense of harmony, form and style.

This combination gave them a deep understanding and appreciation of aesthetics, making each of them an artist of no little skill.

A surprising side benefit Mac learned, was they became experts at doing small, complicated things with their hands, which enhanced their sensitivity to balance and design. The kanji-training conditioned the Japanese to persevere in their goals. The long-term practice, of kanji, thus became a mold, which shaped the Japanese physically, emotionally and intellectually, homogenizing them and binding them to their culture. Learning the skill brought enormous respect from Mac, and taxed even his methodical brain. Few exceptions to the grammar rules made it easier to learn, but he noted, also meant little latitude in speaking.

As Frank acknowledged before him, in learning the language, one as well learned the culture, as they were one, more than Mac could say of English. To him, like taking "Psychology 101 of the Japanese," as he learned their foundation and purpose of control. The arts were *kata-ized* in the *Kabuki* and *Noh* drama forms - the ultimate in method acting. Once the model and order of movements of Kabuki had been established by a master, the style he created became sanctified. Every movement, down to the blinking of the eyes, was minutely prescribed for all of his disciples. Virtually, no personal interpretations were allowed. The challenge for each performer was to follow the kata absolutely. Success was based not only on the artistic interpretation of the plot, but also on how precisely they repeated the set precept.

* * * * * *

Noh, actually, became more stylized and kata-bound than Kabuki. It developed into a crystallized scheme so esoteric, only a limited number of dedicated aficionados were attracted to it. The essence of Noh was for the actor to merge his whole personality into the wooden, face mask he wore. He was to physically and spiritually put himself into the mask, allowing himself to be taken over by the character represented by the mask.

This total sublimation of character and personality into an unchanging wooden mask, and making an art out of it. Then with the mask becoming both the medium and the message, was precisely the goal of all kata, and characteristic of Japanese culture in general. This point was not lost on Mac, as he read as much information as he could. In class, they were lucky to have a professor who showed them films of famous productions. Kabuki and Noh were excellent examples of the power of kata in producing illusions, and giving reality to the unreal - both of which were vital ingredients in Japanese culture.

The death scene - in all classical Kabuki - reflected another kata of the culture. Suicide - what one might think of as the ultimate private last act - had become the kata-detailed ritual of hara-kiri. While suicides in Japan were still common, the only kata left to it tended to be one's age and sex: i.e. a grown man used a special ritual knife or sword and did not take pills - a woman's kata; hanging was preferred by teenagers; while jumping from buildings, cliffs, or bridges, was still open to all, as an *acceptable* channel. Since guns were not allowed in Japan, they were not an option.

* * * * * *

While Mac and Paula had little time, much less the money, for him to explore the arts-realm in person, studying it gave him more inside understanding to learn beyond the basic interactions. Being an ardent individualist, the hallmark of Japan's kata-ized culture from earliest times, the promotion and maintenance of *wa* - harmony, balanced- social accord - just went so against his grain. Not that he did not want 'harmony, etc.,' but Mac was a die-hard of choice, personal choice, and perhaps even timing. He did not like the idea of personal behavior, as well, all private and public relationships to be based on the strictly controlled harmony-consensus of inferior-superior context of society.

One of the most important cultural factors which evolved, came from the need of the Japanese to maintain a facade of harmony- agreement in all things. This was aided again, by the use of ambiguity in speech and nonverbal communication, to avoid commitments, disagreements, responsibility, and to help maintain the appearance of harmonious-accord. As it had become a vital part of the Japanese Way, it was highly practiced within Paula's family. Mac truly felt this ambiguity-enigma was usually helpful in maintaining surface harmony-kinship, and keeping foreigners outside of their inner circle. Frank had lived with it, and Mac quickly learned.

If the Japanese language was an impenetrable barrier keeping outsiders from looking in upon the Japanese people, it was also a barrier keeping them from looking out on the larger world. The restrictions of language did not magically work like a one-way mirrored glass, seeing out but not seeing in. Knowledge of the language erased the translucent or opaque protection. The price they paid for this privacy was high. It was emotionally demanding, at least of those who had become partly 'de-Japanized,' from their foreign experiences, so often frustrating.

The kata factor was applied to everything - down to the arrangement of food on a tray. It fascinated Mac to no end, even the smallest activity was covered by a kata. He also felt it was quite absurd. He sometimes wondered if they were just not logical, or simply chose not to be. When Mac would question some of his older professors, he would hear this strange sound come from them unconsciously, as they sucked air into their mouth through their teeth. after many audible experiences, he finally associated it with his uncomfortable 'society-oriented' questions. Frank had become too Japanized to be interested in discussing the situation with Mac. The philosophy of the *shi-kata* was simply what made the Japanese, so very *Japanese.*

With fresh eyes of a fairly new gaijin, Mac made a point to observe all he could, and questioned Paula either to clarify or confirm his theories. Though Nagoya still had few other gaijin living there at that time - most were there on company or military contracts - those he did run into he questioned. It was easy to surmise, that all the things foreigners found either delightful or deplorable, had emanated from this all-encompassing kata conditioning. This was why when the foreigner tried his/her hand at one of the kata-ized traditions like *ikebana* - flower arranging or tea ceremony, they were hesitantly welcomed, then patronized for participating.

Yet, the Japanese knew no foreigner could ever *really* succeed at their endeavor, simply because they were not Japanese. Every cultural tradition was so tied to *their* lifestyle - balance, patience and thought of reflection - as to who *they* were. How the tea was measured, the water poured, the flowers placed and balanced - it just would be too much for a gaijin to truly be capable of doing, since they just did not have the heritage. It was not unusual for the professors to quote how the great haiku poet, Basho spent his whole life writing a few perfect seventeen-syllable poems. The insinuation, of course, was no other culture or people would be capable, much less willing or able, to socially sacrifice their life for such things. At last, Mac all too clearly understood what Paula had meant about the fake-adulation she'd received.

Yet, Mac did not look for just those things to complain about or criticize the Japanese, he was a fun-loving guy. He found a real good time in the *Matsuri* - Festivals, which went on throughout the year. Mac made a point, as busy and broke as they were, to attend as many as possible. The local, regional, and national Matsuris were some of the most positive things to result from Katas, for nothing was more traditionalized, ritualized and stylized-bound - yet so much fun.

From Celebrating *O-Hanami* - Cherry Blossoms - *Sakura* blooming, to *O-Shugatsu* - New Years, or dancing in the summer in remembrance to *Tanabata* - the "Star-Crossed Lovers," or even flying gigantic kites, there was nothing like Matsuri in Japan. This was the Japanese at their best, almost natural and actually having a good time, even encouraged to do what could be called silly, or absurd things. And, most importantly it was all acceptable to the rest of the society because it was in the name of *Matsuri.* Of course, the *sake* flowed heavily. Again, through learning the language, Mac learned another side of the people which gave him a perspective beyond what was encapsulated in his sequestered-family.

* * * * * *

Matsuris were perhaps the ultimate celebrations, because amid a spectacular display of colorful, ornate costumes, the participants were either satisfying, or summoning the gods down to earth to mingle and rejoice with them. Japan may have well enjoyed more festivals than any other country. Somewhere, from the tiniest hamlet to Tokyo itself, there would be some tradition, be it Buddhist or Shinto, celebrated either on a local small scale, or the grandeur of a national holiday. Though they may have spiritual roots, one did not have to profess any religious identity to join the pageantry, drink the sake, or believe in the any expected results.

While Shintoism was the national religion, and unique to Japan, it was common for the celebrations to be intertwined with Buddhism. In more recent times, the Japanese also encompassed American holidays, though rarely understanding their concepts. They were adopted simply for the fun and excuse to let loose, or buy someone a present. One of their first attempts at an American holiday was back during the Allied Occupation, since they were so into trying to please the conquering hero, General MacArthur. The exclusive Mitsukoshi Department store, for the first Christmas, 1945, decorated their windows with Santa Claus on a cross - a faux pas at its best.

Although a relatively small nation, Japan supports some 75,000 Buddhist temples and 100,000 Shinto shrines of all varieties - large, small, grand and modest. Many of the Matsuris were related through out the seasons to rice - growing, planting, harvesting - as it was the very foundation of the Japanese culture. Then with its recognition and honor given to the deities, who were to be pleased to bring forth the continuation of bountiful crops. Even the Emperor participated in the once-a-year Spring planting at the shrine's sacred rice paddy. There were usually numerous processions around the country, with very specific clothes worn, from headgear to the *tabi* - split-toe socks, and *getas* - wooden clogs or *waraji* - straw folk sandals. Many times one or more *mikoshi* - god-dwelling wooden houses, were carried or pushed on their large wooden wheels from their storage place to the temple or shrine.

Another national celebration is *O-Bon* - Festival of the Dead, when one's ancestors are honored as they returned to earth for a visit. At the opposite end is the *Chichi-Go-San* - Seven-Five-Three, which celebrates the children of those ages. Also, the coming of age, which in Japan is twenty, a day of celebration. Specifically, there is Boys' Day, which has been renamed Children's Day, but the Carp Streamers are still primarily for the boys - it is Japan after all, and still quite a male-dominated society. It was part of Golden Week, a full week of celebration and one of the three official vacation holidays in Japan. O- Bon and New Year's being the others, when the businesses and manufacturing facilities actually closed down for several days.

At the opposite end, and not for children's participation, are the Naked, Fertility, and Penis Festivals, which are usually more regional and one's involvement may be for fun or seriousness. Production of children is expected, usually two, and if not a curse was suspected and a change of partners, also accepted. These are very ritualistic ceremonies and while laughed at by outsiders, they do have deep meaning and participation. Even highly regarded, by the Yakuza.

The men join together to carry the sacred carts, or large poles, or giant penises. The priests do the blessings and walk along chanting to the temple or shrine, with enormous taiko drums beaten, symbolistically, at very slow, then fast speeds. Special flutes and other instruments are also associated with the different events, and it's quite an honor to be chosen to play. For most families, they wear their own *yukatas* or *hapi* coats, so they are in full swing of participating, and enjoying the special food cooked at the various booths. Games and souvenirs are part of the remembrance, as well as the fun the festivals bring to the neighborhoods. Mac made sure his little family attended as many of the local Matsuris as they could afford, so they would have some pleasant memories of Japan.

* * * * * *

Frank had written many English books, which Mac helped sell, along with teaching students every free hour he had away from his own classes. Frank restricted how Mac taught the students in the home- style English classes, because his son-in-law was the only person under his orders. Every time Paula asked for extra money, Sakiko gave her a lecture on the fact she had a husband who could not adequately support her. She insisted if Mac were a decent man, he'd have gotten another job - in other words, a second job besides full time Japanese classes and studying!

It made no sense at all, for if Sakiko paid them both the going rate for a gaijin teaching English, or at least a sufficient wage, Paula wouldn't have to ask for money. Sakiko had no concern or recognition of the time and energy Mac spent on his studies. If he was to be 'family,' then he must contribute. Besides, they both owed her for 'everything' she'd done for them - a very vague subject, of a much bigger picture in her eyes. It was inconsequential that Sakiko was profiting from everyone's hard work, as there was no limit to what she felt she deserved, and continuously spent the money on herself.

Paula was not strong enough to argue and win with Sakiko, so she'd return home to Mac crying and complaining of the terrible things her mother had said. It was a tangled-web, Mac could only see breaking from once he'd earn sufficient money, and proved himself to his domineering mother-in-law. Even after he was able to get a part- time job on his own, she still did not relent. Finally, Paula went to work part-time at her old high school, in order to have a regular paycheck, and relieve some of the pressure of dealing with her mother. There was no way for either of them to totally comprehend Sakiko's need for power and dominance, or expensive items. It was an attitude of arrogance and unquestionable self-righteousness which fed into her other insecurities. They both felt helpless in going against her, when she filtered what they said and then twisted everything.

* * * * * *

Peter had long given up trying to please Sakiko, and they continued to dance with a nightmarish waltz of battles, losses, and standoffs. Peter never really won, but he did manage to embarrass, or cost his mother money when Sakiko rescued him. He still ran away several times a year, drank heavy, and yet, did a variety of work diligently for short periods of time. His reputation ran the gamut depending on who was doing the talking. He had begun working at Nagoya Station at a restaurant in a very fashionable department store. The owner had taken a liking to him, not only because he was so excellent with the customers, but for some reason he truly empathized with his personal turmoil. As the owner learned about Peter's family, he decided to make them an offer to open up an English school on the seventh floor space in his building.

Of course, without acknowledging Peter's influence, Sakiko jumped at the idea. She knew it was an excellent location, and they had become quite crowded in the house. Once it was fixed, she had Paula and Mac giving away promotional flyers. Nothing would sell something quicker than the attention gaijin garnered. Few Japanese, especially in Nagoya, had the opportunity to learn English from native speakers, especially those who could also speak Japanese. The public school system was notorious for its grammar-only approach, rote memorization because of the tests, and lecture style of teaching. Japanese people only developed any speaking fluency by either studying abroad, or working with gaijin. Travel was still quite restricted for the Japanese by the government, and English schools were prohibitively expensive, while the gaijin population was limited to a few dozen in Nagoya.

Sakiko considered her financial prospect growing brighter, and looked more acceptingly on her son-in-law until his visa expired. The immigration department was infamously rigid. Once Mac had used up the six-month extension over his one-year student's visa, there was no allowance given. Paula and Frank begged the staid bureaucrat to reconsider, as they had the new school open and were doing so well. But, the law was quite clear now - gaijin had to have a college degree to teach English full time in a school. Besides, the government official countered with the usual arrogance, there were plenty of Japanese qualified to teach English, as he had learned it. Even powerful Sakiko knew, it would not have been prudent, or successful to argue linguistics with immigration officials, who could not begin to comprehend the meaning of *fluent* English. They had always used 'Japlish' when dealing with any gaijin and it had worked.

On the other hand, to Sakiko, Mac and Paula were just walking out on her when she needed them most *and* after all *she* had done for them. "We started this for you ... now you're going to throw it all away. You could have tried ... there were ways ... and if you really wanted to help me ... and repay me." She tried to get Mac to take more classes in Tokyo, simply so Paula could stay and work at the school in Nagoya Station. The separation would have been more costly emotionally to them, than the financial benefit to Sakiko.

She had literally drained them both, physically and emotionally. Mac was back down to a weight almost as low as when he'd returned from Vietnam, and Paula cried on a daily basis from the frustration of dealing with her unrelenting mother. Sakiko's favorite tirade was, "Mac wasn't as good a husband as a Japanese. A Japanese man never stopped working to support his family. Mac's not a good man because he can't support his family." Sakiko refused to accept any blame or responsibility for their financial woes, or that she had not paid them adequately. Still, she constantly flashed her new jewelry openly and proudly.

The parting was blanketed by bitterness on both sides. Paula insisted her parents take them only to the Shinkansen, and not see them off from Tokyo. Her father was supposed to be parking the car while they waited for their train on the platform. Sakiko was holding the children while complaining, "Oh, how much I will miss them both!" As if she had ever spent any quality time with them at all. She turned to Paula, grabbing another chance at pouring on more guilt. "How cruel to take them away from their grandmother." She kissed them each lightly on their foreheads, trying to portray as much emotion as was possible for her to demonstrate an uncommon act, being in public.

Paula, once again genuinely believing her mother's sorrow, tried to soften the blow, "Perhaps we can return once Mac has his degree." He'd stayed in the background, knowing when it was impossible to referee such intense circumstances in an emotional atmosphere. He also knew his freedom from her was only minutes away, so he could contain himself.

Yet, Sakiko could not contain herself, and sarcastically laughed at Paula's pathetic idea, "He'll never finish, when he has a wife and two small children to support." The train arrived to save Mac from expressing the mounting anger, barely beneath the surface. He picked up the suitcases to board, but Sakiko refused to let them leave until Frank was there to say good-bye. It was a struggle to the last, with Sakiko publicly yelling at Paula once again. "You are the most disrespectful daughter." It did not matter to her they had reserved seat tickets on the train, and a plane to catch on the other end. Paul grabbed the children and stepped inside the train, crying once again over her mother's intolerance of her life choices.

* * * * * *

The return to America could not have been more devastating, or humiliating in every aspect. Mac felt like a dog with its tail between its legs, scooting away after being scolded. They had little money beyond their airline tickets, and nothing waiting for them in New Jersey. They were actually starting over again, but this time he had the added responsibility of a wife and two small children. His happy parents welcomed them back in the beginning, and Mac eventually found a job in a motorcycle shop across from the university. His boss gave him great leeway in his schedule, so he could take classes early in the morning or late in the afternoon. Still being the hard worker, he was soon promoted from clerk to service manager.

It took three months before they were able to move into a little apartment of their own. The struggle continued, but at least they once again had the freedom of their own life. The budget was tight with only Mac's parents to relieve some of the extra expenses of grocery treats and toys for the kids, but he was determined to finish school and get that degree. Once his Veteran's benefits began to come in for school, they were able to buy a TV and get a telephone. Since Paula had never gotten her driver's license, which limited her work prospects, she helped out by taking in other children to baby-sit. Once again a couple on their own and making every decision, they took joy in each little purchase, and every step showed accomplishment.

The biting criticism of Sakiko rang in his ears any time he slowed down, so Mac worked full time, went to school full time and finished a three-year load in two,. Once graduated, he went back to General Motors and worked his way up to a management position. With their joint venture with Isuzu in Japan, Mac also became the official greeter and translator for Japanese dignitaries who toured the plant. He wore the status well and gave the job his total commitment, while trying to convince his bosses to transfer him to Japan to represent them there. When that failed, he began writing letters in Japanese and English to the Japanese car manufacturers, offering his knowledge and services to them.

Mac knew the future would hold many more joint ventures, like GM with Toyota's NUMI - North America United Motors, Inc. - in California, Chrysler's with Mitsubishi in Illinois, and Ford with Mazda. Still, few companies returned the courtesy of a refusal, while others could not imagine their benefit in hiring him. He was a man ahead of his time, being blocked by a limited corporate tunnel-vision that plagued so much of management - American and Japanese. Though Mac was not quite at the same level of influence, the same thing had happened twenty-plus years earlier with W. Edward Deming. While his Quality-Control methodologies were rejected in the States, he was welcomed and made almost a god in Japan. His methods helped hasten Japan's recovery after and beyond World War II.

General Motors continually frustrated Mac with not seeing the advantage in using him to his full potential. With their Japanese connections on a full time basis, he could make a difference in business. Yet each visit, the management always acknowledged the usefulness of his language and cultural knowledge, yet would not budge on moving him to Japan. Time had not erased Mac or Paula's bad memories of their last trek in Japan, he simply wanted to prove he could be successful there. With its continued closed trade practices, Japan was the most closed semi-democratic market in the free world. *"You just watch, I'm going to do it,"* had been Mac's mantra, and was driven to make it come true. He knew, too, the only way to overcome the business politics was to be there to show his determination.

For Paula, returning to Japan was perhaps some absolution. Her mother had continued, through phone calls and letters, to dump guilt on her for whatever personal or business problems they had. She also emphasized Frank was getting old, and he had taken to drinking quite heavily. It was difficult to get good gaijin for the English school, and their pay for teaching English was exorbitant. Every cold, flu, or even minor health problem of her grandmother Haruko, Sack reported she was on last legs, and calling for Paula to come see her before she died. Each new photograph Paula sent of the children, Sakiko complained anew how terrible it was to have to be separated from them. Though Mac denied this to be true, and asked Paula to name exactly when or what Sakiko had ever done with or for the children, and she really couldn't, Paula still wanted to believe her mother loved her children. Though it was Mac who first brought up the topic of going back, Paula quickly agreed, as her parents were getting old and she wanted to spend time with them before it was too late.

The difference, Mac insisted, this time they would be in charge of their lives and the situation. Mac reiterated, "It wasn't the country of Japan that turned me off, it was the circumstances." Paula traveled back to Japan the summer of 1980 with the children to check things out herself, and to see what arrangements she could set up for them. Sakiko then said she and Frank were ready to give up the school in Nagoya Station, as Frank was getting too old to deal with it all. His excessive drinking had taken a toll on his health, and though the quality of teaching was not important to the students, his attendance and attentiveness was. Sakiko insinuated several times they would turn the school over to Paula and Mac, though of course, no specifics. She knew Paula would not question her or ask for the details.

Upon on her arrival, Paula went to the high school where she'd attended and been a teacher. She spoke to the principal to see if he might be interested in having a gaijin work there. He was quite accepting, and she worked out the arrangements with him to be their visa sponsor in Japan. She also contacted her childhood grade school to see if they would be accepting of her children. Though they would not directly refuse her, they had not expected Paula actually would show up sometime in the future with John and Jane, who were now third and first graders.

Since Paula was not certain of their exact arrival back in Japan, she did not want to pay the advance money for a house or apartment. This consisted of not only security money, and two months rent, but also the traditional 'gift money,' a 'present' to the landlord, because of who he was - the landlord, a person of prominence for allowing them to live there. This was not something special gaijin had to pay, though landlords did not hesitate to refuse gaijin. So, Sakiko cooperated, as she knew she could benefit from their return, and checked for them once their arrival was set, and found them an appropriate place. All blocks seemed to be in place for a successful return.

Sadly, but for the better, the new setting in Japan would be without Peter. At Sakiko's insistence, Frank took Peter up to Tokyo to see if he could get some work as a model, as it was quite easy then for most gaijin to turn into a celebrity overnight. Unfortunately, Peter did not last more than a year under the big city pressure, and returned once again to Nagoya factory work. He lived in a dormitory, which was the usual situation for single men. But, this also did not work out because of his years of so much emotional abuse from Sakiko, and it had caused such instability and waves of depression in his life over the long term.

He'd finally come to terms with the idea if he was going to have any life of his own, he must get totally away from Sakiko. Even when not living with her, she'd call and ridicule him for not supporting his family - meaning giving her money from whatever job he had. Though he loved his father dearly, his drinking made him weaker than ever in standing up for Peter, so he could no longer exist under his condemning mother.

Subsequently, he left Japan and went to America, staying with Paula and Mac for a while. Then, understanding their own struggles, he went on to New York where he got a job working for a Japanese shipping company driving a truck. In English school, he met and married a woman from South America. By the time Paula left again for Japan, he had two daughters, and was doing rather well. Their adult separation was replaced by the deep love and support they always gave each other. Peter still drank and escaped when his demons became too great, but he seemed to have finally found love, and occasional acceptance of himself was better.

* * * * * *

Controlling everything and everybody was not just Sakiko's way, but the Japanese mother's way. Yes, she was most extreme in her egomania, and addiction to material things because of her massive insecurities and feeling everyone - family or stranger - owed her. All things were to be fit into neat little categories, rules and hierarchical decisions. In her own mind, she only wanted to give Peter and Paula what she thought was best and most important - to be a successful Japanese. Yet, with her own taunting from her adoption, she feared they would not love her as their true mother. Still, since love was all they needed, it was the one physical and emotional thing she could not give them. Sakiko always seemed to relate happiness and love to success and money, with recognition from the outside. She tried to live too many years in both gaijin and Japanese worlds, where the conflicting constructs of happiness were entirely different concepts.

As for Frank, there was a chink in the armor, or at least a bad fit regarding his niche in Japan. He'd been one of *those foreigners* who fell passionately in love with the 'Mysterious East,' and tried to see in Japan everything they felt was lacking in America, or any other country for that matter. These sentiments last for months or years, but after a lengthy sojourn, the pendulum swung. As they learned more of Japan's language and understood more of its intrinsic culture with its rigid society, most long term gaijin found themselves in a love-hate relationship. They were torn between loving Japan and its people one day, while hating the society and its confinements the next.

Given enough time, most people reached an emotional equilibrium, and accepted their lives as no better or worse than mankind outside the islands. For others, fantasies rudely destroyed, they developed an overt dislike and distrust of Japan and all the Japanese. While continuing to live there, they found themselves hanging out with other disillusioned foreigners grumbling about this or that trait of the Japanese people.

If Caucasian, and unaccustomed to being a minority, they complained about how racist Japanese people were. As a rule, the higher the expectations and the more inflated the fantasies of the visitor to Japan, the greater the ensuing sense of ultimate disillusionment and betrayal. It was perhaps one reason why so many foreigners developed excessive drink habits - to drown out the reality of the unhappiness of their lives in Japan, while rejecting their addiction to the country. Drugs were strictly prohibited, while excessive drinking was widely accepted and condoned. It was by no means a unique or new syndrome. While Mac truly thought he knew what he was getting himself into, he did not really comprehend the depth of it all.

A Letter from Lafcadio Hearn:

With regard to, "The Plight of Foreign Teachers at National Universities," Lafcadio Hearn, the Foreign Instructor at the National Fifth High School (Kumamoto University) from 1891 to 1894, had this advice in a letter he wrote to Basil Hall Chamberlain, Professor of Japanese at Tokyo University, dated June 4, 1894:
I should say these were the general rules for a foreigner in Government service:
- Never to ask any questions concerning business.
- Never to ask why.
- Never to criticize even when requested.
- Never to speak either favorably or unfavorably of other officials, of students, or of employees.
- If obliged to speak, to remember that favorable criticism may objectionable than the other.

- Give no direct refusal under any circumstances, but only say:
1. "It is difficult for the moment …" or
2. "Certainly"- but take care to forget all about it.

Direct refusals are not forgiven. The other devices are respected and admired.

3. Never imagine intimacy possible, - or imagine reserve possible.

Both require impossible; but one must steer carefully between them.

4. Consider that all adverse criticisms upon national or official matters thrown out as "feelers" and that any of sympathy with them is likely to provoke hostility.
5. Do not imagine that the question of application, efficiency, or conduct in relation to students is of any official importance.

The points required from the foreigner are simply two:
    a. Keep the clams in good humor.
    b. Pass everybody.

6. If told you give too high marks, pay no attention - except to give higher still when possible. The suggestion is policy.
7. Be very much afraid if praised, that something awful is going to happen to you.
8. Be perfectly sure that the result of making any complaint will be that you will be responsible for the cause of the complaint - because that is the easiest way of settling the matter.

Other comments by Hearn on foreigners:
9. "The foreigner is treated only as an intellectual machine."

10. "To the Japanese official world, all of us foreigners are mere animated numerals. The salary of No. 7 ought to be reduced because it is larger than that of No. 8. There is no other reason."

11. "The Japanese seem to regard many men who have passed their best days in Government service, as tools merely to work with - to be thrown away when the edge wears off. Did not the Nakamura, who wanted all foreigners discharged as soon as the "freshness" had faded out, really express a national foreigners sentiment?"

12. "I do most sincerely hope to get out of Japanese employ someday before long. The conditions of every employee are bound to become worse. And no effort is recognized, no personality remembered. The indifference shown us is certainly barbarian."

13. "A foreigner among Japanese officials simply a *go-ishi,* a pawn. He has no friend, and no sympathy."

Lafcadio Hearn must have had great foresight, as everything he said at the end of his years in Japan still rang true one hundred years later. Unfortunately, Frank Williams had the Syndrome, but he never heard of, nor read what Lafcadio had written in his later years. The fact still remained and was mirrored often: though Hearn loved Japan from the depths of his soul, he still died a broken, disillusioned, and very bitter old man. It would have been to Mac's advantage, to know and learn about Lafcadio, and most of all to prepare himself for his life as a gaijin in Japan.

A Different Cultural Perspective:

Chapter 6 Growing Up *'Gaijin'* in Modern Japan

Lafcadio Hearn married a Japanese, lived in a Japanese home, wrote beautiful and discerning books about the Japanese. But he confessed at last that he did not know them. In his final book *Japan, An Interpretation,* he wrote: "Long ago the best and dearest Japanese friend I ever had said to me a little before his death: '"When you find, in four or five years more, that you cannot understand the Japanese at all, then you will begin to know something about them"'"

Willard Price,
Key to Japan - 1946

Returning A Hero:

Mac stepped off the Shinkansen at Nagoya Station loaded down with luggage, and said - with as little hostility as possible - directly to Sakiko, with Frank standing behind her, "Was there ever a doubt in your mind we wouldn't be back?!" His great triumphal reentry for sure, for he'd done what he'd said he'd do, and exactly what she'd said he would not. The weight of her stare held then all paralyzed, as if waiting for her to take credit for his success.

As Sakiko realized there was nothing she could say in response, she quietly said, "Welcome back," more directed to Paula and the children, whom she distracted her attention to, in a saving-face gesture. In a negative way, one might believe it was a self-fulfilling prophecy - would he have pushed so hard if she'd not laughed at him? Mac would've made it no doubt, Japan was his destiny, though the time frame influenced in a positive-negative way.

Mac's achievement took less than four years, but most importantly, totally on his own terms. The faces of Frank and Sakiko were easy to read, since the shocked-look showed the disbelief they'd uttered so many times to each other and Paula. The MacAllens returned, and they intended on staying for the long haul. Some may have considered Mac crazy, and others considered him masochistic in wanting to live in a country that historically distrusted and kept foreigners out. Yet, it was Paula's adopted homeland, and while never completely accepted there, not counting Sakiko, she still felt less insecure in Japan than in America.

Yes, she'd come to love America, but could not quite fit in it comfortably. For Mac, Japan had definitely become more than a quest, for him to succeed in proving his mettle. He took it on like an ancient gladiator, slaying one foe or obstacle after another. And, what was to come of all those battles he might win? Was he fighting Sakiko, or the culture? If it was a war, when would he know it was over, or even if he won? This could jump into the not so far future computer game, and someone simply pushes the restart button. Would the battle start all over again?

Mac and Paula were enthusiastic, as well energetic at first, but these positive traits could not begin to overcome the tightly bound Japanese system, in which they intended to live and work. Again for the first month they stayed with Paula's family, crowded into the little house. All too soon, Mac's job turned out to be disappointing. Proudly, it was Paula's contact, but admittedly a rather low level, second class private school with little money, and less interest in their English program. Few of the students were motivated to study English, for they knew there would be limited opportunities to use any language other than Japanese in their everyday, or future work lives.

Right from the start, Mac bucked the system with his methodology of teaching English. He'd taught university students in the States and had the specific training for teaching English to foreigners. But, this *was* Japan. There was the *Japanese way*, and the way of the rest of the world did it. The fact most foreign students, even in third-world countries, learned sufficient English in a few years, did not matter. The Japanese system taught their students a minimum of six years, but usually a handful, or less could utter more than "Hello," or in Japanese English - Jap-lish, "Harro." Yet Mac, like so many gaijin before and after him - particularly those who spoke Japanese somewhat fluently - wanted to be accepted by the Japanese, and not be treated any differently than their native colleagues. Which meant then, he had to reconcile and do everything the Japanese way. It *was* their country, he contended.

Mac worked diligently on his Japanese proficiency, picking up the Nagoya-ben - dialect, using idioms and the common colloquial phrases. At first, the other teachers, neighbors, and new acquaintances constantly complimented him on his progress and earnestness. Mac felt he was truly a part of the society, and not just a typical gaijin living a Westernized Japanese lifestyle. Then a very strange thing happened. Mac began to feel a resentment and sarcasm insinuating he was being haughty, or arrogant in his joking and Japanese slang usage. He questioned Paula, Frank and other long-time gaijin, only to be informed the Japanese *actually* considered it an invasion of privacy, when the gaijin learned about them and their language, too well.

Such a cultural shock, prompted Mac to never look at any Japanese in quite the same way again. Because of Paula and his own earnestness, he had assumed the Japanese wouldn't be prejudiced against him. He soon learned his closest friendships could be developed with those Japanese who had traveled extensively, or actually lived overseas for some time. They had a definite empathy, for they also were not totally accepted any more in their homeland, as if tainted or contaminated. Eventually, he was able to make friends with long-term gaijin, those either married to Japanese, or having been raised in Japan as children of missionaries.

Mac was not alone dealing with the Japanese educational system, since John and Jane soon joined it. He felt he needed to do some research to understand it, and make the best of it to explain more to his children for awareness. He knew he couldn't change the opinions and feelings of the Japanese about him, but he could learn how to best handle their treatment of him, without being rude or insinuating he didn't care what they thought.

* * * * * *

Though the first gaijin teachers came on the heels of the opening of Japan, with the Meiji Restoration in the late 1800s, they were usually connected with the missionaries. Most were sent home with the war, but their numbers grew at a steady pace following the Allied Occupation. SCAP - Supreme Commander of the Allied Powers - MacArthur and the Occupation were one and the same - changed the mandatory free education from six years to nine. They also made it more accessible for females, and encouraged the expansion of the number of universities, so they could accommodate more students with less class division. Equality of the ranks had always been frowned upon in all of Japan's history, as one's blood-ancestry was preeminent in all things.

SCAP also tried to decentralize the system out of Tokyo, but singular control and power was so embedded, the minor changes were immediately discarded once the Allies were gone six years later. The Allies were more concerned in what was being taught, so time was spent eradicating the military drills and Emperor-worship indoctrination, rather than bringing about a more Western approach to learning. Japan quickly grew into a country of 'average people," having the largest middle class in the world - ninety percent.

This would slowly change over time as money and power through manufacturing and business success replaced the required 'right' blood line. Yet, from the Allies changes, virtually every citizen became functionally literate, having the capability of basic math, reading and writing sufficiently to socialize, work together in a group, and most importantly, follow instructions. Imaginative or creative ideas were usually suppressed by junior high, and those stubborn *'artistes'* would be relegated to a very separate group, and wear a beret to distinguish themselves even further from the masses. This restricted development created fewer Nobel Prize winners in the arts, but they weren't much of a concern, as not a lot of money or power was attached to them.

Some 'educators' tried to influence MacArthur into outlawing kanji, and having all Japanese adopt English. Instead, he decided to have the kanji simplified in the strokes needed to create the kanji, and the total number of them to be used reduced. Significantly, MacArthur chose 1945, for the number of kanji to be available for the language function. China had an estimated six thousand kanji, with hundreds complicated by having more than a dozen strokes for their individual creation. The change process, as usual, ended up being fruitless, as the Japanese educators simply gave more definitions to each kanji character, which meant no one's life was simplified.

During the transition time, and to keep the masses informed, the newspapers converted much of the news into *hiragana* - the phonetic syllabary of Japanese, to be able to read their news without kanji. Mac quickly learned, the young people he was trying to teach had come to depend mainly on the hiragana. Few, unfortunately, had more than a basic working knowledge of perhaps five hundred, or at most, a thousand kanji. Nearly forty percent of all books and magazines published in Japan were comic books - *manga,* and printed exclusively in hiragana.

Adults, particularly male, read comic books in public as commonly as the children, but theirs tended to be pornography. No matter how degrading, they had few limitations other than the nipples and genitals not being shown, or just blocked out. The government also did not allow children younger than junior high age to be portrayed in the pornography. The tacit acceptance of pornography, available in reputable bookstores, vending machines - along with 'verified-used' panties for the collector. This practice, of course, was never talked about, simply ignored by women, and anyone else with a concern about it in most other countries. Besides, there was no general sex education, even separately, other than the girls being taught about menstruation, with no sex details connected to it.

* * * * * *

The average Japanese student knew well who Washington or Edison or Ford were, and could probably write in Japanese a pretty good essay on each. Unfortunately, these essays would all be identical, depending on the grade level. They were all taught the same information and expected to repeat it, as such and for answering those questions on tests. The Japanese took pride in their high-scoring students' success in rote-learning, never concerned for the lack of participation, or individual interaction allowed from the students. "Why" was not allowed, so the concepts related to the subject didn't matter, just the rote information.

Mac had a difficult time hiding his frustration. He knew not one of his students would have said something outrageous or obnoxious, like about Washington's wooden false teeth or affairs with his slaves, even if he asked, because of the virtual restriction of questions and interaction. The Gettysburg Address was a standard used as a junior or senior high school speech to memorize for giving in front of the class. Abraham Lincoln was Emperor Hirohito's favorite person, so quite immortalized with his portrait hung in numerous libraries, schools, and public buildings. Yet, no student could give his or her personal opinion as to how, or what the man did, or the beliefs the speech purported regarding the Civil war, or changing history. They only knew rote facts, with no room for interpretation, or reaction to it or him.

The literacy of English, thus, did not mean knowledge, but merely the ability to read and write, without any concern in being able to speak it. Rarely, except in top universities, was there a key to unlock understanding and further inquiry. It did not take long for Mac to see he was not just bucking a single school's set way and pride of doing something. Other Asian countries, with lower literacy, had a higher percentage of individual or creative knowledge. Education in Japan was a system of transmission, mental regimentation, and memorization of *officially* selected facts and ideas. He realized this since, 'officially,' all Japanese public, and most private schools, were strictly controlled by the Japanese Board of Education, the *Mumbusho*, which in turn was a government department.

The local, prefectural, or regional district had no participation or influence in the whole process, except a limited choice of texts in elective courses These were all previously approved - usually edited and changed, by the dictates of the Mumbusho. Most noted in this rewriting was a 'cleansing' of Japan's war role, which in later years brought much criticism, yet little change. MacArthur did make sure the bombing of Pearl Harbor was changed to come before and not after Hiroshima. So, as amazing as it seemed to Mac, all public school students, from Hokkaido in the north to Okinawa, in the south, learned the same subject on the same pages on the same days. Only a natural disaster would be an acceptable excuse for the slightest variation from the set schedule.

This was the main reason most teachers simply lectured the planned information to the students, never slowing down, or allowing questions to digress from the goal at hand. More and more, as time did progress, some private schools purchased the required books, and then used their own choices as well. Students still had to learn sufficient information from the Mumbusho books, so they could pass the national entrance exams for university or even high school.

To Mac's surprise and disgust, dozens of gaijin with Phd.D.s had been known to sell their names to publishers to list them as 'editors' for English texts and dictionaries. Considering the

constant mistakes, few had ever looked at the books, much less checked them for any accuracy of grammar or usage,. It was common knowledge, a gaijin could have the required degree in any subject, not just English, much less a teaching certificate, to qualify for the endorsement. The students then, could not be blamed for their bad pronunciation or grammar usage, when the books lacked support of their meager efforts to communicate. In reality, few of the texts had been updated since the Occupation, although more innovative methodologies had proven their worth.

To many outsiders, it was assumed the Japanese children were incredibly smart in that they could learn everything the first time. Western observers were influenced by their familiarity with their own model of educations, so erroneously concluded if the teacher was teaching calculus, the textbooks were open to a page of calculus, then all the students were learning calculus. Not true, they were just following the schedule. Only a percentage, hopefully at least a majority, would understand and learn the subject - calculus or whatever - being taught. While the brilliant may be catered to by special treatment, as in the States, the slower children were often left to their struggles. Such was the case with Peter after his accident, and his lack of knowledge of anything beyond the basics. But, the Japanese system felt they were not ignored, as the slower children would also have their place in society designated to doing the more menial tasks, that also needed to be done. In this way, they rationalized theirs was a fair and just system. Actually, most of the really intelligent children would have been tested out earlier, and sent to the more prestigious schools, to be with their 'own kind' to not be slowed down, but truly excel. It was perhaps of these the observers wrote their reports, and the superiority of the Asians, particularly how the 'Japanese brain' came into being.

Mac, like many Westerners, looked at Japan's phenomenal, growing economic success in the international market and merely assumed it was the educational system. Considering the shape of the schools and denigration of American youth in the 1970s and 1980s, it was an obvious conclusion. What the observers did not know, did not ask and were not told - though Mac eventually earned - the Japanese textbooks targeted high achievers, in a 'shotgun approach.' It was better to know a little about a lot, and those students who got more were the benefit.

Sometimes, upwards of ninety-five percent of the students did not understand what the teacher was talking about, and a passing score in the prerequisites had been set at only thirty-five percent. Therefore, most students were studying calculus or whatever, without having passed the prerequisites. What the students did not comprehend was basically their problem, and they must sit there not disturbing the others. This may answer the question of why after six mandatory years of studying English, the average Japanese could not speak more than a dozen words, and only a few introductory phrases. Mac's students were not alone in being lost in their limited comprehension of English.

Other misinformation, taken more from statistics rather than their detail, was Japanese students spent more time in school. Granted, they were attending, but not necessarily studying. The three hours of classes on Saturday morning, made up for the non-academic hours during the week spent on home room activities and mandatory club activities. Typically, some sixty-five to seventy days' worth of afternoons were either free time or given over to nonacademic activities. Students were also required to attend school, in uniform for one day in the middle of summer vacation, so teachers could take roll and then send them home. Yearly, three or four school days were devoted to cleaning the school, which students must help and participate in doing real scrubbing, etc. Eventually, Mac learned not to question, just to reconcile to the established practices and unwritten laws. He was constantly reminded that he, a mere gaijin, could not nor was expected to comprehend the system.

The school exams were given nationally three to six times a year on the required subjects, depending on the grade level. Much classroom time was spent preparing for these tests, which meant memorizing facts, and student had the afternoon off on the test days. One or two subjects were tested at a time, so as many as three days were lost with each periodic testing. Yet, in effect, 'testing was the sole purpose or reason for the schools and education. If one could not prove what one had learned, why have education?' It was not a rhetorical question, but a belief. To Mac, and many gaijin, it was a sacred rationalization they challenged.

The infamous entrance exams, not only for the university, but for the better junior and senior high schools were a self-serving entity unto themselves. One's future status was strictly related to the schools attended, as the career or job was the direct results of them. The self-educated or self-made man was a rarity outside of the arts, and the late bloomer was even more of an oddity. So, passing the all-important entrance exams, whether junior or senior high or university, was the goal of every parent - especially the mother, since her main job was the 'education' of her child. Life success and academic achievement were so closely related, the stress or failure attached was the common cause of suicide in the spring, term's end when the exam scores were posted. With such an investment of time and money, failure was not accepted from anyone for any reason.

Most middle class families underwent economic privations, so their children received the advantages of numerous avenues to success

- private kindergarten, jukus - the cram schools, and tutors. No matter how small the family living space, each child had his own desk to study and do homework, which began in first grade. The mother's role in the child's success was a given, and *her reward of being taken care of in her old age was equal to it.* She was expected to stay at home with her children all the time, so her husband attended parties or other social functions alone, where it would not be appropriate to take the children. Her social contact was limited to the neighborhood shops, school functions and other things specific to the children.

Using a baby-sitter, other than the grandparents would be neglecting her duties, and it would be years before day care or nursery school were at all accepted. Educational success was responsible for the initial birth control practices of city dwellers. It was just too depleting, financially and emotionally, to educate well more than two children. Of course, preference was given to the males. In early times, mothers constantly told their daughters from toddlers on, "Nice face and gentle speech," and taught them not to protest against any slights, just be submissive. With time, Mac began to have a totally different perception of Sakiko's obsessiveness, with how she had raised Paula and the investment she felt she made, now deserved unending rewards. What was less known to Mac about the best public schools,

which had the most stringent test requirements, was they were not restricted to the neighborhood area where a family lived, but only to the Ward or county district. Therefore, many of the students were from the more prominent families, or at least those who had the money for special tutoring were accepted. Yet, since the parents still could not depend on the schools to guarantee their child's acceptance into the highest institutions, extensive amounts of time and money were spent on sending them to jukus - the infamous cram schools.

There they were all but guaranteed to pass the exams, since the largest cram schools had the contracts to create the ten thousand question pool, most universities pulled from for their entrance exams.

Simply, in the Japanese Way, the student memorizes the material for the answers, and passed. The system also did not consider sharing information and answers on homework as cheating, but just being polite and helping their fellow student. It was a business after all, and their main job was to serve the businesses of Japan with the best Japanese. The government totally supported the concept, as it kept the economy growing, which they felt benefitted everyone, though most importantly the businesses.

The loss of face in failing a test was the most humiliating thing that could ever happen to a Japanese, for it said one did something the wrong way, went against, or *failed* the kata. For most, those years of junior and senior high school were unbelievably grueling in studies, horrendous in stressful competition, and most dangerous to one's health. Almost all Western teenagers, especially Americans, were running around to school sports games, clubs, dating or at worst, suffering through some mind-numbing part-time job.

Japanese teens meanwhile, were attending jukus three to five nights a week, burning the midnight oil every night doing homework, and contemplating suicide if they floundered. They received support from their parents in the form of demands to try harder and being told, "Six hours sleep, you fail; five hours sleep, you pass." Again, the child's success or failure was direct reflection on the parents, but especially the mother. Since most children, particularly the boys, were totally spoiled when younger, many were not prepared for these years of trauma and punishment in their studies.

In addition to everything else, there was an exorbitant charge for all entrance exams, with the university ones being as much as a thousand dollars for each test taken. The easier schools gave their exams first, then those who passed must pay at least one-*non-refundable* semester's tuition immediately, the minimum usually being five thousand dollars. Parents pursued this process, even when their children were taking several exams at higher level schools, as this thus guaranteed the child had a school to attend.

It was not unusual then, for parents to have paid the entrance exam fee, plus the semester fee for three or more schools. As said prior, like everything else in Japan, education was a business and a very lucrative one, notably when all of the costs of the jukus were added in.. The lower academic level private schools and universities cost more, but 'guaranteed' a diploma, as attendance was the only requirement to receive it. Surprisingly, it was the National, Prefectural (state/region) or large City Universities that were the most difficult to enter, but then they cost relatively little, being covered by the government. They all required the student to actually study and pass real exams after they had entered.

Students at the vocational high schools were mostly male and the academic program was much less rigorous. Many boys, like Peter had so many years earlier, choose the school as much for the sports team as for their connection to a particular industry or manufacturing training. The students expected to graduate, and went on to work as skilled or semi-skilled apprentices. These schools also supported more sport teams like baseball, soccer, etc. and their competitions were followed closely nationally, since they were not '*politely*' rigged like the professional sports. In reality, it was also not unusual for the best sports players to remain seniors for more than one year, to benefit the school. Like so many Japanese stuck in a certain class level, they were bound by group isolation, and the *privilege* of sacrifice for the group.

Though they still had to master the basics, in trade schools they had no 'exam nightmares' for their later school years had them already working part-time for the corporations, so they walked right into their jobs the day they finished school. As always, the government supported the effort of businesses by having paid for much of their on- the-job raining. It also niftily eliminated the role of unions, while building *guilt-loyalty* to the company. The boys did what they were told and were paid what the company chose. Of course, the company in turn became their mother, if not Big Brother - housed and fed them, helped choose a wife when the time was right, and got them a house in the company development, with a company mortgage.

Again, neat and simple, their whole life was wrapped up for them, like the perfect gift packages from the department stores, with their many layers identically folded. It was not as pretty as the white collar-boys, but still no worries, no decision, no problems - the Japanese Way. The lifetime employment was implied, but never actually guaranteed by the company. Yet, their loyalty to the company came before self or family. Still, if one compared it to the large number of those unemployed in Western country ghettos, or rural areas, it might seem utopian. The only thing missing was individuality, choice and personal freedom of expression to do things for themselves. It wasn't quite mediocrity, while you weren't expected to be imaginative or creative, you must do your job well, as you had to sign-off on all work you did daily.

* * * * * *

Mac and Paula had agreed placing the children in Japanese grade school would be beneficial for them learning Japanese and assimilating quickly into the culture. Besides, there was the reality they could not afford the Nagoya International School, for there was no corporation or missionary program to pay their expenses. Since Paula had attended the same grade school as a child, she could relate to the problems and prepare John and Jane for some of the difficulties they might encounter. The teachers were perhaps a little more used to gaijin, and being aware of Paula's family, they were a little more accepting. Every little bit would help to soften the blow, since John and Jane were older than Paula and Peter had been, so their memories of America were more distinct.

Their last home in America had been in a very middle-class neighborhood, insulated even more by the fact numerous other MacAllen-General Motors' families also lived on the same street, or close by. Into this placid picture was thrown the school bussing program for integration of the black city children. Racism was more prominent among the blue-collar families, and its topic was heartily discussed, joked about, and generally batted around in a prejudiced, or at least pejorative way. Although, Mac and Paula did not hold these convictions, between his older relatives and friends at school, John had a negative picture painted about people of color. Fights, slurs and other racially-based problems occurred almost daily in and around his neighborhood school. It was one more item, along with increasing teen-drug usage and violence, Mac had put on his agenda for wanting to leave the States and move back to Japan.

John was a very physically active third grader, who took up boxing to release some of his pent up energy. This influence had come from a cousin five-years older and proudly, at the time, blessed by Mac. But not unusual for John to be encouraged to practice his macho 'sport' on other cousins, schoolmates, or neighbors. John had been training at the gym for almost a year, when it was time to move to Japan. More than anything, John hung onto the memories of that last year, and the actions of those people who had meant so much to him.

It was summer break between the Japanese school semesters when the MacAllens arrived. The children had a few free months to adjust to Nagoya's humid heat, pungent dank smells, and the crowded, identical neighborhoods with their uniform, third-world's living conditions. It was also rainy season, and it sometimes kept a layer of cloudy gloom around them. There seemed to be a permanent scent of sour in the air, as the mold silently grew in every corner of every building. In their houses, Sakiko and Paula used the little, plastic- boxed absorption crystals, which the vapid humidity astonishingly filled up in only days. Deodorizers merely added another flower to the air, hinting they were only fooling themselves, but never the relentless mold growing in the humidity.

The curse of an over active and sensitive olfactory organ was never more true, as every few feet it seemed smells wafted out, as John and Jane walked around their new neighborhood. Whether it was the strange smells from the herbalist shops, wasabi and soy sauce from sushi shops, along with the various fish orders, or just the acrid urine from every hidden corner, or alcove used as a receptacle for the acceptable practice of males urinating in public alleyways.

The kids often spoke of how 'odorless' the States had seemed, since so many places were over-air conditioned, or the disinfectant- cleaned air in grocery stores rarely gave clues as to the products sold. Even the few 'fast-food' restaurants in Japan did not smell the same, and obviously not the same food either. One constant smell, both inside and out, was the smell of cigarettes - their smoke, the obnoxious offense when they had been left burning, and then the putrid, blunt-odor when water was poured over a mass of butts. There was too, that not unfamiliar, yet not as definitely prominent, of alcohol - both beer and whiskey - their grandfather drank continuously and reeked of.

There were no memories remaining of their last visit to Japan, so the culture shock of both smothered like a wet blanket, and intrigued them by its bizarre differences from what they had left behind. The tight-knit living area revealed more than the released wafting of incense from the various shrines and temple, some with only a door front entrance, having sold off the street frontage to shops and restaurants. New Jersey may have gotten hot in late summer, but it was nothing compared to this humidity, so dense and heavy it took their breath away, especially after having emerged from an overly air- conditioned shopping mall. There were still the old market places Paula had know, but the Nagoyans were proud of their new malls.

They made sure they became sanctuaries to the younger, spoiled generations who had no interest in suffering in the heat. The parents had sacrificed much so their children could have everything they did not. Few Japanese ever seemed to show any perspiration, as it was a definite genetic trait. Yet, the government put much pride in their new electronics industries, and encouraged the people to support them by buying the products which were in the malls. No one ever had to tell Japanese children this twice, as they demanded and got every new item their parents could afford.

While so many things were recognizable or similar to America, the dichotomy of the reality imposed on them, kept John and Jane in a constant state of confusion. Logically, in John's mind, he thought the off-colored people would be put into the same category as the blacks back home. Still, it confused him that his grandmother and great- grandmother were both non-white, yet acted quite prideful and authoritatively. Though he had no idea what they are saying, he was quite convinced they had considerable control over his life, and even more over his parents. It was something that just would not fit in his brain - this could not be so, yet it was.

On the first day of school, in the welcome back ceremonies, the principal introduced John and Jane to the whole school from the auditorium stage. It was their first nervous moment in the spotlight and seemed fun. They had both been just like their neighbors back home, but in Japan, they were someone special. It never dawned on John and Jane, it was not *who they were,* but *what they looked like* - Jane's long, blonde, curly hair, John's wavy dark hair, and both of them with blue eyes and very white skin. The belief of being someone special soon turned into the reality of being something odd. In the hall, on the way to their respective classrooms, the other children with no previous up- close and personal experience of being around gaijin, most conspicuously of their own age, kept running around them, pointing and saying strange things which only sounded like noise, and then laughed. John, was sent to third grade, although he had already finished it in the States and Jane, because she was so big and tall, was sent to second.

In the classroom, this commotion was not abated by the teacher, as children from other classes poured in to get a closer look at the gaijin. During the ruckus, one of the kids running around John's desk accidentally knocked over his canteen, and his Coca Cola spilled out over the floor. Unknown to John or Paula, cola was not allowed in the classroom or the school, only Japanese green tea was acceptable. The craziness of the situation shot John's emotions back to the States, he grabbed the boy who had done it and punched him in the nose. Blood instantly spurted-out over his face and clothes.

It was no big deal to John, for that would have been a normal occurrence back home, but in Japan it created havoc and panic. To make things worse, when the boy exited from the nurse's office, and confronted John directly, with words he could only imagine the meaning of, he punched hm out a second time. This time, John was quickly marched to the Principal's office and his parents were called. It took almost a week of apologies, and *'gomen-nasai'* - "I am so sorry" - gifts to everyone involved: the parents of the child, the teacher, and the Principal to soothe over the incident in a satisfactory, Japanese way.

John's home room teacher could actually read English and write a little, but he could not speak any - as usual. The only way John could communicate with him was through a journal the teacher had him begin keeping, and turn in at the end of the week. John was not able to get any answers to his questions - like: "What was he doing there in the first place?" but at least the journal gave him a less physical outlet for his emotions. It would take more than talk and explanations, to make up for the sheltered environment of his previous, large, extended, protective, and supportive American family. Neither could the anxious teacher answer why the replaced surrounding, had not only strangers, but ones who pointed, gawked, and followed him home chanting strange words. John could only think of, and hope to return to his suburbanite citadel, that was so comforting to him to remember, as his resentment toward his parents grew day by each intolerant day. Adjusting to Japan would have been arduous enough, but fitting into a Japanese school was nearly unendurable, even if John had been willing.

The strict, uncompromising rules of behavior throughout all areas of the school were beyond weird, and seemingly stupid as they made so little sense to John. The students had to stand and bow on the teacher's entrance into the classroom, keep there hands clasped behind their back until they would raise their hand to answer a question. Students were not, of course, allowed to ask questions. If chosen to answer, the student then must stand up to speak.

Finally, at the end of class, the process was reversed - stand, bow and thank the teacher for the good lesson. It was, of course, all ridiculous to John from the beginning, but the severity of not following the rituals made the compromise worthwhile. He numbed himself by hours of bouncing a ball against the wall in the playground and at home. He also began to withdraw into himself, becoming more sullen, whiney, and shy to outsiders. His mind would escape in daydreams of the freedom and comfort he'd known so well, yet had not appreciated in America.

Though Jane was a year and a half younger, she was put into the second grade. Images of most things did not seem as strange as they did to John, since Jane had less of a backlog of memory or attachments with which to compare. Every day was a new experience, just as it would have been in the States. One thing Jane liked about her teacher, she was small, closer to her own size, and hence not so scary or intimidating, as a man might have been. She also responded to Jane's special need for learning Japanese, and took the time to teach her in a most tactile way. She'd give the other students an assignment to keep them busy while she took Jane outside. She lead her around the school or classroom, choosing items, then repeated over and over their Japanese name. Kind of a Japanese Anne Sullivan to a language- less Helen Keller, of sorts. She had Jane carry a little notebook, in which Jane would write the item's name in English and the teacher would write in *Romanji* - the alphabetized spelling of the Japanese word, and *katakana* - the more simplified characters for pronunciation. To complete the picture for memorization, she had Jane do just that, draw the item.

Slowly, Jane also built a few friendships, especially with other girls who lived close around their house, and did not treat her like an alien object. Their games were the universal sharing of children almost everywhere - a ball is a ball no matter what its name in what country. And, if one child wants to play with another, the name of the ball will be of the dominant country. So, as Jane taught her new friends American - hide-and-go-seek, or tag, they taught her other Japanese games. At her pliable age, friends across the sea were easily replaced by the here and now of others.

They quickly built their own mixed-pidgin language for playing. Her only vivid memories that brought regret were of her American grandparents, since they'd seen them almost daily, and constant displays of affection were expected. The physical and verbal warmth was missing from these new Japanese grandparents, for Frank was as constrained with showing emotion and caring, as Sakiko was bridled by ritual. Yet, like her mother and uncle Peter's reversed roles before her as children in Japan, Jane's closest ally, confidant, and friend became her big brother John.

Much of the lack of attention that Jane, and John to a lesser extent, received from home was replaced by the constant spotlight from classmates and strangers. Once she saw the fawning for what it was, Jane delightedly basked in her limelight and uniqueness. Almost everyday, one of the students would ask her for a piece of her long, curly blonde hair. She would snicker and laugh at them, treasuring it as if it would turn to gold, or that it was already a priceless commodity.

The girls would put these fine, precious strands in the back of their plastic, pin-on name tags all the children had to wear to school. Once she naturally absorbed the language by exposure, she could return whatever gibes she might still receive from those less adulating.

After the initial positives and negatives of the spotlight cooled down, the realization of his predicament finally clicked in to John - he was now the minority. While not 'bussed' in, they had invaded the placid environment of the Japanese school system. The racial superiority and prejudice he'd seen given out before, he received. A lesson few Caucasians ever learned, especially at such a young age. The first two years John considered a living hell, as his freedom had been snatched from him, without his knowledge of having put it to any good use in the past.

Not just the lack of communication isolated him, for the language ability came quickly as used in survival and comprehension of classes taught. He cherished this memories of life before Japan, as his fears mounted he would never regain them. More frustrating, was the fact any detailed connections back to America for John had to come from Mac, as Paula lacked the long-time experience of the culture or traditions. But the transference, or reassurance of these bits and pieces came rarely from Mac.

Unfortunately, his constant work schedule and obligations to Sakiko's English school limited his access to his children.

In reality, like his Uncle Peter, only through his sports activities - baseball, soccer, and basketball, did John began to blend in on an accepted or peer level. Eventually, over the next two years, friendships developed from club and sports participation. Of course, John learned not to use any of his boxing skills again. An equality of sorts, he was invited to teammates' homes to meet their families and spend some weekends together doing mutually-shared interests. In many ways, because Paula and Peter had been the pioneers some twenty years before, she did watch and even warn her children when necessary, as they quickly assimilated functionally, if not physically and emotionally, into the unwelcoming society. Time, as Paula knew so well, could replace, if not erase, old memories and build new friendships with strong attachments.

Besides attending the local Matsuris on holidays, Mac and Paula did manage to get away to show the children a Japan other than the one controlled by Sakiko. Trips to Kyoto and Nara were not just diversions from the hustle-bustle of the everyday pressures for them all, but to give the children a deeper, broader look at the culture, heritage, and history of the old capital cities as their tradition or foundation of who the Japanese were. While some referred to the simpler palaces and temples areas as the 'belly of the country,' or more politely as the kinder, gentler part of Japan, it had also been built and controlled by the sword. The talk and sites of ninjas, samurai, and shoguns did get the attention of John more than Jane, as he'd heard about them.

Also, after Tokyo, Kyoto was the most conducive to English, simply because of the large number of tourists increasing each year. If this was all many saw, besides the usually quick views of castles, and giant Buddha statues, it certainly was a totally different Japan the foreigners took home with them. It did illuminate in some ways the mysteries and misbeliefs they came with. Yet, Mac knew, it was difficult adjusting to the new life they had not really chosen, so it was important for John and Jane to see this side of Japan, too.

The children had been literally accosted with food they could not recognize. In the States, Paula somewhat introduced them to what could have been called generic-cooked Asian food, because rarely were the ingredients available for any authentic Japanese meals. While the dishes in their Nagoya home were still tempered for their learning taste buds, the food at school was not, and they had to take their lunches to survive. Still, it was not just the smells, but the impact of noise, constantly and everywhere from the density of the living situation. Even the malls and shopping streets had a constant din of music, sometimes recognizable as a tune, but not the lyrics. While John had already begun to enjoy coffee, it was so strong in Japan he had to add large amounts of milk and sugar. With time, he became addicted like so many Japanese, and ate just about everything in his diet with caffeine added to it, except rice.

* * * * * *

Paula's life evolved into a monotonous routine of teaching English at her mother's school at Nagoya Station. Sakiko had promised to turn the school over to Paula and Mac, and in essence she had, since they did all the work. But, all companies and contracts required a Japanese name and a Japanese partner, so it remained in Sakiko's Japanese name, which meant she could still administer the disbursements. As with all business in Japan, there were many middle people taking a percentage. The tuitions from the students were recorded and turned over to the department store manager, which he took his part off the top for rent, utilities, etc. and deposited the remainder in the school bank account, which of course, was under Sakiko's maiden name. Sakiko then took her 'royalty.'

This percentage was never set, merely what Sakiko needed, wanted, or felt she deserved by her selective memory, and only paying Paula when she asked.

The school was open four days a week, mainly late afternoon through evening with adult and children's classes. Mac would return from teaching at the high school, have dinner with the family, then he and Paula would go to the English school, teaching until about nine o'clock, or six on Saturday. There were perhaps five or six adults and fifteen children when they took over from Sakiko. She'd been using Japanese teachers, rather than Frank because of his drinking and the attendance had dropped. Within a year, they built it up to twenty adults and almost fifty children. The more successful it grew, the more money Sakiko seemed to want and then deducted. She said she had accountant expenses, yet took all the business tax deductions for herself. At times, she'd put off paying Paula because she'd overspent on something for herself, she did not want Frank to know about. Still, Sakiko believed Paula's work should be gratis, simply because she was he daughter and it was something she'd do for her mother.

The realization struck Mac, his repetitive teaching year after year was only sightly above Paula's rut - with little change to look forward to except for the faces of the students changing. This total lack of allowable, creative input was obviously turning quickly into drudgery. One small respite was his extended family life had improved with Frank almost his 'buddy,' and Sakiko and her mother, Haruko, actually treating him with appreciation, if not respect. Some of this came strictly because of the Japanese ranking system. Mac, though not the 'son,' but son-in-law and even the son, Peter, had not been a 'Japanese' son. Therefore, their expectations of Mac, were lower than they would have been had he been Japanese. In other words, he got a left-handed compliment: "You did a good job, considering you're not Japanese."

* * * * * *

Mac could not, and had no intention of replacing Frank in the family. His father-in-law was a dedicated scholar of classical Japanese of several periods and styles, including folk tales and mythological stories. Of particular interest, was his historic research into the ancient, national sport of Sumo with all of its religious rituals and psychological ploys. These intricate points made the sport 'god-like' to its followers, who literally worshipped the wrestlers. Frank still loved the fixed kanji characters of the past, as they did not change, rather than the modernized ones, whose meanings had been altered so.

Maybe this was why he had so little interest in speaking the language. He was well recognized by most of his colleagues at Osaka University, yet had the continual frustration of having his manuscripts rejected for publishing in any scholarly journals. Frank just did not have the needed eloquence of expression for his translations. Perhaps he'd written too many dry-English textbooks, which never used any creativity. Because of his own pent-up emotions, which he understood so well, would not flow out for the readers to understand and enjoy, a real futility of the human endeavor.

In many ways, Frank found his odd niche in Japan, yet it never gave him the sense of satisfaction or accomplishment he'd yearned. Some gaijin men who were also fractions of their potential, imagined themselves complete. Frank did not. He knew he was a man out of synch with the changing Japan, a phenomenon not uncommon that he shared with Lafcadio Hearn, though most famously portrayed a century earlier. Frank knew he was no longer advancing in his career, but sinking in the quagmire of the Japanese system. If he could not get published, he would never rise beyond his outsider-gaijin position at the University. The only answer, he contended, was to take his extensive Japanese knowledge beyond Japan, where the students would be more mature and

212

appreciate his reservoir of erudition. After years of negotiations, letters, and references. Frank finally got an incredible offer from a university in Hawaii, and he felt his life reprieved. And, his accomplishments were acknowledged.

He was a loner, but loneliness finally caught up with him and he needed to be around his own kind again. Sakiko previously encouraged Frank to reach his goal, yet when the positive response came, Haruko blatantly crushed down his escape. Sakiko never hesitated to side with her perverse mother. The little orbit of Frank's career was consummately nullified. Haruko, as head of the house, refused to move from Japan and Sakiko, of course, could not leave her mother. It was a simple, common answer that had no allowable discussion attached to it.

Frank's drinking of sake, which had been lacking in his early days, along with the whiskey and beer steadily increased. He resigned himself mentally to his situation, though it was obvious that emotionally the alcohol removed him from its absoluteness. The crux of his frustration with his impediment, lay in the fact of his conscious views of what life ought to be, but did not correspond to what life really was. When the full impact of this was accepted deep in his soul, he drank. Other times, for ego protection from others, he whitewashed or rationalized the chances of its improvement.

Frank, never a mean or violent drunk, was always happy and sometimes cheerful. In peculiar ways, it made his set conventional and orthodox personality a bit more palatable, especially when he would joke or kid around. He loved his grandchildren, John and Jane, who particularly giggled when he would do silly things, or make comebacks to comments made to him by Sakiko and others.

Jane especially enjoyed the time with her grandfather, for she always knew where he was - up in his room. If no students, he usually took time to be with her. The family had no idea how dangerous his weakened health was, primarily from the falls down the stairs, but certainly when they required hospitalizing Paula showed concern.

Rather than not purchase the alcohol, dutiful Sakiko hid it, filling his co-dependency perfectly. Confrontation meant acknowledgment, which would have caused disharmony, so she simply left the house all the time to not see him drink.

For many years, more so after Paula refused the spotlight, Sakiko made Frank the trained performer and attention-getter, she had desperately needed. Frank became quite proficient on the *shamisen,* and took pride in his talent. Dressed in formal Japanese style, he'd dutifully play wherever Sakiko arranged it. She, of course, benignly smiled, humbling to the supposed role of devoted wife, and do all of the translating for the newspapers, and television people. Frank never refused her, and though he knew of her exorbitant spending on jewelry and clothes, said little. She negotiated all of his teaching and personal contracts, controlled all of the family finances, and since the money was either cash envelopes or direct bank deposits, (checks were rarely used) he had no idea of his actual earnings. His generously-large university bonuses, which in the Japanese style came three times a year - spring, summer, winter; were spent by Sakiko before they ever hit the bank.

In some ways, Sakiko wasn't an atypical Japanese woman, particularly of that period. She'd been raised surrounded by a lot of destitution on the Japanese side, and the antithesis later of the wanton- waste of Americans, on the other Occupation side. Yet, more than that, it was the only way the Japanese woman could revenge her second class status of female and wife. Since society accepted the men's drunkenness, and their widespread sexual depravity, control over the family finances was the only reward for the wife's hard work, even if she hadn't suffered abuse. But Frank never spent his money in bars, with 'mama-sans' or prostitutes, so Sakiko could not justify her own need for showy, expensive items to feel good about herself. In many ways, with her rampant insecurity, she justified it all to herself, for she was fulfilling a role expected of a Japanese woman of any ranking.

So probably, more a concern about the loss of Frank's income, than guilt over any contribution she may have had to his drinking, prompted Sakiko to ask for Paula's help. Frank's health, and performance level for teaching were being threatened, as his drunken mishaps, tripping, or other embarrassing gestures became daily occurrences. "Daddy, please ..." Paula's approach was hesitant, but she knew what her shy father needed more than anything. Something he'd never really gotten in Japan, in all his years. She slipped her arms around him, and kissed him lightly on the cheek. "I love you, Daddy

... Please don't drink so much." She kissed him again on the other cheek, as the tears streamed down his face. "I love you, and I don't want to see anything happen to you."

Paula held him closer, as she put her head on his shoulder, and he hesitantly hugged her back. It was the first time, as an adult, Paula had hugged, kissed and told her father she loved him. She could never have done that, if not for all she'd received from Mac's family and her relatives in the States. It slowed his drinking for a while, yet no panacea for Paula could not change Frank's loss of his goal, or what was missing to make his life worthwhile.

Frank, now in his early seventies, had been upstairs in the house teaching some students when Sakiko and Paula, who happened to be there, heard a big bang and crashing noise. Frank had collapsed on the floor knocking over furniture as he fell, and was not breathing when they reached him. Sakiko had the sense to give mouth to mouth resuscitation and it worked, he started breathing again. Paula called for the ambulance and they got him to the hospital.

Because of the high content of alcohol in his system, the medical staff could not decide if he had a stroke, heart attack, or just blacked-out. Once Frank was conscious enough to complain about the pains in his stomach, they discovered some arteries had ruptured and were hemorrhaging into his stomach. Paula called Mac, who immediately contacted many of his gaijin friends to come and donate blood. Many of the family's long time friends also gave blood, but it was all for naught. The long, abusive lifestyle of alcohol and cigarettes made the weakened arteries collapse, each time they were hastily sewn back together.

Frank, a basically good man, had even gone to church when drunk. But the loss of his dream could not be fixed by his religion. The only goal-searching he'd done in those later years was for the hidden bottles of sake. Although a strong, practicing Catholic, Frank wanted to be buried in Japan, Buddhist style. For in this way, he felt he'd not be forgotten. Even Sakiko could not forsake the regular monthly ceremonies the first year, as well the larger, elaborate periodic ones, marking significant years after his death. Almost as if the acknowledgment, respect, and attention neglected or denied to him while living, in Japanese tradition *had* to be paid after death. Maybe it was his own form of retribution, passed under the guise of his *Japaneseness*. The sanctity of it could not be questioned or denied. For all the battles he may have lost, perhaps in his mind the war was won. This satisfaction and price paid for it, was noted by Mac.

His passing caused not only a loss of income for Sakiko and Haruko, but created an upheaval in the family scheme. There was no son to take over the support and panic set in, as Sakiko had expected Frank to live into his nineties. She'd made jokes about other Japanese professors who continued teaching their classes from wheelchairs, and had said, "You'll be like that , too, won't you *Otoasan* - honorary husband?" Her life from the past as a struggling young business woman, had been planned with almost minute detail. She'd taken it all for granted once she married Frank, and then simply enjoyed her momentary rewards of new clothes or jewelry.

Sakiko, not wanting to tempt fate, had also not planned for his burial, so Mac took over and purchased a plot for him. He then arranged for Frank's Air Force pension and retirement fund to come to Sakiko. She was grateful, and it increased Mac's family standing, but he was not building a foundation to take over as the household figurehead position. With the enormous vacuum, Sakiko finally could see how Frank had always spoiled and pampered her. No one else would ever do that again. In the early years, he'd protected her from the Japanese prejudice for marrying him, so he truly gave his life for her happiness.

Sakiko never saved any money and now the well was down to a trickle. Changing her free spending pattern would be nearly impossible. The retirement and insurance monies went as if they would be easily replaced. Strangely, after her loss of who she was, she turned to playing what she'd considered, 'the bourgeois' pachinko almost everyday, sometimes for hours. The refined facade of her position and standing, she'd intricately built up over the years dropped almost over night. It was as if she needed the numbing noise of the pinball parlor, and glitz of the flashing lights to drown out her fear of the future. While she'd not have analyzed her reversed status, it was.

* * * * * *

Mac had been the only one who clearly saw what was coming, and he, himself, had no intentions of living out his life in a dead-end teaching job in Japan. He may never be able to break Sakiko's manipulative obligation-guilt hold over Paula, but he certainly would not become one of her dutiful puppets. The dueling with Sakiko was a parrying game at first he relished, for the challenge, then quickly became tired of, because her relentlessness over the most minor encounters.

Mac had more important tasks to accomplish, which would have greater influence on Paula and his family. Once again, he prepared himself and was in the process of moving back into the automotive business when Frank died. Just as with understanding the educational system, Mac studied the historical background of Japan's manufacturing, so he might use whatever minute details he could find to his advantage. In numerous earlier talks with Frank, regarding the Occupation days in Nagoya, Mac learned the economic miracle did not fall from the sky onto Japan, or just start in the 1960s, as many forecasters suggested. It did not take a genius to see the books had never been closed on World War II, and the ripple effects of the Allied Occupation were still influential.

The Japanese knew they could learn much from their conquerors, for they had never been beaten before, ergo, the Americans must be smart. Clearly, the only country which came out of WWII practically unscathed was the United States, and then quickly became the world leader. So, looking to the Occupation as a positive learning tool first hand, it was their idea to copy the leader, like the adopted son, or step-child searching for praise from its mighty father. If necessity was the mother of invention, then the war-survivors were the most creative, making something out of the throwaways of the wasteful Americans.

Once the Korean War started, Japan was given the opportunity and technical help they needed to produce the military goods for their kind benefactors. That growth step over, they could turn their newly developed manufacturing talents to consumer goods, since Japan did not have to waste time or money on the Cold War and military armaments. The American/Japanese Constitution of no military or weapons was a blessing in disguise for successful business. All their energy would have one goal and direction - products they could produce to sell overseas.

Aa previously mentioned, W. Edward Deming had been given to the Japanese in the late 1940s by SCAP, via the Agriculture Department. He was a statistician, who believed the only way to improve business systems was to use statistical tools, which charted the variations that caused problems, and pinpointed where the difficulties were. Unlike the American managers in Deming's native land, the eager Japanese listened to his lectures on quality. In fact, they were so inspired by their total success when they used his techniques, by 1951, they created the Deming Prize for best quality production.

Everything Deming taught epitomized their 'holy' Kata-system and reaffirmed their Japanese set way of life. He thus became the icon of Japanese quality control management, as the competing manufacturers followed his assessments, leadership, and training. Mac noted when visiting Toyota's corporate headquarters in Nagoya, Deming's was the only gaijin portrait there, and was also the largest. Mac then knew the key to his personal success was to thoroughly learn the Japanese business manufacturing rules, and eventually use them to his benefit.

There were many things Nagoyans were said to be famous for, or perhaps infamous would be better. Their great love of the horse, led naturally to their greater love of a car, and most of the famous carriage or wagon makers went into the car manufacturing business. During the Occupation, under the direction of the Americans, the wide, boulevard streets and sidewalks had been built. Following their benefactors, after the Korean War, to first support their businesses, the Nagoya and Aichi Prefectural governments built more roads and highways before any housing for the families.

Along with their required numerous parks, Nagoya had the largest number of wide, Western-style streets in Japan - unfortunately this encourages reckless driving in the Prefecture, as it was always first or second in accidents in the country. With such tacit government support, not a surprise then, three of the largest manufacturers of cars surrounded Nagoya. Resulting again with the government prescribing loyalty of its citizens in purchasing new cars frequently, to the point to most Nagoyans, it was more important to have a new car than a house. Of course, the oldest son usually inherited their parents' house. Besides the conservative Nagoyans had less hesitation to live with their parents after marriage, than those in Tokyo or Osaka.

On top of this, once the Military Occupation was over in 1952, Japan felt it was finally moving into the Twentieth century, even if it meant economic development took priority over individual freedom. Prime Mister Ikea proclaimed the challenge of 'doubling income in ten years,' which was considered the heart of the postwar economic 'miracle.' The government made the growth-oriented economic policies its prime initiative The actual doubling was achieved in seven years, not ten. It was also the foundation of immortalizing defeat, thus guilt cast upon their former enemies and Occupiers, by using it as a trade crutch.

Maybe winning was only a transient thing, being just a respite from losing in the long term. Quickly, the business leaders learned the newest technologies were in English, and much could be lost, or slowed down by translations or interpretations into Japanese. If they were going to sell to the world, they would have to speak its business language - English, but rarely in the past was a gaijin available they could trust, who was fluent in their language. The Japanese government might have been given its businesses protection - the Anti- Monopoly Law enacted by SCAP was amended three times: 1949, 1953, and 1977. And the expansion by joining GATT in 1955 and OECD in 1964, promising to each country it would open up its trade barriers - but only those companies able to do business in English, would succeed easily, internationally.

Akio Morita, whose family was native to Nagoya, recognized the difficulty of his company's Japanese name

- Tokyo *Tsushin Kogyo Kabushiki Kaisha.* When they shortened it to Totsuko, still few Americans could pronounce it either. "You cannot buy, what you cannot say," Morita reasoned. So, in 1953, the name was changed to SONY, set up like an acronym, but more like a nickname for the Latin word *sonus* - meaning sound, which was what they sold. Once his pocket-size transistor radio was invented in 1955, Morita decided to use an American advertising agency to market it.

By 1970, SONY was the first Japanese company listed on the New York Stock Exchange. Morita truly knew the importance of speaking in the language of the market, something it took decades for most American companies to accept in reverse. Mac knew there were progressive Japanese companies, he just had to connect up with the right one, at the right time. He already had the advantages of having the experienced background from General Motors, as well as a good fluency in Japanese.

Once Japan got its semi-independence from the Allied military, following the Security Treaty of 1960, exportation of Japanese products became the goal of the country. To Mac and most younger gaijin who had experienced negative repercussions, the United States Military had more of a detrimental presence in Japan. The over one- hundred thousand American personnel and their dependents were on bases around the islands, taking up good land, while causing resentment with drugs and sex problems.

Mac was shocked when he learned by the end of the Vietnam War, he'd been one of the over ten million GIs who had passed through Japan since the Occupation. There were no longer white bits of toilet paper on the rice fields from the night soil fertilizer, and the vegetables did not have to be washed in iodine. The country became a leader in the Peace Movement and did not want any military in its midst. Japan was finally moving into real economic development, and though it took priority over individual freedom, it was something the general population never had a real cognizance of anyway.

With every big jump in the Japanese economy, the number of English teachers and English schools in Japan increased, with a few of the more ambitious moving into Japanese businesses. SCAP had set the yen exchange rate to the U.S. dollar at 360, and the government refused to change it until 1971, when President Nixon threatened trade embargoes, because of the severe trade and payments imbalances.

Still, it was only revalued to 308, and the first drop below 200 did not come until mid-1978. This not only began to move Japanese products out of the 'cheap' price range, it made it much more lucrative for foreigners to work in Japan. Previously, their yen only had real buying value in Japan, or other poorer Asian countries. With business and trade first and foremost in Japan, a more aggressive stance was taken as China opened its market in 1972. Japan, not having a moral issue with discrimination, Apartheid was ignored, making Japan South Africa's largest trading partner. They had never stopped trading with North Korea or Vietnam, so Prime Minister Miyazawa later referred to it as, "A foreign policy lacking in moral values." It was said they would sell to the devil, if their price was paid.

Mac studied every vital piece of information in formulating his plan to move out of teaching and back into industry. He followed up on every opportunity, no matter how remote they might have appeared at the time, from going to speak to different groups on obscure subjects, to attending functions which only pandered to him because of his gaijin-Japanese speaking status. Mac doggedly pursued every lead, as it expanded his knowledge base and experience in dealing with different Japanese groups. Just in time, the right doors opened and Mac walked into a management position with the largest Japanese auto parts manufacturer. Everything he had ever worked for, and worked at, came together to make him a valuable find.

The company was at a point of development, just broken away to expand from the mother company. They thus needed a gaijin fluent in Japanese to help them compete internationally. Not a quick decision, as it never happened in Japan. After thoroughly investigating Mac, with Paula's background a significant, decisive positive influence, the job opportunity came to fruition. Mac played the game to the hilt, not only a significant salary, but compensation for John and Jane to go to the International School. A new, much better life now started for Mac in Japan. He had dreams being fulfilled, Frank could never have even imagined. Sakiko was furious at her loss, laying even more guilt on Paula's lack of concern for her mother's well-being.

A Different Cultural Perspective:

Chapter 7: Torn Between Two Worlds

To live like an American - at any tine in Japan - has a great number of advantages. One of the joys is that you're considered so strange, that any extra amount of strangeness doesn't make any difference. You could wear almost any kind of clothes and behave in almost any manner. Whereas, the Japanese have the weight of the society on them in the sense that it is an invisible, intangible, yet very real police state, very much alive and controlling almost every facet of their lives from morning to night.

Donald Ritchie,
Japan As We Lived It

A "Bubble" Like No Other

Japan shot fully into its famous "Bubble Economy" by 1985, taking Corporate America by storm. Most American companies were ill- prepared for the dire competition, and turned on each other to see blame. Managers accused the lazy workers, while the unions pointed their fingers at ivory tower management, and the public suffered the 'lemon' consequences of having more cars recalled in 1977 than were even produced. During the Reagan-Bush Administrations, forty- percent of the manufacturers moved out of the country, and Japan became the world's banker until 1991, holding one-third of the United States' debt, which gave it tremendous leverage over Washington. In 1988, ten of the largest banks were Japanese, and there were no U.S. banks in the top twenty-five. While the U.S. was bogged down in recession and unemployment, Japan led with twenty-five of the thirty- four vital technologies. The little country grew up into a mighty machine, and had not slowed down or stopped mass producing.

Japan had long replaced the United States as the most affluent nation, while still riding behind archaic trade agreements, and with West Germany reuniting with the East, the New Germany was hardly a current competitor. Japan was buying-up Australia and North America, like they were minor real estate pieces of a global Monopoly game. Even when they knew they were being swindled or cheated, the Japanese paid the inflated price rather than question. They'd never lose face as being thought of not being able to afford the price, or to look cheap to the seller. The more they paid, the more proud they were of their purchase.

Ten million Japanese began to travel every year overseas. Though they usually had short vacations of five to ten days at most, they would cover several countries in Europe, or cities in the States or Australia. Most traveled in groups, on a tightly, escorted itinerary in a variety of tours (even sex-tours for men) covering every age or purpose, including honeymooners. The most important aspect was shopping, since they could buy duty-free the designer products they craved. And, *Omiage* - souvenirs - for friends, relatives and co- workers were required of all who traveled.

These group-traveler-shopping addicts, soon became the butt of countless jokes, while being taken advantage of by the shopkeepers. Since most Caucasians could not tell the difference between the Asian races, the Japanese were thought to be the only rich ones. Other negative characteristics of rudeness and arrogance were attributed to Japanese men, when there were many Korean, Taiwanese, and Hong Kong Chinese traveling, too. After the new job, Mac and Paula took the kids back

225

for the Christmas holidays. Stopping in Hawaii on the way, they could not believe how 'Japanese' it was, and also how cheap, of course, in comparison to Japan, With the 'Bubble' expansion, many Japanese corporations were sending thousands of workers to various overseas countries to work in their newly expanded factories - basically to train the foreign workers - either for short periods of months or longer stays of three to five years. Through a series of sometimes quite, embarrassing disasters of sending single men, who had little experience of the freedom of these countries, especially the U.S., companies began restricting the long term stays to married men with families. The men over thirty benefited the most, as they were guaranteed promotions on their return, they would not have been able to secure otherwise. However, sometimes many of the wives did not want to give up the large house and yard wth so many conveniences not typical in Japan, as well their own newly acquired freedom and equality. Yet, there were the few who just couldn't live without their Japanese rice or their mothers.

The children returning from overseas, particularly from English schooling, quickly learned they would be the subject of *ijime* - bullying in the typical Japanese school, and sometimes led by the teacher himself. They had to be careful in English class, where the teacher's spoken English was almost nonexistent, while they'd obtained an excellent command of idiomatic English.

They were expected to follow unquestioningly, the *Sensei* - teacher - their mistakes, poor pronunciation and all. They even hesitated speaking to the gaijin teacher, should the school have one part-time, as they'd be targeted. The Confucian philosophy, which so strongly influenced Japanese thinking, along with the kata, preached great respect should be shown to teachers, no matter how inept or wrong they were. This respect turned into ultimate, unchecked power and corrupted the teachers, just as surely as it had the politicians from the economic success.

Most students capitulated, and resigned themselves to the system, doing whatever was necessary to get through it all. It was sad, their teenage years were stolen from them, as they went through all the necessary movements with a blank, despondent veil on their young faces. The only other alternative, and one the corporations were eventually forced to pay for, was sending these 'returnees' as they were called, to the International School, which most of the large cities now had. They were not cheap, and may not have had the best education, since most of the students were transient, but they were the only place accepting everyone with an 'international' or unusual or 'mixed background.

A Little Bit of America in the Middle of Japan

To John and Jane, the move to the Nagoya International School (NIS) was like taking another culture shock trip, along their already bumpy existence. It had the tremendous benefit of giving them back a form or framework of American holidays, traditions, and the more casual lifestyle of education in their own language. The broader spectrum of current topics and classes were taught interactively, without the usual Japanese way of memorization of facts for testing only. The drawbacks were not as visible immediately, for they were the subtle, subliminal influences. They catered to transient children of corporate gaijin, or wealthy, spoiled Japanese who lived for the newest fad, for the sought- after attention they did not receive at home.

The oddball dichotomy of the other students included the extreme contradictions, of many Mormon Missionary children and those of the Yakuza - the Japanese Mafia. Most of the foreign children came and went, as a result of their parents' work contracts, so no seriousness was attached to their studies or friendship. John and Jane's knowledge of English, grammar, as well as conversation and slang, had become limited, so naturally associated more comfortably with the Japanese teens.

Great embarrassment came to Jane, when she learned her English ability was so low they transferred her into the seventh grade remedial, or ESL - English as a Second Language class. The only gaijin there, an anomaly caused by her being away from English schools since the first grade. Japanese had become her more comfortable speaking language, as it was spoken with fluency in and out of her home. Jane simply never thought about picking up a book in English to read for pleasure, though there were many in their home. Since her English ability was sufficient for family life, it never dawned on Mac or Paula, that her reading or more sophisticated vocabulary comprehension was non-existent. Changing to NIS, brought home to Jane, more so than to John, she was an American, not a 'white' Japanese like her mother, the aberration she'd come to think of as herself. The first year she spent hours after school being tutored in all of the basic subjects but math, since it didn't really require English.

The instant freedom at NIS astonished both children and caused still more confusion for Jane. For the past six years, school life had been so structured, limited and restricted, not only from activities like chewing gum, but to personal things like hairstyle, clothes and even underwear. Now amazed to see all the girls with makeup, jewelry, or nail polish, she had to question, "You can do that?" only for them to respond, "Sure, why not?" From the duty-laden responsibility of taking care of themselves at tender ages - riding the subways alone, diligently doing homework without questioning its purpose, or any other rote action - the new liberty went beyond license. How far could she take the carte blanche, and not be chastised, or punished?

The gaijin in her grade were the minority of about five, while the fifteen majority were either Japanese or Korean. Most of them had attended NIS since grade school, or they lived overseas themselves, so were not typical Japanese. There was also a plethora of Japanese girls wanting to have the Westernized experience, as the society did not judge the girls so harshly on the schools they attended. NIS was an oasis for children of divorced or mixed marriage, too.

For there, they would not be taunted and teased, as they would be in the Japanese system, that abhorred non-conformity. As the cliques formed, Jane chose the mixed and divorced Japanese ones, whose defiant stance was easily recognized. Consistently, the only gaijin in her circle of friends, while she did well with her grades, many of them did not and later had to drop out. Jane's gregariousness bloomed, then swung beyond extrovert to an exhibitionist, as she got addicted to the attention. She learned to use her unique blonde looks as a status symbol.

Tuition, per student, ran approximately ten thousand dollars a year, with another three thousand for bus transportation. Not cheap by any standard, at that time of the late 1980s. NIS was simply open and accepting to whomever could afford it, as well met their minimal educational standards to stay. Now Jane could wear regular clothes, instead of a uniform, so they became more than basic covering, but a statement. Her outrageous and grunge outfits shouted loudly to the rigid Japanese society, which previously controlled her. Her education concentrated now more on activities, parties, fads, and what was popular or 'the thing to do.'

School studies overall were minimized, since few of the gaijin students would spend more than a year there, so why not have a fun experience? There was little concern for the local Japanese students, as they would be learning more cultural information and English than those attending Japanese schools anyway. These non-truadional Japanese would either attend a college overseas, or go into their family's international business. As drugs were becoming more popular and available in Japan, even the Yakuza saw the benefit of their next generation speaking English to their overseas Mafia counterparts and suppliers. Another kind of 'Allied Cooperation.'

John's group of friends were more mixed, with some being older gaijin boys he knew through his sports activities. He attached much sentiment to them, as it brought back his younger days when he'd spent so much time with his cousins and learning from them. These other gaijin helped John recapture his culture, while they also showed him how easy it was to break the rules by drinking and smoking on sports trips.

By the time these friends left Japan, he had a definite attitude problem towards the teachers and the administration, as he looked for every opportunity to harass them. Few of the staff could speak or understand Japanese, so the language became John's favorite weapon of choice to frustrate or make fun of them, causing the other students to laugh. What had been done to him as a child, he relished doing to the teachers, even though they weren't the ones who had castigated him in the past. He was expelled, not knowing where to draw the line, but winning the game of words convinced him he was much smarter than any of those in charge.

By their third trip back to America, the summer after Jane's ninth grade, she felt she could no longer fit into her native culture or lifestyle. Being at NIS had become such a quasi-substitute, the real things no longer had appeal. What was hot or popular in the States, had not hit Japan yet, so had no meaning. Most importantly, she could see her cousins had to live with more restrictions than she did, at home as well as at school.

Yet, what she missed most was, in America she was just another pretty, blonde teenager, not the star, model or center of attention which came so easily in Japan. She had little interest in what was happening to these relatives, their personal lives, or feelings for her. She whined continuously to return to Japan, her friends, and their activities. She feared, if she was out of the Japanese-International scene too long, she'd miss some important fashion trend or statement, party, or hip happening.

John, on the other hand, savored each trip back to compare and impress his friends and relatives with his life in Japan. He loved their attention to his stories and tidbits about school, food, or whatever. He liked it so much sometimes he began to stretch details and make up his own information. Since there was no one to challenge him, he became dependent on the habit, to the point he began to believe whatever he said himself. When Mac and Paula would catch him in one of his exaggerated ramblings, he'd adamantly defend it, swearing its validity.

A warning flag, about which Mac had concerns, but he made no connection to the source of the problem. John was tall and had dark, good looks, but did not have the star-status of Jane in Japan from her friends. With his hesitant English, he needed more attention to soothe his insecurities, as it was not a real life and he knew it. Also, it was Mac's first clue that while NIS had given his children back some of their culture, it may have given them too much freedom.

To rock Mac's socks off even more so, fate affected their lives in the most scariest way of all. When the time came, their return to Japan was to be on Korean Air Lines flight 007, which was shot down by the Soviets, creating a huge international incident. With some family delays, Mac had rescheduled them just the day before to a different return flight. The shocking reality of how close they had come to all being killed, made him rethink many things about their lives and their living situation in Japan.

Unfortunately, John's expanding pathological-lying continued even more so after their return to Japan, as he began to rely on the lies rather than dealing with reality, or fulfilling his obligations. Even as his parents, friends, and teachers began to catch on, John became more accustomed to living-life through his alternative way, bypassing the truth whether or not it was easier or necessary to lie.

It seemed nothing would break the habit - not embarrassment when caught, anger from others, or punishment from teachers. He was good looking, likable, and seemed to be comfortable with his life, so there should have been no reason for him falsifying it all. Eventually, those around him just accepted what he said could not be counted on. The bonus that kept John addicted, the Japanese would never counter what a gaijin said, or reveal they had been gullible enough to believe a lie. More important to them to prevent loss of face, than to confront a liar. John's psychological enslavement could not have been surrounded by a more conducive society.

Jane, conversely, became more mischievous as she participated in the pranks and escapades of her Japanese cohorts. Being active in the sports at school was not enough to keep her interests and energies occupied. "TP-ing," or toilet-papering someone's house, particularly one of the teachers, was a favorite diversion, especially just before rain. Once, some of John's friends did their house, Mac was so furious any future adventures were immediately curtailed.

Jane and her friends then took to roaming the underground shopping malls of Nagoya on Saturdays. Since they did not have to suffer through school classes, like the average Japanese teenagers, they cruelly laughed and pointed rudely, calling out to the other students. Pajama parties became the norm, as the girls got together to talk, eat, watch videos, and secretly smoked cigarettes, as marijuana and other drugs were quite rare in Japan. Yet, the new pastime quickly became passé, as they wanted more stimulation for their boredom.

John wanted more freedom with his money, so convinced his parents to let him work part-time. He quickly got a job as a disc jockey in one of the discos. Again, his good looks and natural Japanese was a drawing card, while his being underage was not a subject matter to the business or the lax law. Also, it paid much better than a convenience store job, had they even considered hiring a gaijin.

The drinking slipped into Jane's activity program naturally, since it was a common and acceptable form of entertainment for the teenagers, as well as the rest of Japan. With the ubiquitous vending machines on every corner, offering alcohol along with almost anything else, it delivered instant-gratification to whomever had the money. At least, until the magic hour of eleven o'clock anyway, acquisition was not a problem. But soon the sneaking of liquor into the mutual houses also lost its luster, so time to venture into the public with their random quests for more kicks.

The blanket monotony of the Japanese society was smothering, though it barely touched or affected their rarefied lives. Japan, conversely-known to have the most neon-flashing lights in the world - Nagoya included, despite its conservative nature - they were a beckoning beam to all. The indifference, to what was going on around them, was a common malady among the youth of Japan. Raised in the great affluence, at the height of the "Bubble Economy" of the late 1980s, as naive teens they thought it would never end, so only some new stimulus could keep their attention.

Individual thought was not connected to something new, untried, or outrageous. A psychologist might suggest they were not only lacking attention from their harried, success-seeking parents, but needed control or limitations representing love, care, and concern. One could also say they had grown up too fast, with too little family interaction, and surrounded by too much city.

Under the guise of staying over at friends' houses, Jane went into bars and the discos. When her parents caught her, John jumped in and said, "Don't worry, I'll watch out for her Mom, and bring her home when I come." Their lifelong, quasi-symbiotic sibling relationship took a new twist, and while John tried to warn Jane about her actions, she raced ahead. The bartenders and business owners could have cared less about age limitations, since these patrons had money. English was used among the girls or guys only for privacy, when surrounded by other Japanese clientele.

Once they learned the scene, it was easy to figure out they could get away with almost anything. The managers could not call the police for any disturbance, for they would receive a larger fine for letting them inside in the first place. John now a senior, and Jane a junior, had unlimited independence. Though Paula and Mac had said little to them about leaving Japan, they knew it could not go on forever, so they lived it up. They were gambling on the infrequent punishment of restriction or confinement from their parents, which kept them going every direction experimenting, as they played for the fun of it all.

John and Jane became notorious in their small circle of bars and friends, which had expanded beyond the confines of NIS students. They were both dating Japanese who moved well in their moneyed- circles, which meant neither of them needed money themselves - female Japanese frequently paid the expenses of her date. While John worked, Jane invented new brazen antics for attention, like burning holes in the clothes of the other Japanese women on the dance floor.

Dancing with a constant cigarette in her hand, it was easy to take an apology and when they got away with it, her friends would compete, like counting-coup on the enemy. The cost of the clothes, most pointedly a disco outfit, made them relish the vile joke more than any repercussions. The need for attention became more a need to destroy, ruin or disrupt other people's lives. If caught for repeated acts or complaints, Jane, unlike some of her Japanese accomplices, escaped chastisement because of her 'star' status.

She'd not been sitting back on her laurels just partying or acting out, but Jane had done extensive modeling and been on TV shows regularly. The opportune, talentless fashion-fad of gaijin celebrity worship, could only exist in Japan. Maybe out of sync with other Asian countries, but not as warped when compared to the fanatical praise of James Dean, Marilyn Monroe, and Audrey Hepburn, as if all were still young, alive movie stars.

There was no reality in these beliefs. In Japanese eyes, Jane's distinction made her exempt to criticism and created envy, for she was doing what they could only dream of - a license for unbridled lawlessness in Japan, going against the rigid system. Luckily, Jane had the perfect formula - a pretty blonde, Japanese speaking gaijin, who actually was alive and acting out constantly, for whatever audience she could find. With arrogance and youth, she spoke often of marrying a very rich Japanese man, who would keep her on a pedestal and shower her with attention, as the trophy she'd become to believe she was.

Mac and Paula were not totally ignorant of what was happening, yet with their own schedules, it'd not been easy to maintain discipline at home. Personally knowing the kinds of repression the society dealt on most, they implicitly ignored the actions of their children. They were a tight family, despite whatever problems were encountered, for interdependence was the foundation of any long term gaijin's successful stay.

In the traditional way, Paula felt it was more Mac's job to speak to John and Jane, or restrict them somehow. Yet, he empathized with their having to live in Japan, so hesitated to do more than warn them about the gaijin legalities involved, if they actually got caught breaking any laws. Rarely speaking of his own pressures on the job, he chose more to remain in the dark, rather than question or challenge their whereabouts and activities.

The late hours, especially on weekends, became habitual and once John could see his father's weakened position on their activities, it was pushed to the limits. Since not difficult to maintain grade requirements for NIS, Mac reminded John an American college would not be so lenient on him.

John's inflated self-importance, added to his native quality Japanese, he felt would be his ticket to success, without enduring any further schooling, he surely believed. He certainly was not blind or stupid as to what was happening around him, in an economy fed by conspicuous-consumption, with people throwing out any product the minute a new version hit the market. People did not look to save money on discounts, they were proud of the inflated prices they paid, believing the exorbitant spending gave them a certain status symbol.

Already savvied by years of observance of the wealthy bar crowd, John kept a keen ear to his father's new found experience in the Japanese automotive industry. He just knew there would be an easy niche for himself, among the group of business power brokers constantly surrounding him. He would never have to lower himself to the position of being just an English teacher, as his father and grandfather had. Being raised in Japan give him a definite leg-up on a Japanese dominated world, for he arrogantly believed his native- quality speech surpassed his father's slightly accented one.

Enter the Gaijin Teachers

John may have made fun of the gaijin English teachers, and thought he could look down on them in disdain, but during the Bubble Economy there were not much better jobs for gaijins to be had than in Japan. Since most of the countries the gaijin came from were in bad economic recessions, life could be lucrative, if not truly good in 'Bubble' Japan.

To those who could escape, only a bachelor's degree from a university or four-year college, was all one needed to make the 'easy money' in Japan, doing what came naturally - speaking English. The hundreds of Japanese who owned English teaching companies, with thousands of schools scattered from one end of the country to the other, were waiting with open arms for the *Eigo Sensei* - English teacher. Learning English had gone beyond the six mandatory years at school, or the corporate need to have English knowledge to send employees overseas. English was now *trendy*, the magical word which also made it a big business. How big? At its peak in 1988-90, it racked up fifty billion dollars (NOT yen) a year, with English classes at specific English schools, not colleges or universities, including text book sales. That kind of money attracted two-legged sharks seeking naive fresh blood, and easily found it.

The Japanese rarely needed to speak the foreign language when they traveled in their group tours, but just in case they got a chance-opportunity, they wanted the knowledge. Studying English became the most popular hobby, ahead of the other fads of driving a car or golf for men, and shopping or going to American movies (which were subtitled in Japanese) for women. Gaijin who could not get jobs in their own countries kowtowed to flippant, young people, who were more into the snob-appeal of attending expensive language schools, or taking private lessons. The gaijin would joke at getting paid twenty, fifty or even hundred dollars an hour to talk to a student, who most likely understood perhaps thirty percent of the English spoken. There were no real conversations about emotions, feelings, or opinions on current topics, as it was an amusing recreational game and a highly lucrative one. Few gaijin had any qualified credentials to be an honest English teacher, and frequently the immigration tracked down those who had their degrees from the College of Xerox.

Some of the young Japanese women in their early twenties, had nothing better to do with their father's money, and they loved the allure of a fairy tale romance with a gaijin man. For those gaijin who could not have gotten a date with the most average plain-jane, had quite pretty, Japanese girls falling all over them, wanting to have sex with them. Sex appeal was blatantly advertised to attract both sexes, with young blonde or bosomy females emulating the party atmosphere, most language schools had developed. Photos of the white, male teachers always showed them smiling at the girls surrounding them. While in reality, teachers were of all ages, and sometimes colors, though most schools were rather slack on their policy of 'no fraternization with the students.'

If you had the money and wanted the experience, lessons were given in limousines, always with the opposite sex as the teacher, or on yachts, or holiday trips with gaijin escorts. The actual English success of many of these schools was not the issue, and the government had no standards set to monitor them. Besides, they were in the *business of entertainment,* not education, all only a guise to make it acceptable to spend thousands of dollars - paid in advance, often dropped after a few visits, like a difficult diet or exercise plan.

There were rip-off artists on both sides - Japanese and gaijin. Bosses who did not pay on a regular basis, or promised pay, and teachers who did not have real degrees, or showed-up drunk on the job. Some of the gaijin-dregs used the students, especially the female ones, like they were a private harem. Likewise, the Japanese-dregs tricked female gaijin teachers into more personal kinds of leisure, or outright prostitution. Often, not a pretty picture in person, or blabbed on TV talk shows, as the money attracted more riffraff, and the Bubble's growth increased the money being paid almost monthly. Everyone seemed to be racing to get as much as they could before it all burst, which rudely happened in mid-1991.

The universities and colleges were not far behind the tacky English schools, yet putting on a facade of respectability by hiring only those gaijin with a Masters or Ph.D. The market was soon glutted with highly educated people, who had been unable to get employment in their own countries - as England, Australia and Canada suffered recessions along with the States. With so many qualified gaijin to choose from, the most insignificant junior colleges were arrogantly being selective with whom they would reward with the 'baby-sitting' job of the spoiled students.

It would be impossible to calculate how much talent, education, and experience was wasted on the ninety percent of the students who could have cared less, who stood before them spouting English. Most, still never learned to speak with any competency. This too, like the semantics of referring to the geisha as a cultural tradition, when they were really just another name for high-priced entertainment and prostitution. Likewise, few Eigo Senseis would have admitted their uselessness, yet grateful for the exorbitant paycheck.

* * * * * *

Mac learned the hard way never to take anything for granted, and nothing was ever as simple as it seemed. He knew to do his homework, as the knowledge gave a confidence in being able to handle whatever surprises came at hm from left field, which was the standard, not the exception in Japan. Pioneering a gaijin achievement in Japanese industry had a long and illustrious past, if not a questionable one. Mac did his job with dedication beyond what was required, to quell any taint other gaijin had brought upon the scene. Still, there was an accumulation of stress nothing seemed to relieve. Just too many years, of too many crowded trains, subways, and general traffic on the sidewalks, or just about wherever he went, with never knowing the glory of silence. The trudging up and down commuter station stairs while being jostled, pushed, squeezed, and breathed upon, as well as coughed and sneezed on. It was the phenomenon of the masses.

Apologies, forthwith, it was a cache stockpiled to the point, where an amicable person as himself, knew his limit was coming really soon. No doubt, there was a vibrancy to the city life, and truly Nagoya did have an easier pace than Osaka or Tokyo. Mac could not conceive of how people kept their sanity in those places. He had close friendships of Japanese people, and he could not imagine knowing or finding better friends. He had years before learned Sakiko was an enigma, created from her historical, fated-circumstances, and thank God he met no others with the likes of her obsessive, narcissistic, cruel self-indulgent persona. This surveillance of reality, also made him acknowledge John and Jane had become frenzied-souls, whipped around in a freak-show world of decadence, which existed in few other places in the world. Mac hoped it was not too late for them to accept a more grounded-atmosphere, to mature into adults who would be able to clearly incorporate their bicultural/bilingual experience into a fulfilling life.

The timing was ripe once again to make a move, both up and out. Paula and Mac wanted to keep their family intact, while making a smooth transition. Mac knew he had risen about as far as he could in the corporation, being a gaijin.Though many of his colleagues had lived overseas, or had some schooling there and were more open- minded or non-traditional, their support could not get him much further in Japan. He'd become the assistant Manager of his extensive international department, and most importantly, the *first non-Japanese to go on the organizational chart of any major Japanese corporation.* He dealt mainly with their European clients, and sales continued to go through the roof, yet he knew he could only hit those 'home-runs' for just so long. A drop in sales was never considered a normal run of things, but a mistake on the part of the manager.

As well as Mac had done in the International Sales Department, it had not gone unnoticed by the Vice President himself. Since Mac sat in front of him for years - in the Japanese office system, most department employees are placed in one large room with no walls or partitions. Therefore, it did not take any great investigating on the part of the V.P. Mac diligently followed all of the Japanese 'salaryman' rules: "Don't be late, don't take time off, and especially, don't do any real independent or impressive work - particularly if it showed up your superiors or other coworkers in a lesser light." Mac never hesitated, when he was instructed to go with part of the office group, to pray at *Atsuta Jingo* - a National Shinto

Shrine in Nagoya - at New Years for the company's future success each December. He followed the status quo on the group harmony: after work drinking, consensus agreement, and most of all waited for his turn for recognition, promotion, and transfer or *nimawashi* - cultivating the ground for better relations.

Transfers were the basis of a well-functioning Japanese corporation, for they kept the employee's talents generalized, as he moved from department to department, or branch to branch, while specializing him in the ways and methods of the company. It made it virtually impossible for him to leave the company, as he'd become a 'moveable asset,' and only fit well into the cogs of that company. The employee in return, was given an implicit guarantee of seniority promotion and lifetime employment.

Granted, this may encourage ineptness in a few who continued to collect a salary, while their underlings or coworkers did all the work. But, it was considered the reward for his having done the same for his predecessor. Should the older employee become totally useless, he was simply put into a corner, and considered a loss-factor in doing business. The younger employees continued working exorbitant hours, most in what was called 'service overtime.' They were expected to work, but did not get paid for any of it, because of loyalty to the company and expected promotion. It was the normal way of doing business in Japan, and kept the cost of a competitive edge much lower over foreign producers.

Karoshi - death from overwork, was a very real thing in 'Bubble' Japan, with an estimated - by private organizations - 10,000 men and 1500 women per year from the late 1980s through early 90s. The government refused to even acknowledge karoshi's existence, so they would not have to pay death benefits, as they *never* supported an employee over a company. The government also depended on the fact that lawsuits were considered 'rude,' and the family ungrateful for the years the employee had worked, though rarely paid for any of the extensive overtime which killed them. Still, when the topic was covered on American television by ABC's *20/20* show, people began to get attorneys and sued the companies and the government. It did not however, slow down the long hours or company loyalty requirement. But it did make some people have an awareness, it just was not right, or usual for some in their forties to die, literally at their desk.

* * * * * *

Mac, in a more advantageous position, for not only was he bilingual, but knowledgeable with manufacturing experience in the American car market, from his years at General Motors. His boss really did not want to let him go, not even to Tokyo, much less overseas to Europe or America, where they were expanding so rapidly. But, Mac was concerned about his children, for he could see Japan was now the negative influence, just as how he'd felt America had been before. He felt John needed American university training, whether or not he decided to return to Japan in the future.

The fact most Japanese private universities were nothing more than reward-playgrounds, for those who passed the entrance exams was well known, if not acknowledged. So, attending them would only be beneficial to John in Japan. Jane needed the realities of what other American girls were doing at her age, instead of the more adult status and solicitous activities she'd acquired. If Mac was not eager to discipline his children regarding their environment, removing them from it would be a bonus to his career move. Probably, without realizing it, he was taking the pure-Japanese tactic of having the job make the change, rather than him taking direct action.

So, Mac did what he knew was the proper, Japanese way of handling his transfer desires, he put it out into the office grapevine. The purest form of non-committal, ambiguous, enigmatic, and Japanese vague-way to inquire as to the remote possibility, for his turn at a transfer. An observer could only say 'touché,' for he had obviously given up the ugliest of American traits - straight-forward talking about what one wanted. Mac knew the dynamics were all in place when the VP uttered words he'd never spoken before, "What are you going to do for lunch today?" So simple, so Japanese, and if one could understand their inference, no translation was needed.

With the genial conversation flowing, Mac let him know his concern for the transfer was not for himself, but for his children's future education. Again, a perfect tactic, for it would be rude and selfish to ask for something, simply for one's self. Also, most importantly, education was the most valuable thing in a child's life in Japan, for it determined one's job and station in life. Of course, the idea of a mere change or more challenging job might sound good in America, but did not buy much sympathy in Japan, where martyrdom, stoicism, and capitulation were as common as the rice they ate daily.

It just so happened the VP already had a scheduled business meeting in Detroit. Upon his return Mac learned, not from him, needless to say, as it would be too direct, but from Mac's immediate boss, he would soon be transferred there. After a thorough search dependent upon Mac, his successor, another gaijin, was soon hired, trained, and personally informed as to steps of decorum.

In this way his leaving, as the Japanese said, "…wouldn't make a ripple in the water on his departure." The Sayonara parties were held, the traditional gifts given, and each ritual was very carefully followed. Mac may have stumbled into Japan the first time an inept, unprepared gaijin, but truly leaving an unprecedented, conquering hero. He'd accomplished more than even his dreams could have foretold. It could be said Mac left an indelible mark on Japan in a very positive way blessedly, for many gaijin had not. To many other Japanese co-workers, neighbors, and friends, he would long be remembered. Of course, Sakiko would always be another story, for she saw financial stability leaving her when she needed it, and had most definitely expected it - in her old age.

* * * * * *

Obviously, Mac's arrival in Detroit would be a totally different thing than Japan. He left the beginning of April, the Japanese traditional start of a new work year, so Paula remained in Japan while Jane finished her school year at NIS and John graduated. A family disorientation for each of them, shared on very different personal levels. Change could take a distinct stance or face, depending how one approached it, whether it was wanted or not - one could run away, play avoidance, take it as a challenge, or charge head on. The only irrefutable thing was, change was inevitable, at least in most countries. Mac knew no one in the Detroit office, for his area had been Europe. Over the years of trying to fit in, he'd become totally engulfed in the traditional Japanese office way. Though he was now surrounded by Americans, which he kept repeating *were supposed to be like himself*, he could only relate comfortably to the few token-Japanese in the company. He was shocked and dismayed at the infighting going on, as well as the constant, petty arguing with the Japanese coworkers. The disorganization was disheartening. And, he was surprised at the overt political maneuvers on the part of some Americans, thinking they could take the company over from the Japanese. The ridiculousness of this was stupid enough, but the time wasted was infuriating. To think how he had complained about the time-consuming Japanese meetings.

Previously, Mac reeled from acquiescing for group harmony, obviously not conducive to new ideas being brought forward, but this new individual competitiveness and independent cliques, did not create much receptiveness either. He saw continuous excuses, rationalizations, and laying the blame on one another for their lack of performance. Suddenly, Mac was feeling more Japanese than American, for everything the Japanese had said about Americans' work performance being poor, stood before his eyes. His adjustment back would definitely be more than just counter-culture shock, at having been away from the American system for so long.

Disappointing too, the Americans who were above him were merely no more than puppets, making the movements their Japanese bosses wanted. In many ways, Mac was caught in between the levels of authority, for though he was capable of reporting back to Japan in Japanese, he had to refer his information to the Japanese bosses for them to do the reporting. This not only justified their being in Detroit - for most overseas management positions in Western countries were *plums,* awarded to loyal company managers - but fulfilled the protocol of hierarchy. There would always be a fine line between the finesse of handling something well, while being a team player. At leaset, Mac had the challenge he was looking for, and perhaps his having lived on both sides would bring the balance needed for success.

In reality, by early summer 1991, reluctant, yet fearful economic analysts were reporting the long running Bubble Economy had finally burst. Its devastating affect, and denial on the part of the government, would not be totally felt or accepted by the general population for another year. The over-inflated real estate prices of Tokyo, heady over-priced foreign purchases, stock investment, and banks backing them all would be the first to go - hundreds of *billions of dollars* would eventually be lost. Their tab, paid by taxpayer money on insistence from the government, as if the people had a choice - would produce scandal after scandal for the rest of the decade.

Paula and Mac had no idea of knowing they had gotten out just ahead of the economic crash, and the cushy, affluent lifestyle taken so for granted by all, was coming to an abrupt halt. Though Nagoya would be the last, large city affected, because of its solid industrial and conservative base, the glory days were definitely going to be screeching to a shocking close. Thousands of lives technically would be lost in battles, for suicide was as common as alcoholism, with jobs dissolved. The devastation would cause rancor toward the government only slightly less than World War II, with corrupt politicians and political parties tumbling into a crevasse of distrust. To many Japanese, their success of being on top of the world, had run out as one depredation after another fell upon them.

Around the edges, after 1991, Japan went from being the fashion-center-name-brand-designer-wear market (*more Louis Vuitton bags were sold in Japan than all other countries combined*) to having *visible* homeless in the streets. These were not the few alcoholics who had lurked in corners and under stairways hidden from the public, but the vast number of tens of thousands causing general embarrassment to the country. There were thousands living in the subways by night, and the parks during the day day, while being fed by garbage picking, or gaijin and Japanese church organizations. With no actual welfare system to care for them, and no government to support them from being fired, most were over-fifty males with a full variety of skills. When push came to shove, in the die-hard competitive world of Japanese business, the 'lifetime' employment was not worth the paper it was never written on.

The women went first, of course, delegated to part-time, or no job at all. Men who had sacrificed everything for the company were transferred to jobs in some obscure location, and then did work they had absolutely no training for, or embarrassingly menial labor work. The epitome hit, when others admitted they would have rather died from *karoshi*, than be disgraced in some job of insignificance. Since many Japanese married later ilife to give their future families financial stability, these fifty-year olds probably had children in high school, or just entering college. When their highest salaries were needed more, they would not be there for the family.

Still, when scraping the bottom of society, their lives kept the Japanese kata form, as each homeless had his own domain of a cardboard box, with a newspaper floor, for which they removed their shoes before entering. With limited unemployment payments, to everyone's surprise, the Japanese Christian churches were the ones who came forward to help feed the homeless in the train, subway stations, and public parks. Asking for assistance was just not within the Japanese society the thing to do, as it would mean a tremendous loss of face. The other national faiths of Buddhism and Shintoism, being so deeply culturally embedded like the government, simply did not participate in the process of acknowledging 'homelessness' even existed, or that a need was there.

In dire straits, many men took jobs they had only looked down upon before, or had been most recently filled by the imported foreign workers. With the usual exorbitant cost of advertising in Japan, many small and a few large companies took to hiring these displaced men to be their advertisements. Like the *Chindonya* - traditional vaudeville- type advertisers of the past, these men walked around in costume, playing instruments: drums, bells, etc. under a bright colored umbrella, as they chanted a song espousing the product or company. For many remembering, a scary-ring of old Japan, and those days following the war with starvation, just not as much physical destruction.

* * * * * *

By the time June rolled around, Mac, with Paula's consent, had purchased a large four bedroom house in the far suburbs of Detroit. No easy chore, for either of them, with the emotional upheaval, as Paula packed and shipped their belongings gathered over the past ten years. Sakiko, of course, felt like she was being abandoned to destitution, losing her cheap English teachers, while Haruko was simply sad, at once again losing her granddaughter. With failing health in her later years, Haruko intuitively knew she would never see Paula again.

Paula promised to send Sakiko money, though she really did not need it, but again expected it. Paula even strongly suggested Sakiko sell the school to someone, since she knew her mother did not want to pay the current price for gaijin teachers. The Japanese came to expect them, and a school without gaijin teachers was doomed to the massive competition from the numerous English teaching schools which had popped up all over, during the past lucrative years.

John and Jane had mutual trepidation over the move, and it was not just the loss of their Japanese friends. Though John had finished high school, he really did not look forward to going to college. He'd not been accepted by any American university, so the two-step process would be junior college, with a hopeful move into a good university, once he'd proven himself. Mac felt his children needed more language skills, with general American communication and cultural knowledge, which college would give them. Yet, John did not want to wait any amount of time for his financial success.

He and Jane both wanted the instant-gratification that had come so easily to them in Japan, solely because of being gaijin and expecting it. Jane naively thought she'd maintain her status of modeling, and perhaps, as if it were her choice, become a famous model. It would be a devastating shock to find out she was not only overweight by American model standards, but just another pretty blonde. Unfortunately, only the first step on a long road of bumpy disappointments waiting for them both, as they returned to the States.

Having become accustomed to the city life of stores and shops on every corner, suburbia loomed like a desolate desert of boredom. Jane's night life, consisting of disco parties till the wee hours was over, since it was rare for the average adult to consider going into downtown Detroit after dark for entertainment. Her rejection of her new life was so strong, she did not even want to adjust from the jet lag. She stubbornly kept to the Japanese time zone, not changing her watch, sleeping days and staying up all night. Paula still did not drive, so John and Jane soon felt more isolated, angry and resentful at being dragged from their home in Japan. John finally got his license and began driving Mac into the office, so he could have the car.

Though he often took Jane with him, it had been his initiative to learn how to drive, so he did not hesitate to leave her behind, as he explored what was available. John still felt slightly uncomfortable in his English ability to communicate in public, as if he were some alien- anomaly - a supposedly-educated American who made strange grammar mistakes. Some were very simple like - 'yesterday night' - a direct Japanese translation, instead of 'last night.' He was not used to hesitating when he spoke, and now his most basic responses had to be planned in advance.

Paula pushed Jane to meet a few of the neighborhood girls her own age, and reluctantly she agreed to go out with them one evening. "I'll take you to meet some of my friends I hang out with, and we can all do something together." Driving off, Jane perked up a little thinking she and John just had not found the 'in spots' for action, or maybe better, they were actually going downtown. When the neighbor girl pulled into the convenience store parking lot, Jane was expecting it to be a stop-off, not the destination. Getting anxious to move on, yet not sure what was happening, Jane finally questioned, "Is this it? I mean, is this all you do?" Her put down was so derogatory, it was not surprising neither pursued another jaunt together. Amazingly, there were not more venues for the young people to patronize, yet hanging out at the shopping malls or going to movies were basically the extent of their activities. Like most Americans, the teenagers had their friends over to their houses for parties, and the alcohol restrictions were also more controlled in the States. Having played the adult for so long in Japan, Jane did not want to go back to being a teenager.

Things did not improve for Jane after school started, for she was going into a rather upper-crust high school, where the cliques had long been established. The few Japanese students, whose fathers were mostly working in the automotive industry, quickly became her choice of friends. Jane began to float through her senior year with little cognizance of her own presence, much less those around her. She settled into marking time till she could get a life of her own. The bitterness built up, feeling herself a prisoner of her parents and the educational system.

Paula loved her new home in the suburbs, as it reminded her well of her first move to America with Aunt Marge. Though the non- driving was a challenge she was going to have to conquer. She particularly liked their older home in a more settled area, with lots of trees and a real backyard, rather than a new development. As she attended Mac's company picnics and co-workers' barbecues, they both gravitated more to the Japanese attendees.

It was a mutual comfortableness among them, and Paula soon learned the grade school near her had quite a few Japanese children. When she called to volunteer her translating and teaching services, they jumped at the offer. Paula's foundation and support in Detroit was her love for Mac, just as it had been in New Jersey. Likewise, she had been his in Japan. One moment cannot be truer than another, since those moments were theirs. It was love, and being together which made them survive any turmoil or stress.

John went to junior college halfheartedly, but when opportunity knocked for him to return to Japan, he quickly jumped at it. Some of Paula's Japanese relatives needed an interpreter to handle a business deal which was going sour, and offered a considerable sum of money for Paula or Mac to handle it. Though it was only supposed to take a few weeks, Paula had no interest and suggested John. He didn't hesitate, even joking to his father, his Japanese knowledge was more valuable than a college education. Only a few weeks later, Sakiko called Paula, saying ninety-one year old Haruko was truly on her death bed, so off she flew to Japan, too.

Jane, alone with her father and stuck in the house, whined, complained and carried on about the inequalities in her life. John's interpreter job stretched from weeks to months, as he lived the high life on an expense account for his hotel, restaurants and bars. Jane's envy sky-rocketed when he called home to tell her the happenings in the bar scene they had left behind. Paula's experience was less joyful or free, as she returned to Detroit by Thanksgiving, having gone through the full rituals of the Buddhist funeral for her grandmother.

She tried to get Sakiko to consider at least moving to Hawaii, where a friend had moved, if not America, but she would not think of such a move. Her life was virtually free from all obligations, yet she refused to make any changes for the time being. Finally, a close friend insisted Sakiko join her and her husband on a trip to Australia. Sakiko found it to be incredibly boring, for she had no interest in animals, the outdoors, or strange food. She felt comfortable in the familiar, closed- in buildings, street noise, and socializing with commoners in her old neighborhood bars and *karaoke*. The mind-numbing addiction to pachinko became a regular, ever-expanding part of her new life. Sakiko had truly become one of the minions she'd ridiculed so often in her stately past.

* * * * * *

A few months before graduating, a new girl started attending Jane's high school. She had an African-American mother and Caucasian father. She and Jane quickly became fast friends, and were soon inseparable, for they had a similar mindset for partying. Finally, Jane learned the downtown scene, for her new friend had a car, and was not afraid of the action. Once high school graduation was over, Jane's life improved greatly in her eyes, as they got an apartment together, she got her driver's license, and she was able to get a job at an exclusive Japanese restaurant. She stayed a year and a half, and made many Japanese contacts. But, hough the money was quite good, eventually she decided she did not want to be a waitress the rest of her life.

Then, as if her old magic was back when surrounded by Japanese men, Jane only had to ask and she had a high-paying job with a Japanese trading company in their Detroit branch office. She then thumbed her nose at her father's insistence she needed a college education to develop a career. Within six months, she was asked to go to Japan to handle some business for the company. The moment she stepped off the plane, it was like she'd never left, and picked up the phone to call friends she'd not seen in several years. She was instantly back into the bar scene, going to all the most trendy ones and being the center of attention. The crowds certainly had thinned, with the recession so rampant from one end of the country to the next. But, certain groups of people always had money, and were even happier to spend it, to show their status. Her mind was set, as to what her future destiny would be.

When Jane returned to the States, though it had only been a few weeks, it was culture shock all over again. This time she would only work long enough to get money to move back to Japan permanently. She knew where she belonged, where she fit in, where her greatest, easiest spotlight and rewards were. There would be nothing to it, she'd simply marry a wealthy Japanese man, have children, and be a happy Japanese wife. Being s second-class citizen to a Japanese husband did not even enter her picture of thought. It was only right, Jane thought, the man should make all the decisions, as it was less she had to contend with or process her brain. Her uniqueness of appearance and speech, could only be rewarded in the one place she knew so well.

John's interpreter job, in the meantime, had stretched to almost a year and he was getting quite bored, though flushed with money, and rightly arrogant for his accomplishment. One night while talking with a Japanese bartender friend, he met a young, beautiful Japanese girl named Mariko. What swept him away, was she simply complimented him on his Japanese, without any of the usual questions of why a gaijin could speak so naturally. He innocently thought she was treating him as an equal Japanese, not a gaijin.

In fact, Mariko could not have cared less, or had any curiosity as to why a gaijin would be speaking with native ability. She was simply vacuous, spoiled from a wealthy family, and spoke absolutely no English, and no interest in learning to do so. None of her actions, or what she said daunted him at all. It was a whirlwind affair, that neither of them considered any need for accountability. When Mariko became pregnant, she guilelessly got an abortion. John was somewhat stopped in his tracks by her coolness, for he felt he loved her. This might be his chance for happiness, though she'd never uttered one word of encouragement to him with similar feelings. When she became pregnant again, less than a month later, he insisted they get married, so Mariko, matter-of-factly produced the child he seemed to want shortly thereafter. Motherhood never quite entered her picture, much like sex, it was simply a biological function to her.

With no plan whatsoever, John returned to America with his new little family. Mac, as the concerned and reality-based parent he was, helped him get a job at the same trading company Jane had worked with. John knew nothing of doing business, but at least all the interpreting negotiations had taught him how to do the communicating for both sides. He quickly learned the art off deal-making. While work success seemed to fall easily into his lap, his new personal life was anything but, what he'd expected. Though he tried to take on his responsibilities as a father and husband, they lived with Mac and Paula, who welcomed them.

It could not have been a more perfect environment for the totally Japanese Mariko, as she soon connected up with the young Japanese female scene in Detroit, lunching and partying. She'd only seen America through Japanese television, which painted it as an alternate picture of either Disneyland from coast to coast, or crime and drugs everywhere. The real thing was a bit much for her to handle, so she stayed in a Japanese-bubble never interacting beyond a Japanese speaking circle. In flippant slang, she referred to her son as *'hafu'* - meaning a child of half Japanese and half gaijin descent.

John's promises of how their life was going to be in America soon began falling by the wayside. The stubborn, spoiled girl was not the typical, acquiescing-Japanese. Mariko saw through her husband's lies and was not about to capitulate. John had finally been caught in his own web of fabrications, where he was the biggest victim of misbelief. With her own frustrations of living month after month basically with only a room of their own, she was not accepting of his excuses, and confronted him badly when she caught him in repeated lies. Obviously, neither one was ready or old enough to handle marriage, and this was certainly not what she expected her life to be. Mariko could not be left in the house alone, for she could not answer the telephone, or call 911 in English for any emergency. Yet, she never hesitated to leave the baby with Paula to go shopping, or spend time with her Japanese friends, rather than study English. John and Mariko were in a quandary, where neither was adult enough to admit their own contributions to the mess their marriage had become.

When Paula needed to return to Japan to help Sakiko move out of the old house and into a new condo, Mariko jumped at the chance to go back herself with the baby. It was a chance for space, perhaps they both needed to reassess their marriage. Paula did not interfere or question, as it gave her more time with her grandchild, as well an opportunity for Sakiko to see him, as he was beautiful.

Sakiko sold the old house and property to the funeral home next to her for almost a million dollars, so finally she had no limitations to her spending. Frank may have paid for the house and expensive furnishings, but of course, Sakiko kept all the money for herself, never even offering anything to Paula from her father's estate. Still, not the closing chapter of her life, as once again Sakiko reinvented herself, trying to fulfill the illusive-quest of having prestige and recognition.

Like a modern day, Japanese version of Scarlett O'Hara, who had survived war, famine, reconstruction, and invalidation, as well as encroachment from the conquering forces, she'd manipulated her way out successfully at every juncture. But, she was no longer a young, strong, and vibrantly beautiful woman, so whatever recognition she got would be more of the second class variety. This was not a cathartic period of reevaluation, acceptance or regret; she was what she'd always be. Sakiko was shallow, even by Japanese definition, and self- centered beyond defense or rationalization. But, just as Frank had run out of excuses for drinking, she'd run out of dreams, yet she never let any regrets of her own doing enter her mind, just those of what others had or hadn't done for her.

And, a life without illusions was just not acceptable to her. The little tinsel and glitter of the karaoke bar, or pachinko parlor could not suffice her needs any longer. Sakiko was more than alone, she was lonely, for she had never taken the time to appreciate what and who surrounded her, only how to control them to her benefit. She was a financial success story, who had missed loving someone unconditionally - a major point of life. Her closest friend was a retired Geisha. They had more in common than she would have recognized, for they'd both been playing a role for accolades, without any deep meaning or feelings.

On her own, with no one to answer to for anything,

it did not take long for Sakiko to succumb and be bilked by a rogue in a karaoke bar. He convinced her he had musical talent, missing out on success only because he needed someone to support and guide, his promising career. Almost thirty years her junior, he knew how to play to her ego and desire of bright lights and adoring attention, while posing her as the benevolent guide behind the discovered talent.

Besides buying him a new, flashy, sports car, and of course, the required wardrobe for stardom, she invested heavily in promoting him with demo records, trips to Tokyo, as well as the best voice coaches. Once Paula and Mac became aware of her flamboyant-fling, they tried to reason with Sakiko. Mac tried to emphasize the need for her to invest some of the inheritance, which was not replaceable. It all fell on deaf ears, as Sakiko dropped a considerable amount of weight, with a complete make-over, grabbing at the youth and beauty she'd once known. This was her one last chance at celebrity status and the spotlight. So, no monetary limitation would be put on it. Obviously, it did not take long for him to disappear, as fast as the million dollars.

* * * * * *

In the weeks Mariko was in Japan, she was never home when John called, and she only visited Paula and Sakiko once. Jane saw her often in the discos, as she herself flitted from one Japanese man to another, but she never revealed to John what Mariko was doing. When it came time to return to the States, Mariko told John she wanted to spend more time with her parents. John fearing she'd leave him permanently, insisted she come back to Detroit. While granted, a spoiled girl, she still felt the obligation of the obeying-Japanese wife, so she returned most reluctantly. Yet, in her own streak of defiance, she brought her brother back with her, saying she had needed help traveling with the baby. He moved into Jane's empty room, and Mariko went out with him every night.

Arguments with John ensued, for he had to be up early each morning for his job. Soon Mariko began sleeping on the couch in Jane's room, while her brother slept in the bed. Eventually, over weeks, Paula complained Mariko was never taking care of their son. When John's furious blow-ups and physical threats came, Mariko decided to return to Japan again with her brother. She promised to return in a few weeks, but the months dragged on until John, once again traveled after her to Japan to bring her back. Not until she was once again pregnant, did she finally agree to return to Detroit, and the built-in-baby-sitting grandparents would not turn her away. Apparently, her parents had no interest in her, or her children.

A more honest man, might have been broken-hearted at his sad excuse for a family life and marriage. In reality, John thought he'd found the perfect solution in Mariko. She'd been like 'his little piece of Japan,' who'd always be close to his heart, always reminding him of his life there. He believed only a Japanese woman could understand him, for he'd never been successful, or comfortable dating a gaijin. John felt totally out of sync with assertive American women, who expected so much from a man, and would never realize he was somebody special. It would definitely take a Japanese woman to recognize, he surmised, and therefore accepted the situation with Mariko living her own Japanese-style life, in the suburbs of Detroit.

Perhaps, like Jane, too many of John's formative years had been patterned by the Japanese cultural ways, traits and beliefs. Yet, Paula had lived more years, and under stricter Japanese tradition. Her success, along with her determination to adjust to life in America, could only have been from her love for Mac and his understanding support of her. Although John continued to work for the Japanese trading company, making more than adequate money, he and Mariko did not move out of Paula and Mac's protective domain.

Jane eventually married, and had the two designated children, like the Japanese family she tried to be. But unfortunately, a depressed economy limited the choice of wealthy Japanese men. Her life did not turn out like the dreams she had painted. It actually looked more like a cheap version of a pair-by-number impression, barely a recognizable copy of the famous artwork it was supposed to be emulating. Clearly, to anyone who knew her, she'd taken the easy way out of accepting her position in Japan, rather than creating a new one in America.

Jane's looks and uniqueness would still get doors open for her in the meantime. Anything too far in the future, might be too frightening to want to create any more dreams. Interestingly, she did build a whole, new relationship with her grandmother Sakiko. They had more in common in keeping each other company, than just smoking and enjoying spending money to have a good time. Paula had always been too 'good,' maybe even *too* traditionally Japanese. It was something Sakiko played at, only when required, but was never part of her soul. Jane became Sakiko's mirror image, and in this way they validated each other and their existence.

After only a few short years, Sakiko had wasted all of the property money she'd gotten. Too much spent on jewelry, gigolos, and their expensive trappings. She eventually lost her condominium and with great complaint, came to live with Paula and Mac, continuing to make their lives miserable. She never quit playing upon Paula's sympathy, while draining her of money, and then returning to Japan at every chance to visit friends and party, as if she were a young woman. Actually, in Japan, such a generational family living together under one roof, and basically being supported by only the male head-of-the- household, would not be considered strange. Sakiko had no concern for what was accepted in America, for it would not be her norm.

Who could say, if Sakiko had not gone through what she had suffered with the war and then her involvement with the Allied Occupation, would she have been a different, more loving and empathic person? She did try her best to copy those Americans around her, and some of them were not the best role models for kindness and generosity. Not that Sakiko ever rationalized, and used those experiences or sufferings, as reason for her actions or behavior, since she did not see anything wrong with herself, because of her blinding ego. Other Japanese, surely had more devastating experiences and losses from the war, or deprivation, even after the Occupation, yet perhaps had not become as hardened as Sakiko. One cannot say what it was which contributed to her personality, or persona or character. It's always a personal choice of what one makes of their experiences and changes. Sakiko, of course, never felt she needed to change.

* * * * * *

Opportunity does not knock just once, but continually, and Mac jumped to recognize and act on it each time. For Paula, she had to create it. They now lived this life they had chosen, and worked so hard to make happen. What dreams Mac, and even Paula, still wanted to fulfill one could not say. He was still listening for more knocks - as perhaps someday England, or somewhere else in Europe to work and live. Acceptance was a big challenging part of life, while searching for love was another, and neither was ever easy. Yet, Frank to Sakiko, and Paula to Mac, love had come the long way around. They knew, while you could give something without love, you could not truly love without giving. For Jane and John, love snd the life they wanted were more illusive in its true meaning. Like for many of their generation, maybe some things *had* come too easy, and thus no interest in working for a better life or love.

Epilogue: *How It All Ended*

A Truly Different Cultural Perspective Lived

"I see nothing mysterious about the Japanese," says the visitor who has been in Japan for a week. "They talk just like Americans." That is a Japanese talent - chameleon-like, to take- on the color of the person they address. But the mystery gathers as one remains in the country. After five, ten, twenty years what seemed simple upon arrival had become complex. A missionary after long service sagely comments, "First impressions are very deceitful."

Willard Price,
Key to Japan - 1946

After the 'Bubble:'

It was easy to get rid of the unemployed, gaijin English teachers, as the language schools began closing and going bankrupt, almost as quickly as they had sprouted. The work visa was needed to stay in Japan and required a contract. Those who had become addicted to the easy money and cash payments from private students, took jobs as bartenders, cooks, or waitresses - depending on their level of Japanese - just to remain in the country. Many gaijin men - and a few women - married their Japanese students, as the "Golden Spouse" visa was easier to get, and they could work part-time for any English school. It became a mutual-admiration society, as then the schools did not have the obligation of sponsorship. The part-time teachers were cheaper, too, since a monthly guaranteed salary was not required for the immigration department.

It didn't take long for the gaijin men to learn, they were put on a higher pedestal than Japanese men, and the Japanese women were attracted to even the ugliest, and most inept gaijin, who simply paid attention to them. It was probably the biggest advantage to the gaijin, not having to go to a juku, like the Japanese men, who never really learned how to interact or socialize with women, as the gaijin had. Then their Japanese marriage allowed for their escapism to a free, gaijin-lifestyle of drinking and carousing also continued. The Japanese wife *never* questioned the activities of her husband.

But other gaijin problems the government ended up with, after the recession were the illegals - most Middle Eastern men from Iran, Pakistan, and other countries. They had come as the lowest-level laborers during the bubble, when few Japanese wanted to do the dirtiest jobs. These illegals now congregated in the parks, train and subway stations selling drugs and fake telephone cards. Since they were supported by the Yakuza, the police did little to stop them, and few Japanese women were interested in marrying them, as Muslim.

Life was not a party for the illegals, as few spoke much English or Japanese. There were a few horror stories of Japanese women who did marry, as well converted to Islam. When they traveled to their husband's country with their child or children, they were never heard from again. Violent crimes, which except for rape - though rarely reported - had always been a blessed-rarity in Japan, now slowly began to rise with the economic chaos. Not so much the increase in the number, as the bizarre brutality of some crimes, and the perpetrators came from the benign masses.

Prior history had shown, Japanese modern social order had been maintained by equitably sharing sacrifices, and the fruits of good economic growth. It emphasized social consensus and community solidarity in a crowded environment, by a relative upright police force, and by strict handgun control. But they did not come by this process of socialization by genial origins. Shortly before his death, Lafcadio Hearn hinted at a greater realization of the complex roots of the graciousness and good behavior of the Japanese he admired. "Such manners," he wrote in 1904, "need not cease to charm us because we know that they were cultivated, for a thousand years, under the edge of the sword."

During the Edo period (prior name of Tokyo), 1600-1867, a nearly flawless system of totalitarianism developed, which permeated society all the way down to the neighborhood level. The *goningumi* - neighborhoods were originally formed of village households by the feudal authorities to help stamp out Christianity and control *Ronin* - the masterless-Samurai. Like tinges of Nazism or Soviet Communism, they developed into a means of strongly 'encouraging' shared community responsibility and solidarity. It was, of course, a way of controlling society at the grassroots level.

Something as humanly basic as smiling was still considered frivolous, even for family pictures, while totally out of place in the work environment. Clerks gave a hearty *"Irasshaimase!"* - Welcome!, to entering customers, but never a friendly grin, much less idle chitchat. The client was waited on with almost embarrassing- assistance, showing or demonstrating numerous items as expected, and a profuse 'thank you,' whether buying or not, but they never got a generic, "Have a nice day."

You could say, it's a cultural requirement to suppress all emotions to keep the *wa,,* as group harmony was above all. The formal society restricted the touching or display of physical affection among family members, especially in public, even after long absences. Strangers may push, or weave their way passed acceptably, as log as an 'excuse me' accompanied the rudeness. Older people still believed, it was not proper to move the face or body itself too much. Yet, in the totally opposite vein, men commonly fondled the young school girls on the crowded trains or buses with no intervention. If the young women were to say something, thean would lose face at the accusation or acknowledgement of the indiscretion. Above all, it's a male society whose rights were preserved and respected.

Outright feudalism was abandoned in Japan with the Meiji Restoration, and then again in detail during the Allied Occupation in the American drawn Constitution, but it lived on in soil hierarchy and business organizations. One could say, the success of modern industrial Japan was due in part to the grafting of feudal traditions onto a modern corporate structure. There were those who felt, it was not a morality conflict for the Yakuza to do 'collection money' from small businesses for the Shinto Shrines after the war. This was nothing less than 'protection' money the Mafia in the States would have done, except the 'state' religion - Shinto benefitted somewhat. The ends justified the means with great rationalizations, when related to some obscure feudal tradition., *Shikata-ganai / Shogan-nai* - it was what it was, and cannot be changed - accept it.

One reason why outside religions, like male-dominated Mormonism - Later Day Saints, fit well into their society was it had strict rules and regulations, which could not be questioned - so it was respected. With the Mormons, they cleverly learned it was best to convert in one's own language, and only sent over Male Missionaries fluent in Japanese. Without personal knowledge, they would refer to Buddhism as a pagan religion. Also, they did not hesitate to insinuate, if not directly said, a more modern religion like theirs, made the Japanese more accepted to the outside world. Very basically, this filled especially the male insecurities to convert.

Little overt coercion was required to maintain the modern social order, because most people instinctively knew their limits. Unlike in the United States, with its wide-open physical and intellectual spaces, there was nowhere to hide in the crowded, island Japan. Family registers maintained by the local authorities, provided a means of tracking the population and updated address files - rather Orwell-shaded. They were used extensively from corporations to marriage-arrangers, for the screening out of those with mixed-blood of minorities, and other undesirables like the *Bunraku* - traditionally 'unclean' because of their work in the killing of animals.

With its rise in the mid-1980s of AIDS - HIV, the people infected were almost openly discriminated against, and there was no American Civil Liberty Union to lend them assistance. Neighborhood vigilante groups, and blatant signs advised citizens to call the police if they saw 'anyone looking suspicious' to prevent 'unacceptable or deviant' behavior. Of course, if one's neighborhood contained gaijin, everyone knew who the troublemakers were, for they rarely tried to follow the rules, or even respect them. While at the same time, many gaijin who had been in Japan any length of time learned, they would be blamed for things, or ignored when they made mistakes. Many took on the attitude of - "Oh, well, may as well be hung for a sheep as well as a lamb," and went on to create more havoc. Japan has often been called the most xenophobic of Westernized countries, but usually only by those gaijin who have lived there any length of time.

Occupied Hearts -
Love the Long Way Around
Japanese Vocabulary List

Prologue:
gaijin - foreigner *Shinkansen* - bullet train futons - sleeping mattresses
juku - the necessitated cram school for junior and senior high school students.
Sayonara - going away party or sale

Chapter 1:
No Japanese used

Chapter 2:
furoshiki - the wrapping cloth the Japanese use to carry
something
Shikata ganai or more colloquial *Shogan'nai* - Don't
question - that's how it is
getas - wooden clogs
tatami - rice straw mats
tokonoma - an alcove designed for seasonal art work
Kempeitai - WW II Military police in Japan
Miso - soybean paste - mix for soup
shoyu - soy sauce

Chapter 3:
Kata - the Way things should be done
wa - harmony, balance, social accord in the society
honorifics - hierarchical speaking - different suffixes
and prefixes for levels of people

jishuku - restraint in all emotions, sometimes called 'the soul of Japan'
tonkasu - breaded and fried pork or chicken covered in
a thick, dark sauce - soy based
pachinko - a mindless kind of pinball game, requires no skill
soroban - abacus study
omiai - the marriage-arranged process
O.L. - Office Lady - the ubiquitous, uniformed female
servant of the office men

Chapter 4:
O Shou gatsu - the Japanese New Year *hakama* - male
traditional dress *shamisen* - a three-stringed instrument

Chapter 5:
Yakuza - the Japanese mafia
yukata - robe
Kabuki and No - Japanese drama forms
ikebana - flower arranging
Matsuri - Festivals
O-Hanami - Cherry Blossom Festival *Tanabaka* - festival for the Star-Crossed Lovers *tabi* - split-toe socks
waraji - straw fold sandals
mikoshi - god-dwelling wooden houses
O-Bon - Festival of the Dead
Shichi-Go-San - Seven-Five-Three Festival
go-ishi - a pawn

Chapter 6:

hiragana - phonetic syllabary of Japanese
manga - comic books
Mumbusho - the Japanese Board of Education
gomen-nasai - I am so sorry
Romani - the alphabetized spelling of the Japanese
word *katakana* - the simplify characters of
pronunciation *Otoasan* - honorary husband

Chapter 7:
Omiage - souvenirs *ijime* - bullying *Sensei* - teacher
Eigo Sensei - English teacher
Atsuta Jingo - a National Shinto Shrine in Nagoya
nimawashi - cultivating the ground for better relations
Karoshi - death from overwork - at one's desk
Chindonya - traditional vaudeville-type advertiser of
the past
karaoke - singing to recorded music
hafu - meaning a child of half Japanese and half gaijin
descent

Epilogue:
goningumi - neighborhoods
Ronin - masterless Samurai
Irasshaimase - Welcome to entering customers
Bunraku - traditionally 'unclean' - workers who kill
animals
genkan - entry-way for house where shoes are left
gyoza - Chinese sautéed dumplings *yaki-soba* - soy
fried noodles *nantoka* - whatever
Sakura - Cherry Blossom time

Acknowledgements

To all those courageous friends and associates - gaijin and Japanese, who shared their memories and experiences with me, over my seven years in Japan. It continues to be, the most important pivotal time in my life, as to cultural awareness, growth and change.

Thank you also to Pat Brown for being my Beta-reader, and Patrica Dahlke for final editing, along with her own experience of years in Japan.

www.ingramcontent.com/pod-product-compliance
Lightning Source LLC
Chambersburg PA
CBHW070911120626
46546CB00001B/224